CONTRADICTIONS OF CONSUMPTION

concepts, practices and politics in consumer society

Tim Edwards

OPEN UNIVERSITY PRESS
Buckingham · Philadelphia

In memory of my mother
Delia Edwards
(1935–1996)

Open University Press
Celtic Court
22 Ballmoor
Buckingham
MK18 1XW

email: enquiries@openup.co.uk
world wide web: www.openup.co.uk

and
325 Chestnut Street
Philadelphia, PA 19106, USA

First Published 2000

A catalogue record of this book is available from the British Library

ISBN   0 335 19917 8 (pb)   0 335 19918 6 (hb)

Library of Congress Cataloging-in-Publication Data
Edwards, Tim, 1963-
    Contradictions of consumption: concepts, practices, and politics in consumer
    socity/Tim Edwards.
        p. cm.
    Includes bibliographical references and index.
    ISBN 0-335-19918-6 (hb) – ISBN 0-335-19917-8 (pbk.)
        1. Consumption (Economics) 2. Consumer behavior. I. Title.
    HC79.C6 E38 2000
    339.4'7--dc21   99-056453

Typeset by Type Study, Scarborough
Printed in Great Britain by St Edmundsbury Press Ltd, Bury St Edmunds, Suffolk

CONTENTS

ACKNOWLEDGEMENTS

Acknowledgements, like books themselves, are a product of their time and context. I have particular reason, then, to thank Justin Vaughan for his easy-going and understanding support in completing the project. The work was often completed under immense duress, not least of all the death of my mother, and I give the most profound gratitude to Mark Solomon, to Sheila Marsden and to Colleen McLaughlin for their support in helping me through that time. I am also grateful for the friendship, laughter and constructive comments of Sam Ashenden, Shirley Beller, Simon Hardy, Philip Hoggar, Hüseyin Tapinç, Jörg Spitzer and Carla Willig. I also remain indebted to my students at Leicester University who, for the past five years, have provided the forum for my explorations, and to the staff of the Department of Sociology for their support. Most of all, though, I thank my mother who somehow, in all the adversity, gave me the life and the strength to move on and who continues to provide so much inspiration for the ideas presented here and the fire to see through the tears . . .

INTRODUCTION: CONTRADICTIONS OF CONSUMPTION

> In the modern world, it has become a cliché to suggest that we inhabit, are even victims of, a 'consumer society'; that 'consumerism' is rampant; that we are dominated by 'consumer culture', having passed through a 'consumer revolution'.
>
> (Fine and Leopold 1993: 62)

Consumer society, as concept and practice, is now a matter for some consumption in itself. Recent years have seen a steadily increasing interest in the ideas and activities of consumption in the fields of academic and popular discourse alike. Television and newspapers now produce regular reports on spending patterns and talk in endless psychological riddles of consumer confidence; and the exploding profusion of lifestyle magazines incessantly advise and direct their readers in matters of style and taste. Similarly, a rapid expansion in academic attention to questions of consumption has taken place across the entire canon of the arts and social sciences, from psychoanalytic interpretation and textual analysis to the further development of economic histories and the production of anthropological ethnographies and sociological narratives (see, for example, Featherstone 1991; Shields 1992; Bowlby 1993; Fine and Leopold 1993; Lury 1996; Slater 1997b; Miller 1998).

What is at stake in all cases is a concern with what the apparently now exponential growth in the significance and importance attached to consumption actually *means* for society as a whole and for the individual. Are we heading over some precipice into uncontrolled hedonism, experiencing new forms of plurality and expression, or walking with eyes closed into worldwide plundering and exploitation of natural and human resources on a scale hitherto unseen – or even all three? These are the contentious if not inflammatory questions that inform the following discussion. Consequently, it is my foremost intention to map out, document and put into perspective some of these questions and their supposed answers and, perhaps more importantly, to ask some new ones concerning the direction and limits, and indeed potential, of consumer society early in the twenty-first century.

Questions of definition

Despite the aforementioned contemporary plethora of articles and texts on the concept and practice of consumption, no adequate definition of consumption or its related concepts yet exists. Notions of consumer culture, consumer society, consumerism, the consumer and consumption itself are often thrown around with abandon and with apparently little concern for their exact meaning. In addition, the expansion of interest in matters related to consumption, allied with its increasingly interdisciplinary significance, have in all likelihood added to the confusion surrounding its definition and done little to pin it down. Although some elements of openness are easily applauded, and indeed necessary, much of the slipperiness of the concept comes from sloppiness in its analysis.

Historically, consumption has been understood in a variety of ways. These have included seeing it as central to the maintenance of status and class positions, as a mechanism for fantasy and day-dreaming related to the rise of city cultures, or as a modern form of justification for economic exploitation through production (Veblen 1934; Adorno and Horkheimer 1973; Benjamin 1973). And, more recently, attention has focused on consumption's role in the formation and maintenance of identities as part of the development of style cultures (Ewen 1988; Featherstone 1991; Lury 1996).

This diversity in perspectives raises a wider question concerning the role and function of consumption as a means of empowerment and expression on the one hand, or manipulation and exploitation on the other. Formulating answers to such questions is difficult, yet the study of consumer society, like consumption itself, is of necessity multifaceted and often apparently contradictory as an equally cultural and economic phenomenon that seemingly empowers and exploits consumers, often simultaneously. In the first instance, then, I wish to try to pin down some of the parameters of the study of consumer society and consumption *per se*.

At its simplest, there are essentially three elements to the practice, and our contemporary understanding, of consumption. The first and clearest of these is the notion of *consumerism*, which focuses on the more organized practice of consumers, often relating most directly to various forms of collective consumer resistance, including the formation of such organizations as the Consumers' Association in the UK. The clear emphasis here is on shopping as the linchpin of consumption and consumer society and, more theoretically, the relationship between subject and object or the significance of the commodity. The second dimension of consumption relates to its definition as *leisure* and, more widely, as the conceptual flipside to its supposedly opposed notion of production, or work. Incorporated in this definition more particularly is the consumption of services as well as commodities, including holidays, sporting activities, and the arts and cinema. This leads to the third and widest element of our understanding of consumption, which relates to the activity of *consuming* itself, whether through, most fundamentally, eating and drinking or, more fuzzily, through viewing or listening. Thus, watching television, reading magazines and generally wandering around looking at things are also incorporated into this widest dimension of consumption. What perhaps underpins the definition of consumption in all cases is the notion of commodification, as walking along city streets or using a park still incorporates some element of monetary exchange, if only the cost of a travel ticket or deckchair rental.

The key distinction that arises at this point concerns the interpretation of more *collective* patterns in the practice of consumption on all these levels. An analysis of consumer practices as matters of style, taste and identity formation or maintenance often informs a more poststructural analysis of consumer culture; and a consideration of the more historical or economic underpinnings of consumer practices or their more overtly political implications tends to inform a wider analysis of consumer society. Clearly, it follows that these two notions of consumption are not entirely distinct or disconnected. Yet there remains a different emphasis on styles and texts or on history, politics and economics. The analysis here leans towards the latter, while incorporating some analysis of style and texts where appropriate, and thus uses the term consumer society to indicate this, rather than the more ambiguous term of consumer culture, which can apply equally to consumption as a set of aesthetic styles or as a way of life. This reflects the dual connotations of the concept of culture more widely and is explored in detail in Chapter 1. More significantly, it also starts to inform some of the dominant themes and arguments of the work.

Consumer society: summary of themes and arguments

Consumption is clearly not simply a matter of style. It is also a matter of money and economics, social practice and social division, and political policy and political implication. In short, it is a matter of consumer *society*. This notion in itself starts to open up questions concerning power and inequality, individualism and identity, and social and economic stratification. This is not to exclude questions of culture or cultural practice, nor to undermine their importance, but rather to put them in perspective or context. For whatever the meaning of our patterns of seamless and repeated shopping, consumption of the media, or participation in leisure, none of these activities exists in a vacuum.

Similarly, many more economically determinist analyses of consumer society, such as those associated with Marxism, have tended to neglect an analysis of the consumer *per se*, who is often rendered passive and plastic, if not redundant, in the grand scheme of things. Moreover, even the most demand-oriented analyses of economic history tend to elide detailed consideration of the consumers' motivations and the particularities and contradictions of the meanings of consumption practices (McKendrick *et al.* 1982; Campbell 1987; Miller 1987). What this starts to create is an oscillating concern with *consumers* on the one hand and the history and development of *consumer society* or *consumer culture* on the other; while an analysis of *consumption* as an economically founded, socially practised and politically contradictory phenomenon tends to remain unproblematized and invisible. This is also a reflection of the wider sociological problem of action and structure whereby the individual and the social are set up in opposition with one another.

As a result, there are three key themes to this work. The first is that consumption, and our understanding of it, is multifaceted and integral to contemporary society. Although some consumer practices are indeed then concerned with questions of style, identity and culture, others are more economically rooted, politically divisive, socially cohesive or simply mundane and routine matters of necessity. Thus, the meanings of wandering lazily around fashion stores on holiday are not easily equated with the tiresome trip to the supermarket watching the rising prices, and nor is the aestheticization of everyday life necessarily easily related to questions of poverty and policy.

This leads to the second theme of this text, which is that the practice of consumption itself, and consumer society more widely, is often socially divisive and iniquitous. The most fundamental factor in this is, of course, economic: if you do not have the money you cannot have the product or service and you cannot partake in any activity that costs more than you can afford, at least not indefinitely. The expansion of credit during the late twentieth century has increased many people's access to much they could not otherwise afford. However, credit levels are under increasingly computerized surveillance, and poverty all too easily ensues when they are exceeded – often as a result of the high interest rates on the sums owed. The situation is further complicated by questions of more physical access. Lack of transport and physical or psychological impairment of any sort exclude many people from the consumption practices they might otherwise undertake. Consequently, the target of most consumer promotions remains the affluent, gainfully employed and physically unrestricted or socially mobile person, whoever he or she may be.

More problematically, consumer society *seems* largely uninterested in questions of class, race, gender or sexuality, other than as niche markets or selling points. Its interests are still overwhelmingly related to profit. However, this tends to mask the continuing significance of indicators of oppression, such as class, race, sexuality or gender, which are often hidden in discourses of consumer choice and consumer democracy. This is not necessarily to imply that all consumers are somehow ruthlessly exploited against their will or knowledge. Indeed, one of the strongest contradictions of consumer society is that we often know all too well when we are falling for the hard or soft sell, yet fall for it anyway and often quite willingly. A good example of this is the sale of anti-ageing products, which are routinely marketed as transformatory of personal appearance. Few people truly think such products will work, or even have any significant effect, yet they still enjoy the idea of using such items and purchase them anyway. Similarly, few people truly know or care which washing powder washes whitest, yet demonstrate extraordinary levels of loyalty to particular products.

This taps into the third and most fundamental theme of this work, namely that consumption, in all its forms, is increasingly important and expanding in its capacity to dominate our individual lives, and indeed the entire development and direction of contemporary society, nationally and internationally. Few areas of everyday life are now not affected or linked to the processes of practices of consumption – from image-making and advertising, or the simple organization of activities and leisure time, to the formulation of worldwide economic policies – as societies, rich and poor alike, are caught up in processes of buying and selling. These developments apply most notoriously to such issues as the provision of health, welfare and education or to the privatization of various service industries (Cahill 1994; Keat *et al.* 1994; Sulkunen *et al.* 1997).

However, they relate most widely and importantly to the everyday lives of individuals, who are increasingly caught up in processes of commodification where difficulties and dissatisfactions with appearances are fixed through plastic surgery, and all manner of anxiety and stress relievers are put into potions and sold on supermarket shelves. Even the most deeply individual of issues, such as love, happiness or personal fulfilment, are increasingly caught up in processes of consumption that now incorporate dating agencies, weekend courses in personal fulfilment and a vast array of counselling services. Even churches now often vociferously request voluntary donations from all visitors. Consequently, in contemporary society, almost no human need or activity avoids commodification, and consumer society, despite its internal contradictions, is increasingly all-encompassing.

Contradictions of consumption

One of the key themes of this work is that consumption, and indeed consumer society, is centred on an inherent series of contradictions on several levels. This is not intended as a controversial polemic, rather it is used to inform what is hopefully a fairly open and dynamic interpretation of consumption, consumer society and their importance and implications. It is also important to point out that this sense of contradiction is not easily resolved, even if that were the intention, and requires acceptance and openness in viewpoint, rather than an attempt to stamp it out or override its significance.

First, there is clearly a sense in which consumption taps into a wider question of structure and action or, to put it more simply, power. Popular culture and the media tend to dictate that consumers are increasingly powerful and in particular adopt a pursuit of choice which is, in turn, increasingly reinforced at a political or ideological level. However, it is also quite clearly the case, as is powerfully implicated in the work of many more classical scholars, that this sense of consumer power is as illusory as it is real, if indeed it is real at all. This then starts to lead to a dialectic where consumers either actively make their own destinies or are duped into thinking they are doing so when they are not all.

The difficulty here, and indeed the contradiction, is that neither is truly the case and much also depends on a second theme of social division. The contradiction is that consumption of any sort does not have a simple relation to any indicator of oppression, such as class, race or gender, and indeed starts to blur these indicators according to its own determinants of income and access. Nonetheless, these factors do still strongly interrelate with pre-existing and long-standing mechanisms of stratification. Consumption in this sense, then, neither overrides nor succumbs to historical precedents in inequality.

Third, and perhaps most profoundly, consumption activities, and particularly shopping, are also inherently contradictory in their nature and meaning for the population as a whole. Although it is sometimes claimed that some people hate shopping (for example, men) and others simply love it (for example, women) much depends on the type of shopping involved: shopping *around* for luxury items or shopping *for* staple goods (Radner 1995). However, what confounds this resolution is the sense in which the most rapturous form of shopping, for example clothes purchasing on unlimited credit in a shopping mall, may equally turn into the most tortuous as the shopper tires, the clothes don't fit, the car park is cramped and so on. Consequently, there is no unequivocal sense in which consumer society is either the hedonist's delight or the *bête noire* of the poor, but is often both and sometimes the opposite of what is expected by logic. As a result, consumption is often as deeply individual and personal as it is social and structured, yet these two perspectives often contradict.

There is also a wider knock-on effect in terms of the prevailing systems of consumption. For example, fashion, which is considered critically in Chapter 7, forms one of the most outmoded and exploitative modes of production that renders the consumer dissatisfied and disempowered, yet creates an unparalleled rate of consumption, enrapturing primarily, though not exclusively, female shoppers at every turn. None of these contradictions is easily resolved, if at all, and they are often reinforced through popular (the consumer as king, the consumer as victim) and academic (pleasure-seeking identities in the shopping mall, the oppression of poor and elderly people on trips to the supermarket) discourse alike. Consequently, it is to an unpacking of these perspectives that the rest of this work turns, suggesting some signposts in the maze of studies of consumption along the way, but no easy exit solutions.

Synopsis of scope and content

As stated previously, the primary focus of this text is sociological. Consequently, while questions of the history, psychology or economics of consumption are incorporated at various points in the analysis they are secondary to more *directly* social questions concerning the nature, meaning and development of consumer society. Although the study of consumption and consumer society is now overwhelmingly interdisciplinary, incorporating anthropology, economics, politics, psychology and cultural studies, differing foundations in perspectives are still easily identified. The key difficulty here, however, is that what constitutes the sociology of consumption remains open and loosely defined, and the recent conflation of the arts and social sciences under the auspices of cultural studies in particular has fuelled this sense of diffusion.

Controversy concerns the extent to which such openness is positive or negative in its effects. As I have mentioned already, a multidisciplinary study of consumer society is necessary to understand consumption as an equally multifaceted phenomenon. However, differences in the theoretical and even empirical foundations of perspectives and disciplines remain fundamental. For example, a psychoanalytically informed analysis of cultural texts is not easily equated, or even connected, with an orthodox Marxist economic history. Thus, although openness and interaction across disciplines is easily supported as important, this is not to be confused with an uncritical or unproblematized conflation of subjects and boundaries.

There are eight chapters which are ordered loosely chronologically in relation to the study of the past, present and future of consumer society. Consequently, it is possible to approach the chapters in a different order, yet most sense is made if they are read in order. In addition, although the text is pitched at a post-foundation level and assumes some grounding in social science or knowledge, it is not raised so high or controversially as to require strict adherence to an overriding argument for the reader to make sense of individual chapters. A few suggestions for further reading are given at the end of each chapter.

Chapter 1 is concerned primarily with the question of definition of consumption, its semantic associations and linguistic connections. In particular, contrasts in the implications of use of the terms 'consumer culture' versus 'consumer society' are illustrated as well as the overall discursive construction of consumption itself and its meanings and implications. In addition, various more classical perspectives on consumer society are evaluated critically, including those associated with Marxism, the Frankfurt School, Walter Benjamin, Georg Simmel and the work of Thorstein Veblen. Having problematized various definitions and interpretations, the second chapter takes a slightly more empirical slant on the development of consumer society, particularly in the light of its perceived connections to the wider formations of modernity, and includes a critique of some more contemporary theorists including Zygmunt Bauman and Pierre Bourdieu. Chapter 3 investigates the construction of the consumer *per se* and our contemporary interpretation of her or him as a rational actor through an analysis of marketing and advertising strategies. A consideration of the advertising and associations of the modern car provides a more empirically driven summary of these processes at the end of the chapter. The theme of the power, or not, of the modern consumer is taken up more explicitly in Chapter 4, which looks at questions of the social policy and social divisions surrounding the differing positions of various consumer groups in contemporary Western society. More particularly, the chapter has a dual focus on the constraints placed on consumers on the one hand, and their active resistance to, and reconstruction of, their positions on the other. This theme also underpins the analysis of shopping which forms the foundation for Chapter 5 and a wider consideration of the inequalities and contradictions of consumer society. The politics of consumer society are addressed most directly in Chapter 6, which considers consumption's potential to empower or oppress various groups according to class, gender, race and sexuality. This theme of the politics of identity starts to open up a more speculative question concerning the direction or importance of consumption and its implications for society more widely. Chapter 7 acts as a case study for a wider analysis of consumption's more contemporary importance and implications, through a consideration of fashion as the epitome of some of its most important elements. This also informs and underpins the final chapter, which raises the spectre of consumption's conflation, or not, with wider questions of postmodernity. This simultaneously opens up an analysis of its future potential and limitations, and a wider assessment of its politics. The conclusion provides a summary of key themes and arguments of the text and attempts to provide some critique of the current position of the sociology of consumer society. It also returns to the underlying sense of contradiction that underpins equally our practice and understanding of consumption alike.

1
CONCEPTIONS OF CONSUMPTION

What is consumer society? We commonly talk of consumer rights, the expansion of consumerism, consumer culture and even the consumerist revolution, and yet no concrete definition of consumption seems to exist. More importantly, are we perhaps not even talking about the same thing when using such terms? Does consumption actually have the same meaning as consumerism and is consumer society easily equated with consumer culture? These are some of the questions I hope to explore and unpack in this first chapter, for it is of primary importance to clarify exactly what is at stake when talking about consumer society. It is also necessary to analyse some of the earliest scholarly work on consumption in order to understand the origins of some of these more contemporary concerns and, perhaps more importantly, to realize that consumer society is not necessarily as new as it sometimes seems in the popular consciousness.

Consequently, there are three sections to this discussion: first, a consideration of what consumption means semantically and, importantly, perhaps implies more discursively; second, a critical discussion of some of the earliest attempts to document the rise of a consumer society or to theorize the social practices of consumption; and third, an initial development of the perspective used in succeeding chapters and, more particularly, some support for using the term consumer society rather than consumer culture.

Questioning consumption: meanings, myths and implications

> In all of its meanings, consumerism is neither ethically nor politically neutral, and is therefore a terrain to be contested and argued over.
>
> (Gabriel and Lang 1995: 9)

At its simplest, consumption refers to the process of consuming or, more simply still, using up, devouring or even eating. There are strong associations with food and drink and with love or passion. It is common, for example, to talk of consumption in terms of desire and there are many analogies made with sexuality: 'look at that *tart*', '*feast* your eyes on that', 'do you fancy some *crumpet*', 'he's a real *dish*', 'I could *eat* him', and so on. In this sense, there is an immediate connection with the more psychoanalytic dimensions of the question of consumption and a direct parallel between desiring goods or services and wanting sexual gratification. It is, then, perhaps no quirk or contradiction that there is such a strong connection between eating and drinking and sex, or that a date for dinner is often seen as a recipe for the food of love. Furthermore, the recent pop psychology concerning shopping, women and sex conflates notions of consumption, shopping and sexuality even more strongly.

However, this concept of consumption also has far more negative connotations, for to consume also means to waste or to destroy. The same sexual association, interestingly, still applies here, as passion is seen to consume the person, override their defences and render them helpless. There is again a strong sense of connection with questions of consumption where the hapless consumer is seen to fall victim to the lures and allure of the advertising, the packaging, or the seduction routine of the sexy salesperson. More importantly, this more destructive or manipulative sense of consumption taps into wider environmental concerns and the politics of the Western world's exploitation of the developing world's natural and human resources alike. The case of the fashion industry is a classic example of all of these elements, where the consumer is apparently prone to fickle fads and trends and yet is seen equally as an active and desiring agent the industry can never outwit; and high prices are seen to reap enormous profits for Western company moguls who ruthlessly exploit manufacturers and Third World workers.

What is clear immediately is that consumption semantically has much connection with consumption as practice and that, perhaps more importantly, its meaning is neither singular nor simple but multiple and complex. What is also perhaps less explicitly apparent is that its meaning is also sexualized, gendered and racialized: for the consumer, whether active or passive, desirous or victim, is often perceived as female, whereas the exploiting company managers and sexy sales representatives are stereotypically seen as male and, in all cases, dominant white culture is seen to plunder oppressed Asian, African-Caribbean and Oriental culture. This is one aspect of the politics of consumer society, and these are points I wish to explore more fully in Chapter 6.

Some of this complexity of meaning and contradiction of implication concerning consumption are more easily explained or explored when considering perceptions of consumers themselves rather than consumption practices or consumer society. As I have outlined, these meanings and implications are multiple and diverse, almost infinite. Part of this is due to the very wide use of terms relating to consumption in vastly varying contexts, from common parlance and the mass media to cultural studies and academia. Yet, in all cases, what is often lacking is any clear definition of what is actually referred to or the terms that are used. As a consequence, it is one of my primary intentions in this first section not so much to define consumption as to unpack its meanings or associations and, more importantly, to point out that these multiple and complex uses of sometimes differing concepts do in fact simultaneously construct and reflect the reality of consumer society as equally plural and contradictory in concept and in practice.

Gabriel and Lang in *The Unmanageable Consumer* provide an interesting and unusual explication of the various discourses surrounding consumption, amounting to no fewer than nine different notions of the consumer, including definitions centred on choosing, communicating, exploring, and more politicized concepts of consumer hedonism, activism or citizenship (Gabriel and Lang 1995). Although ultimately limitless, some of these notions overlap. For example, consumer activism and consumer rebellion are often variants on a theme of consumer *power*, which contrasts sharply with the notion of consumers as victims (the consumer as power*less*). Similarly, consumers seen as choosing, exploring and identity-seeking are often variants on a theme of consumer *pleasure*. As a result, I will propose that there are, most fundamentally, five dimensions to the meanings or implications of modern consumption which I wish to explore further in relation to contemporary perceptions of the consumer. More importantly, I will then seek to illustrate how these different representations of the consumer relate to varying views of consumer society and, in fact, lead to the use of different terms to depict its practice or theorize its development.

The first of these perceptions of the consumer is that of the consumer as *king* or as some kind of victor over primarily the producer and retailer alike. It is now common to talk of increased consumer power or consumer rights, where the consumer is no longer the dupe or passive victim he or she once was but the determined shopper wearing out shoe leather in search of price cuts, making critical comparisons or endlessly complaining, returning items and writing letters. This is the perception of the consumer promoted through the mass media in endless consumer affairs programmes and magazines, which is, not surprisingly, gaining much support from struggling retailers and manufacturers. More importantly, it taps into a wider and more political ideology of economic utilitarianism: the consumer as an unconstrained rational actor seeking to maximize positive personal outcomes. Consequently, it is also a view that has found political sympathies with the New Right of the 1980s in the UK and USA particularly, and other varying forms of neo-liberal individualism (see also Chapter 4).

This first view of the consumer contrasts sharply with, and conceptually mutually depends on, the second view of the consumer as *victim*. There are essentially two dimensions to this perception. First, that the consumer falls helplessly out of control or is duped and seduced through processes of advertising, selling and promotion into spending money they don't have on things they don't need – or, more simply, the consumer is seduced into making the wrong decision for them, which is the right decision for the all-too-victorious salesperson or retailer. Second, there is the conception that we are all somehow increasingly sucked into the world of consumption, whether it is appropriate for us or not, and where the poor, in particular, come off worst. This is the view in the world of social policy, in welfare agencies and the Citizens' Advice Bureau in the UK, although moral boundaries are often added, as the debt-ridden and overspending consumer is often seen either as some kind of helpless fool who needs to 'get a grip' or as a hapless victim of circumstance, particularly unemployment (Cahill 1994). At the centre of this, not surprisingly, are concerns relating to access and credit. Allied to these perceptions is the shopaholic, or kleptomaniac, increasingly a contemporary pariah who just can't help (her)self from helping (her)self, for the kleptomaniac is almost never perceived as male.

This more moral dimension to contemporary perceptions of the consumer taps into the third area of increasing concern, which sees the consumer as *criminal*. The helpless kleptomaniac partly comes into this, but it is the perception of the professional shoplifter who fulfils it completely: the consumer who no camera can stop or who is known by the police to make endless thefts in pursuit of self-profit, yet who, through some legal loophole, still roams town centres like a particularly rapacious vulture. This is the perception that comes from shopkeepers and security companies alike and that seeks to form moral campaigns where the interests of the community are at stake in the overestimated costs passed on to the morally correct consumer in the form of rising prices; while the wider community's net curtains are kept twitching in neighbourhood watch schemes.

A fourth arena of perception contrasts sharply yet also links with the third: that of the consumer as *anti-consumer* promoted in environmentalism and linked to wider social concerns. Here the consumer tries to undermine consumer society through the practice of anti-consumption in campaigns, demonstrations and boycotts. The clear paradox here is that such consumers equally endorse other products, particularly those related to environmental, ecological or health-related concerns, stocking up on water purifiers, health foods and Body Shop products for example. An important point here is that consumption becomes all-encompassing: how does one partake in Western society or even survive without consuming its products? These are questions that partly inform my discussion of social policy and social divisions in Chapter 4.

In a strange way this question also underlies the fifth and final perception of the consumer as *voyeur* or pleasure-seeker – the enraptured window shopper. Not surprisingly, this is the perception of the consumer that finds favour and promotion in cultural studies and psychoanalysis, where people are seen to drift through stores and shopping malls in semiconscious and dream-like states. This is also, then, the most academically driven of the five perceptions of the consumer I have outlined, relying most strongly on a series of highly articulated concepts of audience reception and psychology. It is also strongly tied to arguments surrounding consumption's role in the formation of identities, a contested issue explored further in later chapters.

All of these perceptions of the consumer are, to some extent at least, stereotypes, yet like all such presentations they contain a grain of truth and they are all valid to varying degrees. Admittedly, the difficulty here is that some are seen as more valid than others and each would, and does, demonstrate its own importance over and against the rest. Certain factors still emerge as important in relation to these perceptions of the consumer as a whole, however. First, there is clearly a sense in which the consumer is increasingly seen to exist at the level of discourse as opposed to practice, constructed across a contested terrain of competing definitions, while consumption as practice increasingly takes up part of all our daily lives. In this sense, we are all simultaneously consumers and not consumers. None of us completely fulfils the outlined perceptions of the consumer, as we are all far more complex and, in particular, we are workers or producers too. Yet equally, consumption activities increasingly take up some part of all our daily lives, from leisure activities to traipsing around shops.

The second, and important, point, which slashes through this discussion, is that we do not consume so equally, or even very similarly, for what undercuts contemporary perceptions of the consumer is a sense of social, economic and even political division and, most importantly, a question of power. The consumer may well fulfil the criteria of a king if he or she is affluent, mobile, literate and living in Western society; and, similarly, the consumer may well look like a victim if he or she is unemployed or mercilessly exploited in the Third World.

Third, an added difficulty is that perceptions of the consumer as voyeur, pleasure-seeker, criminal or even as anti-consumer are less easily classified according to demography or culture and this raises additional questions of the wider connections of consumption to more historical developments in meaning and, most importantly, morality. To make these points more clearly, it is worth discussing conceptions of consumer society as opposed to perceptions of the consumer, although these are, of course, interlinked. A further issue concerns all of these discursive constructions of the consumer as a whole. What is raised here is the increasing sense of contradiction that exists across all of these definitions of consumption. Consumers cannot truly be rebels *and* victims or rationalizing bargain-hunters *and* dreaming pleasure-seekers – or can they?

One perspective on this conundrum is proposed by Gabriel and Lang who, following their detailed unpacking of conceptions of the consumer outlined earlier, argue that this plethora of media-driven and academically produced discourses is, in its entirety, increasingly divorced from the reality of consumers' own experiences, which are often much more mundane and clearly structured (Gabriel and Lang 1995). A second dimension to this is the question of social divisions: consumers are kings or victims precisely according to their economic and demographic status. The difficulty in either case, though, is that discourse and practice do, to some extent at least, interlink, so the poor may well try to access what limited pleasures they can in consumption, if only in terms of treats at the local supermarket, while the affluent may feel so pressured to keep up appearances of status that their apparent power as consumers is effectively undermined. It is at this point, then, that wider notions of consumption as empowering or exploiting, active or structured, open or closed are apparent and important and which, in turn, tap into notions of consumer society.

Consumer society has, historically, been considered in essentially three interlinked lights. First, consumer society is often seen as capitalist society dependent on the development of industrial capitalism for its expansion if not its making. This is, of course, the perspective most strongly associated with Marxism and variations on more structurally oriented or class-related theory. It promotes a perception of consumer society as profit driven and ultimately exploitative in maintaining social divisions or in providing the ideological justification for mass production and the exploitation of the workforce attendant with it. Such an approach not surprisingly tends to use the term consumption as the conceptual coin's flipside to production.

Second, consumer society is sometimes seen as rational or utilitarian society made up simply of consumers practising consumerism. This is essentially the view of consumer society that comes through economic theory and, more particularly, marketing and advertising. It promulgates the notion of the consumer as an unfettered rational actor and contrasts sharply with the former perspective in its comparative underplaying of wider social, economic or political factors – at least in terms of their importance in shaping and constraining consumer practice if not in terms of their provision of a launchpad for consumer society. It is important to point out here, then, that in either case we are talking about industrial capitalist society.

A third perspective on consumer society, though, stresses its more recent or contemporary, postwar or even post-industrial importance, seeing it as symbolic society or as a society of signs and meanings, stressing the significance of identity, psychology and the unconscious. This is, not surprisingly, the perspective associated with cultural critics who talk of consumer style cultures or some more extreme forms of the theory of postmodernity. The implications in either instance are a question of emphasis on historical and economic developments or social structures in the first case, on consumers themselves in the second, or on the contemporary practice of aesthetic style-setting in the third. In addition, although the validity of these perspectives individually may vary in differing contexts, none is essentially of truly greater significance than the other and consumer society is most fully understood and explained as a sometimes contradictory mixture of all three elements. The importance of this will become clearer through my discussion and critique of early perspectives on the development of consumer society, and more fully through my discussion of more contemporary theory in Chapter 2.

From production to conspicuous consumption: early perspectives on the development of consumer society

Prior to a discussion of early perspectives on the importance of consumption, it is worth pointing out that what these viewpoints have in common is a concern with late-nineteenth and early-twentieth-century social and political transformations in the wake of economic expansion and the rise of industrial capitalism, thus tapping into a more structurally driven set of concerns, sometimes contrasting sharply with more contemporary perspectives on matters of style, taste and consumption practices. This is most simply explained as a result of contextual considerations – the works are in essence products of their time and place. What is perhaps interesting, though, is that the seeds of many more contemporary, and more culturally driven, perspectives are also sown in these analyses and this is a point I shall explore more fully in the final section of this chapter. As a result, this section is organized crudely according to a documentation of the increasing attention to more cultural and stylistic questions in the wake of a re-evaluation of more orthodox Marxism. More specifically, I will then examine the work of a series of highly influential scholars in the formation of early perspectives on consumption and consumer society, including Benjamin, Simmel and Veblen. It is necessary to start with Marxism as perhaps the most fundamental, and indeed earliest, perspective on the development of consumer society.

Consumption as production: early Marxist perspectives on consumer society

A commodity is therefore a mysterious thing, simply because in it the social character of men's labour appears to them as an objective character stamped upon the product of that labour; because the relation of the producers to the sum total of their own labour is presented to them as a social relation, existing not between themselves, but between the products of their labour.

(Marx 1975: 77)

Despite the recent plethora of works on consumption, Marxist analyses of consumer society have, with some exceptions, tended to stand in the shadow of more directly postmodern perspectives. Don Slater's return to the fundamental themes and concepts of modernity in relation to consumer culture, Daniel Miller's attempt to reapply the Hegelian theory of objectification to what he terms 'material culture', and Martyn Lee's resurrection of the commodity form as the linchpin of contemporary cultural politics represent recent and varied attempts to reincorporate Marxism into the theory of consumer society (Miller 1987; Lee 1993; Slater 1997b).

Such perspectives have developed against a mostly poststructurally influenced questioning of the extent to which there is sufficient attention to consumption in Marxism to warrant its consideration as a perspective or theory as opposed to a set of minor addenda. As is well known, Marxist theory, and particularly its more orthodox variations, has commonly come in for criticism for its economic determinism and, in particular, a simplistic underplaying of the complex importance of individual and group variations. More importantly, and stereotypically perhaps, the question is also sometimes raised as to Marxism's neglect of more social and cultural factors in favour of economic and political polemics and, in particular, this includes an apparent underplaying of the role of consumption as opposed to production.

It is clear from Marx's own work on consumption that he saw it as fundamentally inseparable from production. In addition, the study of consumption is, as it were, subsumed within a wider analysis of production. This presents us with something of a conundrum for if, as Marx himself once wrote, 'without consumption there can be no production', why has the consumption side of the equation remained historically so neglected in Marxism relative to the study of production (Marx 1975: 361)? Part of the explanation for this lies in the conception of consumption itself, which is, for the most part, perceived solely in terms of commodities as part of a wider working out of a theory of alienation. Consequently, this tends to leave out the question of services or other less easily or directly commodified forms of consumption, and it also elides discussion of the personal and social significance of consumer *practices*. The Marxist defence of this position is twofold: first, that attention to more individual and varied forms of consumer practice tends to miss its wider and general significance; and second, that the primary importance of consumption is precisely its relationship to production.

Theorists are therefore divided as to whether the study of consumption lies outside the confines of more orthodox Marxism or, alternatively, whether its frameworks can still provide the potential for its incorporation.

In addition, certain concepts do stand out as of importance for this discussion and start to provide an insight into what constitutes a more orthodox Marxist perspective on consumption. More contemporary and neo-Marxist perspectives are considered critically in Chapter 2.

The starting point for a Marxist analysis of consumption is the theory of value, which is itself part of a wider analysis of alienation. For Marx there were essentially two dimensions to this question: first, a notion of use value, which is most simply explained in terms of functions of commodities; and second, a more complex concept of exchange value, which sees commodities themselves as products of monetary exchange and, more significantly, sees the worker as caught up in a process of commodified exchange of his or her own worth in terms of production. To put it more simply, the use value of a washing machine is that it cleans clothes; its exchange value relates to its cost for the worker to produce it versus its cost to purchase. Importantly, then, commodification forms one key mechanism in the creation of alienation. The worker is alienated from his or her own labour which is itself bought and sold and further separated from the means of production and the commodities that he or she produces. All of this stands in sharp contrast to the rather romantic ideal of the pre-industrial agricultural or cottage worker who produced his own goods to his own ends.

In addition, a further twist of the knife here is that consumption is also seen to effectively sell, at a price, the satisfactions the worker lost in the first place. Consumption is therefore perceived as primarily palliative in relation to production, offering rewards for hard labour. The additional problematic here is that it is precisely the modern form of the worker's labour that takes away the rewards and, in doing so, produces an endless series of insatiable needs. It is indeed the issue that although consumption *seems* to provide the solution to the worker's dissatisfactions, it does not in reality. The difficulty, then, is that the worker, caught up in multiple processes of false consciousness, cannot see this at all, or only partially, for himself or herself.

More importantly, this then informs a wider Marxist analysis of the concept and process of commodity fetishism. There is some confusion here, though, as commodity fetishism does not, as some people might think, apply simply to the implications of commodities. Rather, it applies to social relations and, in particular, how these relations are hidden via the values of commodification in order to maintain practices of exploitation, particularly in relation to production. Interestingly, though, this does still raise the question of the importance of monetary reward in maintaining power relations. The key issue, then, is that consumption provides the motivation for the otherwise immiserated and exploited worker.

What is often more contentious is the question of whether this then means that consumption is a form of false consciousness. For Slater, Marx's consumer culture becomes doubly false as a misrecognition of commodities and their meanings *and* a misrepresentation of them as means of satisfaction

(Slater 1997b). For example, a colour television is not only misrecognized as the product of exploitative relations under capitalism, it is also deemed to give status and satisfactions it does not itself have. This tends to leave orthodox Marxism at least open to criticism for constructing workers as passive victims. However, on closer investigation, the connections of consumption and proletariat politicization are significantly more complex.

More importantly, it also has other connections with the question of consumption, as one clear aspect to the significance of crude cash nexus is not simply that it renders the worker worthless in other than monetary terms, thus fuelling a sense of alienation, but that it also encourages him or her to perceive themselves and others in terms of monetary value and promotes a perception of the importance of money *per se* and, in particular, its value in terms of commodities or consumption practices. This is a point taken up by Simmel, whose work I will consider shortly.

A second, and allied, concept to that of commodity fetishism is that of reification, more commonly linked to the work of Lukács, where social relations are themselves also increasingly commodified (Lukács 1923). The clear difficulty here is the application of such concepts to *all* relations in capitalist society – such as those which are neither exploitative, such as those within the same class – or relations which are not simply centred around the means or mode of production, although an extreme Marxist perspective would assert that such 'uncontaminated' relations do not exist outside the forces of production. The role of women in *re*production is also not included here. In conclusion, then, the prognosis of Marxism for consumption is decidedly gloomy: 'They may be poor or rich, but their capacity to transform the world has become a mere means to the end of buying goods; whereas their own needs and desires, the basis of their relation to the world, have become a mere condition for the making of profit' (Slater 1997b: 115).

Perhaps the most important point to come from such a discussion, however, is the realization that consumption in all likelihood is neither the politically neutral nor separate entity divorced from production that it may sometimes seem, and it is this more ideological dimension to consumption that underpins the Frankfurt School's perspective on its development.

Control culture: consumption and the Frankfurt School

If Marx was, in a sense, pessimistic concerning the development of consumer culture, this reaches a near nihilistic nadir under the auspices of the critical theory developed by the Frankfurt School. Theodor Adorno, Max Horkheimer and Herbert Marcuse, to name only some, were highly critical of more traditional Marxism's lack of attention to the question of ideology and, more critically, cultural practice. At the centre of Adorno and Horkheimer's concerns was the rise of the arts, the mass media and the leisure industries, all of which were seen to put nails in the coffin of the exploited worker or consumer as: 'The culture industry perpetually cheats its consumers of what it perpetually promises' (Adorno and Horkheimer 1993: 38).

This concern essentially arose out of a wider critique of the Enlightenment as part of an overall project in critical theory and praxis: 'The point is rather that the Enlightenment must examine itself, if men are not to be wholly betrayed' (Adorno and Horkheimer 1973: xv). Consumption, particularly in its mass form, thus becomes a form of propaganda and a linchpin in the ideological maintenance of capitalist society. Film, radio and television, along with the overall rise of commodified culture, effectively act as a form of social control in ameliorating the lives of tired and exploited workers and in constructing them as consumers of endless commodities, which are produced in increasingly diverse forms as technological expansion. Therefore, the modern consumer not only wants a television set to watch television, he or she wants one with Nicam stereo or a further small one for the bedroom, or another one to match the kitchen, and so on. For Adorno and Horkheimer, this sense of difference is simply false as it masks a more fundamental principle of similarity in the maintenance of capitalist expansion. Consequently, the clear difficulty here, and the cause of much contemporary complaint, is the tendency towards a patronizing view of consumers as cultural dopes who either cannot or will not see what is 'really' happening to them.

Underlying the development of this nihilistic vision was the welding of the newly growing interest in psychoanalysis to a Marxist sense of political economics. Marcuse's work in particular took Freud's concept of psychic repression and applied a politico-economic dimension to it in an almost apocalyptic perception of complete capitalist control or exploitation of the working man whose libidinal energies become channelled into work and production (Marcuse 1964). The key principle was the near-dialectical relationship of what Marcuse called 'the reality principle' to 'the pleasure principle' which, put simply, applied to the management (the ego) of libidinous pleasure (the id) and the conscious attempt to defer gratification (the super-ego). The application of this perspective to consumption is aptly summarized by Slater, who states: 'both desire and satisfaction are allowed only to take their most limited and repressive forms: the lust for commodities, satisfaction *within* the system' (Slater 1997b: 125). Interestingly, galling as Marcuse's sense of doom and gloom may be, his observations of modern masculinity foreshadowed much of the later discussion of male sexuality as goal-oriented, self-destructive and riven with values of productive performance (see, for example, Tolson 1977; Hoch 1979; Reynaud 1983).

Although this vision has been criticized widely since for its near-Armageddon killing of, if not simply undermining of, the human subject, a couple of wider points still stand out as of importance. First, the definition of consumption is widened to include the leisure industries and the consumption of the arts and sport, a definition which still holds today; and second, the doomed sense of the consumer as a passive dupe or victim of wider economic and political processes raises the more nefarious side to consumption perhaps underplayed in many earlier and later analyses alike, although constantly fuelled in discourses of consumers as victims. Interestingly, comparisons with various postmodern perspectives, and more specifically Baudrillard's conception of the implosive 'death of the social', stand out somewhat ironically as particularly important (see Chapter 8). In particular, Adorno and Horkheimer's damnation of style as obedience to the social hierarchy almost exactly parallels Baudrillard's condemnation of the system of objects (Adorno and Horkheimer 1973; Baudrillard 1988). In either case, the sense of differences between commodities is seen to be illusory. However, whereas for the Frankfurt School this leads to social control; for Baudrillard it simply becomes a black hole. This sense of movement towards a more unconscious form of understanding in relation to consumption leads us directly to the work of Walter Benjamin, for whom the challenge was precisely to 'wake up' . . .

Waking up consumer culture: the work of Walter Benjamin

Many of Walter Benjamin's ideas, and in particular his overall methodology, have tended to foreshadow much of the later and more culturally driven work that has thrown light on consumer society since. Hannah Arendt, who edited the highly influential collection of Benjamin's work, *Illuminations*, notes that his work is particularly difficult to classify, often crossing differing disciplines such as history, philosophy and art criticism (Arendt 1973). More importantly, perhaps, his relationship to the Frankfurt School, and particularly his more personal relationships with some of its proponents including Adorno and Horkheimer, were somewhat uneasy and he was in particular criticized by them for insufficient engagement with the more material dialectics of Marxism. This tends to render Benjamin's ideas in relation to consumption simultaneously fascinating and infuriatingly difficult to interpret. It is, in effect, as if the so-called 'lack' of a dialectic actually exists within the work itself.

Of primary relevance to the analysis of consumption is his study of arcade cultures, documented in Susan Buck-Morss' rigorously scholarly *The Dialectics Of Seeing*, which is built around Benjamin's *Passagen-Werk* or Arcades Project (Buck-Morss 1989). Buck-Morss adds an important dimension of her own to his work, which is that of reflexivity, as she is almost excruciatingly aware of her own influence in the reconstruction of his work and asserts with some force that the Arcades Project as a cohesive study does not, in a sense, even exist. What does exist is an immense series of unfinished yet systematically filed notes and reference points accumulated over a period of several decades, starting in the 1920s and ending abruptly with Benjamin's suicide in

1940. The Arcades Project, such as it is, acts effectively and simultaneously as a visual ethnography of nineteenth-century arcade culture, particularly in Paris, and as a far wider materialist philosophy of history, as Buck-Morss illustrates:

> The Passagen-Werk was to be a 'materialist philosophy of history,' constructed with 'the utmost concreteness' out of the historical material itself, the outdated remains of those nineteenth-century buildings, technologies, and commodities that were the precursors of his own era.
>
> (Buck-Morss 1989: 3)

As a cultural and artistic critic, in particular, Benjamin illustrated the importance of nineteenth-century arcade cultures as dream worlds in which the rising ranks of middle-class women in particular could not only shop, as much as socially engage with the ethos of visual consumption. The profound and important point that emerges immediately from his discussion is a strong sense of the aesthetic significance of department stores, arcades, shopping practices and consumers alike. Most importantly, it was the artistic links with surrealism and the overall aestheticization of city life that informed his analysis, and the European influence of style cultures centred on arcade and boulevard developments is clearly apparent.

This went in tandem with Benjamin's wider thesis of historical materialism and his critique of the Enlightenment, and it is at this point that differences with the Frankfurt School are particularly clear. Whilst for Adorno and Horkheimer the Enlightenment unequivocally destroyed the pre-industrial dream of contentment explicated in the work of Marx outlined earlier, for Benjamin it created in consumption its own dream from which the modern world needed to 'wake up': 'The covered shopping arcades of the nineteenth century were Benjamin's central image because they were the precise material replica of the internal consciousness, or rather, the *un*conscious of the dreaming collective' (Buck-Morss 1989: 39, original emphasis).

The political task, then, for Benjamin was to increasingly connect with this unconscious potential. This leads Buck-Morss into a highly elaborate schema of Benjamin's philosophy around the commodity, which is seen to be situated between two axioms of waking and dreaming, and petrified (or fossilized) and transitory nature. This then informs a dialectic of seeing located in the philosophy of history, where the role of myth and the unconscious are critical. The dialectic of seeing is precisely that we are never quite fully aware nor totally blind but held between the two; while the world we perceive is equally neither truly known nor unknowable, past or present, alive or dead.

This is clearly difficult to grasp and one good example that repeatedly springs to mind is that of the *Titanic*, also temporally not irrelevant to Benjamin's work, which now exists as a monumental ruin at the bottom of the sea yet is constantly 'brought to life' by myth, history and literature. James Cameron's recent film, which itself interestingly overlaps layers of reconstructed Hollywood glamour with documentary footage of the wreckage, thus welding and unifying the ship's demise into its mythic status as the symbolic hubris of twentieth-century technological and economic progress, illustrates this well. The overlaying of the documentary footage of the wreckage with a detailed reconstruction of the ship's original image shows both Benjamin's method as it were 'in action' and the importance of myth itself to our understanding of consumption.

In light of all this, Benjamin's influence across philosophy, literature, history, cultural studies and, most recently, consumer culture is easy to see. What is more difficult to understand is the sense in which his engagement with more Marxist questions of political resistance, dialectical materialism and human alienation has equally been lost in a sea of primarily more poststructural analyses of shopping malls and department stores (Miller 1997). Of particular significance is the role of the stroller or *flâneur*, whose purpose in window shopping and displaying stylish purchases, including clothing, was nothing more than to see and to be seen. The *flâneur* illustrates the intense processes of voyeurism and exhibitionism that for Benjamin characterized many of the major cities at the turn of the century.

On a slightly more contentious note, his paralleling of the processes of shopping with the equally highly visual or even surreal world of the carnival has since stood out as particularly important. Not surprisingly, it is at this point that links to postmodernism are increasingly apparent and indeed taken up in many more contemporary analyses of shopping malls (Shields 1992). Benjamin himself, however, was highly critical of the simple equation of consumption with pleasure, or the notion of consumer sovereignty, to which I will return in later chapters. Similarly, the *flâneur* is *not* simply seen as some kind of pleasure-seeking hedonist, but rather as an empty-headed, disenchanted and cynical consumer in vain search of satisfaction. Nevertheless, it is Benjamin's concern with the visual, symbolic and near unconscious which has been most influential here, and their links to the study of the modern metropolis open up wider questions of the connections of the commodity, consumption and the city considered in more detail by Simmel.

Objects and subjects: Simmel and consumption

The German philosopher Georg Simmel is most widely and famously influential for his important work in developing a more phenomenological approach to the social world and sociology, in contrast to the positivistic influence of Auguste Comte and Emile Durkheim. Put simply, this means that for Simmel the world, and our understanding of it, is as subjective as it is objective. Moreover, this is fundamental, for the most important element of Simmel's analysis of consumption, which is also present in the work of Marx, the Frankfurt School and Walter Benjamin, is an analysis of the relationship between the human subject and the object world of the commodity.

What all these theorists have in common is the view that the rise of industrial capitalism leads to an increasing objectification, and simultaneously commodification, of human life which renders the relationship between the subjective and objective worlds more problematic. In Marxist terms this becomes alienation, for the Frankfurt School it creates false consciousness, and for Benjamin it becomes a state of semi-consciousness. For Simmel, it becomes a social and psychological struggle and consumption becomes a primary site through which that struggle is played out.

There are, in content terms, three dimensions to Simmel's work on consumption, which are his analysis of metropolitan life, his philosophy of money and his study of fashion (Simmel 1904, 1950, 1990). These elements have now been brought together very usefully by David Frisby and Mike Featherstone (Frisby and Featherstone 1997). They are also strongly interlinked in the analysis of the subject–object relationship, which is perhaps most explicit in Simmel's analysis of the psychology of the city: 'The deepest problems of modern life derive from the claim of the individual to preserve the autonomy and individuality of his existence in the face of overwhelming social forces, of historical heritage, of external culture, and of the technique of life' (Frisby and Featherstone 1997: 174/5).

For Simmel, therefore, space and place become as much psychological realities as they are objective worlds. However, the rise of metropolitan life is seen to affect this psychology fundamentally, at once creating enormous opportunity for stimulation through its very complexity and differentiation while putting the modern mind under enormous duress to process more and more information. This becomes a dual situation of mental overload amounting to a modern form of neurosis, which is then offset by an increasingly calculating or distanced attitude that reaches its nadir in the role of blasé. The parallel here with both Benjamin's bored *flâneur* and Weber's iron cage of rationality is clear but, by the same token, not as certain in its outcome. Consequently, Simmel writes: 'A life in boundless pursuit of pleasure makes one blasé because it agitates the nerves to their strongest reactivity for such a long time that they finally cease to react at all' (Frisby and Featherstone 1997: 178). However, at the same time: 'It is the function of the metropolis to provide the arena for this struggle and its reconciliation' (Frisby and Featherstone 1997: 185).

Much the same sense of ambivalence underlies Simmel's analysis of the philosophy, and indeed the psychology, of money. For Simmel the key value of money is precisely that it is valued in itself. In an analysis not dissimilar to the Marxist one of commodity fetishism, this is seen to elevate money above the value of both the object or commodity, which is now valued in purely monetary terms; and the human subject, who is seen to increasingly engage in an impersonal and objective series of monetary interactions which reach their ultimate degradation in the form of prostitution. In addition though, and less negatively, money is also seen to enhance independence and freedom in precisely the same separation of subject from object: 'In this way, money produces both a previously unknown impersonality in all economic ownership and an equally enhanced independence and autonomy of the personality, and the relationship of personality to associations develops similarly to that with property' (Frisby and Featherstone 1997: 244).

The reconciliation to this situation forms a near Durkheimian sense of organic solidarity, as modern monetary life is seen to foster a mutually supportive interdependence. In relation to consumption, this also forms the basis of the modern exhibition, the 'shop window quality' of which forms a dazzling diversity of commodities which are in essence simultaneously produced under a single mechanism of industrial capitalism (Frisby and Featherstone 1997: 257).

This tension of the individual and the social is similarly held together in Simmel's analysis of fashion (Simmel 1904). Commonly known as the trickle-down theory, it starts to tentatively set up the parameters for much succeeding discussion of style in consumer society. As a theoretically driven article centred on his perception of how styles and particularly fashions mutate across class divisions, it produced a sense of consumption that was at once more dynamic and also fixed. At the centre of this are the two key concepts of the processes of 'imitation' and 'differentiation'. To explain it very simply, the lower or working classes try to imitate the higher or middle classes, who in turn try to differentiate themselves from the lower or working classes. Moreover, imitation acts as a form of social adaptation or conforming, whereas differentiation acts as a form of individual separation or distinction.

It is a very interactive and dynamic model that sets up a paper chase of endless style-centred circles, and yet it is also effectively very static, in creating a near-functionalist sense of convenience. At the centre of criticisms of this perspective is the clear point that styles may equally trickle up as well as down and that lower- or working-class groups may in particular seek to react against rather than dumbly follow dominant patterns primarily through more subcultural styles and consumption practices. Of wider importance to consumption here, however, although rather implicit in his analysis, is the sense of struggle that takes place concerning definitions of 'in' and 'out' or style correctness, and it is not a long step until we find ourselves on the contested terrain of more contemporary work. One parallel is the work of Pierre Bourdieu in *Distinction*, which is considered critically in Chapter 2 (Bourdieu 1984).

An interesting example of the more contemporary applications of Simmel's ideas on fashion is also given in Grant McCracken's *Culture and Consumption* (McCracken 1988). McCracken criticizes the simplicity of Simmel's analysis and, in particular, asserts that the processes of imitation and differentiation apply to more groups across more factors of stratification, including gender. In considering the style cultures of the 1980s, he sees women's executive dress, as exemplified in the heavily shoulder-padded suit, as imitating that of men's more traditional work attire; while men's increasingly 'heroic look' of double-breasted power suits, braces and pin-stripes is perceived to form an attempt at differentiation. The conservative, if not reactionary, sexual politics of such an analysis are clear, and this is a point I contest in Chapter 7. However, Simmel's analysis has still seemingly influenced many later studies of the interaction of subcultures and dominant culture (see, for example, Hebdige 1979; McRobbie 1989; Polhemus 1994). Moreover, Simmel's attention to the more conspicuously style-driven aspects of consumption also, somewhat indirectly, informs one of the most famous early studies of consumer society.

Conspicuous consumption and the work of Thorstein Veblen

Veblen has often been heralded, perhaps somewhat notoriously now, as a pioneer of the study of consumption. His primary work in relation to con-sumerism, *The Theory of the Leisure Class*, was partly a critique of late-nineteenth-century North American middle-class society and partly a development of an economic history (Veblen [1899]1934). It is worth noting that Veblen was never truly allied to any tradition of social science or social theory and was, in essence, a fairly prolific social critic. His comments on the middle classes have none the less since come under very serious scrutiny, not least due to his development of the term conspicuous consumption, which has passed into common parlance.

Put simply, the perspective he developed states that, as society increases in affluence, through the advance of factors such as technology and mass pro-duction, there develops a middle or leisure class defined and maintained according to its consumerist as opposed to, or as well as, productive prac-tices. Interestingly, it is the concept of leisure, and its connections to con-sumption practices, which is at the crux of his analysis. As Western society increases its wealth as a result of capitalist expansion and mass production, he asserts, so leisure comes to form a signifier of pecuniary status. His thesis starts with raising a question of definition concerning the leisure class, which he defines as follows: 'The leisure class as a whole comprises the noble and the priestly classes, together with much of their retinue. The occupations of the class are correspondingly diversified; but they have the common econ-omic characteristic of being non-industrial' (Veblen [1899]1934: 2).

Consequently, leisure itself is quite precisely defined as non-productive work, which also invokes its connection with consumption. What is per-haps less clear is the extent to which the leisure class, and its attendant con-sumption practices, is truly connected to the rise of industrial capitalism or, more simply, the importance of ownership and a wider process of com-modification. What also comes under scrutiny here, and is also sometimes the cause of some confusion, is the strong association of consumption with wastefulness and idleness, which clearly has a somewhat pejorative slant to it that is equally easily overestimated. At the same time, Veblen's analysis also quite strongly invokes the sense in which consumption practices are, on occasions, strongly linked to questions of extravagance or perceived as having high status for no reason other than that they are a waste of time and or money. The enormous cost of *haute couture* or some forms of lavish entertaining are prime examples.

More importantly, at the centre of his analysis of the values of consumption are leisure- or middle-class women who, in their role as wives, are seen to perform a primarily status-maintaining function. Interestingly, Veblen is sensitive to the sense in which women are themselves owned and commodified through their consumption practices, which they are seen to perform in maintenance of the status of their male counterparts. At the same time, however, he is scathing of their activities in themselves. Moreover, his association of what he calls 'new woman', broadly equated with first-wave feminism, with some kind of earlier 'barbaric' culture is, to say the least, a little unfortunate. However, given his ambivalence, this does not entirely add up to the sexism that Elizabeth Wilson accuses him of in her work on fashion (Wilson 1985).

What is also at stake here, however, is the adequacy of his theorizing, which often amounts to little more than a simple form of structural functionalism. The analysis starts with some stronger foundations in a fairly unilinear form of economic history, but following an interesting analysis of fashion and some insights into pecuniary questions of taste, drifts off into a scattered collection of articles on various throwbacks to 'barbarism' in modern life – from gambling and feminism to, more convincingly, the predatory nature of commerce. As a consequence, any strong sense of direction or conclusion is sadly lacking. Most significantly, the analysis is focused exclusively on the USA, whose cultural history of consumption is particularly early in its expansion and development on a mass scale.

Importantly, though, Veblen's ideas have since underpinned many, if not all, analyses of consumer society. There are three key reasons for this, which also give some credence to ideas themselves. First, his account of the middle classes makes the important point that many consumption practices or indeed purchases are not explained solely in terms of utility or practicality, but rather in terms of their symbolic significance. Second, the concept of conspicuous consumption in particular highlights the significance of consumer practices as a routine source of social cohesion or community on the one hand and a form of social division or individualism on the other. Third, his perspective also perhaps unintentionally taps into the importance of wider vectors of oppression and particularly the significance of gender in consumption. Thus, outmoded as much of his work may now seem and woefully short of more contemporary sophistication or political correctness, the seeds of some of the future analysis of consumer society were all too well sown in his studies.

In conclusion to this section, then, we are confronted with several interesting and significant points. First, while some of these analyses seem somewhat unsophisticated if not anachronistic to the contemporary reader, this is for the most part explained as a result of historical circumstance. Apart from any consequence or implication, the immense changes emerging as the result of the rise of industrial capitalism and the modern metropolis, including the rise of new social divisions and a conspicuous consuming middle class, were clearly of overriding importance to theorists of the late nineteenth century or early twentieth century in ways that are perhaps now difficult to conceive. Similarly, these theorists could hardly have foreseen the developments of the 1960s which spearheaded so much concern with issues such as race, gender, sexuality or lifestyle politics, and their attendant difficulties, which inform so much of contemporary theory and particularly cultural studies. Interestingly, though, the gendering of consumption in primarily feminine terms does float, in sometimes ghost-like form, through many of these early analyses of consumer society.

Second, their coining and developing of various concepts and tools that remain in the kit of any contemporary theorist are easily undermined, as what now seems so clear and commonsensical was then often misty and distant. The notion, then, of a radical split with such approaches is clearly nonsensical as there is much, sometimes ironic, parallel with the work of contemporary theorists. For example, the work of Pierre Bourdieu, as well as that of Jameson or Baudrillard, shows more affiliation with that of Veblen, Simmel or the Frankfurt School than may at first appear. Some of these connections are considered more critically in Chapter 2.

Third, and perhaps most importantly, most of these analyses provide a more than knowing and sometimes warning tap on the shoulder of some more optimistic analyses, which seek to divorce consumption from its economic, political and even social constitution in talking of the cultural as a separate entity or sphere of activity or in asserting the overriding significance of consumption in the formation of identities and the pursuit of personal pleasure. I am in particular thinking of much of the pioneering work linking consumption to poststructural or postmodern ideas and the frequent take-up of this in many analyses of identity politics or style and the role of shopping (see, for example, Tomlinson 1990; Featherstone 1991; Shields 1992; Radner 1995; Lury 1996).

However, interestingly, as the study of consumption progresses through these early studies, its significance as a social practice increases and its analysis is tied less to critiques of production, of which the contrast between the early Marx and later Benjamin is a good example. The concept of conspicuous consumption proved axiomatic in this respect, as what this highlighted so critically was the importance of consumption practices not only in maintaining class distinctions but in undermining once and for all the strictly monetary notion of the value of commodities and exposing the complexities of meanings surrounding commodities and consumers alike. Simmel's influence in the formation of a more interactive or phenomenological understanding of consumption practices is also important in this respect. However, what is easily lost is the sense in which many of these early analyses of consumer society were, to all intents and purposes, not entirely positive concerning what they saw, often questioning the consequences of consumption more politically, and it is perhaps this sense of caution that remains the most important lesson. It is at this point that I wish to return to the question of the definitions and conceptions of consumption and the development of the perspective taken in this text.

Consumer society/consumer culture

Recent studies of consumption have often conceived of consumption in terms of consumer culture rather than consumer society. This is often summed up in the very titles of many works. For example, Mike Featherstone's *Consumer Culture and Postmodernism*, Celia Lury's *Consumer Culture*, Daniel Miller's *Material Culture and Mass Consumption*, Frank Mort's *Cultures of Consumption* or Don Slater's *Consumer Culture and Modernity*, to name only some (Miller 1987; Featherstone 1991; Lury 1996; Mort 1996; Slater 1997b). There is clearly some variation in the way these authors conceive of concepts such as consumption and culture, constituting in some cases an almost diametric opposition in emphasis on the aesthetic and stylistic in the case of Featherstone and Lury or the material and economic in the case of Miller and Slater. This tends to inform or illustrate a wider tension of emphasis on the cultural, in terms of art and style, or on the economic, in terms often of historical materialism, that now exists within and across differing studies of consumption.

Following this, the concern I wish to raise at this point is that the term consumer culture is itself often diffuse in relation to its meaning and association and, on top of this, I wish to support a return to the use of the term consumer society instead, itself sometimes used in earlier studies, as a clearer indication of the content and perspective on consumption taken here. This also highlights an increasing difficulty concerning the definition of consumption *per se*, and its study more widely, which now sprawls across such differing disciplines as art history, literature, anthropology, sociology, psychology, geography and economics, referring to everything from visual culture to household shopping and from eating customs to marketing techniques, with seemingly little attempt to pin it down. This is a point I have already explored in the Introduction and will return to in later chapters.

Much of the recent emphasis on more aesthetic or stylistic aspects of consumption comes from the influence of various, mostly French poststructural or postmodern theorists such as Baudrillard and Jameson, who have used differing aspects of the question of consumption, and particularly its aesthetic practice, to support the development of wider social, economic or political theories. Another dimension is the conflation of social scientific analysis with disciplines including literature and psychoanalysis. Rachel Bowlby's complex interweaving of both of these in *Shopping with Freud* is a prime example (Bowlby 1993). It is not my intention here to document the development of these perspectives or to provide a critique of them, as this is examined in Chapter 2, nor do I intend to unpack the relationship of consumer society to postmodernity or poststructural theory as this is the focus of Chapter 8. It is important here, however, to unpack some of the most immediate implications of these differing conceptions of consumption and, in particular, to start to spell out the perspective taken here, which will then inform the rest of the text.

In the first instance, the concept of culture has two not unrelated aspects: first, a concern with ways of living linked to wider questions of social practice, attitudes and anthropological or historical variations; and second, a concept of culture as linked to art, invoking questions of style, design and aesthetic content or meaning. Increasingly, and particularly in the wake of poststructural theory and cultural studies, these two aspects of culture have collapsed or imploded into one or a sometimes confused mixture of each. As such, if we take the example of consumption, much mileage has come from the mixing of aesthetic concerns in the style, presentation and aesthetic meaning of goods (culture as art) with wider questions of the social practice of shopping, consumption's importance in the formation of identity or even its psychoanalytic significance (culture as way of life).

Of underlying importance here also is the sometimes explicit and sometimes implicit thesis that changes in culture as art tend to reflect or impact on culture as way of life, or vice versa, and in these cases the confusion of the two aspects of culture is quite intentional, particularly in relation to some wider poststructural or postmodern analyses. For example, the increasing emphasis on the importance of image in relation to cars, whereby the status attached to BMWs is becoming almost notorious, is seen to reflect a wider aesthetic commodification of everyday life (Featherstone 1991).

As I have already stated, it is not my intention to question the validity of such assertions. I do, however, wish to question the degree of emphasis placed on such an analysis, for – to return to my unpacking of the differing meanings and angles to the conception of consumption – an investigation of the more cultural and artistic dimensions of consumption *can* lead to an underemphasizing, if not necessarily an undermining or exclusion, of the other dimensions of consumption raised previously, namely its connection to economic systems of provision and production and its importance in terms of the maintenance and construction of social practices and social divisions. This last aspect is often incorporated directly or indirectly into more culturally driven analyses of consumption, yet often under the auspices of an identity politics (see Chapter 7).

There are, of course, some exceptions, as in the work of Scott Lash and John Urry, which is considered critically in Chapter 8. But even their perspective on the development of consumer society remains quite positive (Lash and Urry 1987, 1994). Social divisions are then often conceived as existing at the level of stylistic rather than structural differences. In addition, underlying much of this discussion is the implicit assumption that more cultural dimensions of consumption are at least semi-autonomous, if not necessarily separate from, the more economic or political motors of its development. The relationship of consumption to developments in modernity or postmodernity, industrial and postindustrial capitalism, is indeed complex and considered critically in Chapter 2 and Chapter 8.

However, I wish to assert here that consumption is most fully explicated and understood as a multifaceted concept and practice that does indeed incorporate more stylistic, artistic or cultural elements, yet does so alongside its ongoing economic and political importance. For example, the development of affluent and fashion-conscious Western consumption practices in fancy shopping malls across Europe and the USA is operated at the expense of, and was facilitated through, the development of increasingly international and racialized work practices, in turn assisted technologically and often justified politically through a lack of protectionist sanctions (Phizacklea 1990).

In addition, consumption practices in affluent Western societies are highly socially, economically and politically patterned, if not determined, where the elderly and infirm, and the low paid in particular, are excluded from many consumption practices through various mechanisms from transport to credit control. The consumption practices of many young people, including those from racial or ethnic minorities and the unemployed, in mimicking, stealing or aping the style cultures and commodities of their more affluent counterparts may undermine any sense of simple economic determinism, but still supports an analysis of consumption that incorporates a conception of its economic importance, political significance and social divisiveness.

Ultimately, then, this also forms a major part of my argument for using a conception of a consumer society rather than a consumer culture. Although consumer style cultures may well thrive in affluent circles in Western cities and are all too real to their active participants, and indeed are also worthy of serious study in those contexts, they do so equally at the all-too-real social, economic and political expense of other groups and other areas of society, nationally and internationally. Consequently, the concept of consumer culture, with its open-ended tendency to incorporate such developments *or not*, according to each individual case, leads me to prefer to use the term consumer society as a clearer indication of an intention to incorporate consumption's economic and political significance *alongside* its more social or cultural importance.

Conclusion: conceptions of consumption

In conclusion, throughout this chapter, it is immediately apparent that consumption is a plural, multifaceted and often contradictory phenomenon in concept and practice. This was explained initially as a result of the meanings of the term itself and the more contemporary discourses, particularly in relation to the consumer, that now surround it. In addition, early perspectives on the development of consumer society often allied its analysis to the study of production, social class or more economic developments. Yet, within this, the gradual move towards a more social or culturally driven analysis of consumption was already present, particularly in Simmel and Veblen's work on conspicuous consumption's importance to the formation and maintenance of social class positions. In addition, Benjamin's formulation of the importance of the unconscious in relation to consumption opened up some of its less predetermined elements to critical scrutiny. This shift in emphasis has started to lead to the formation of a tension around consumption as class driven and economic versus consumption as individually or group driven and stylistic or cultural. At the risk of sounding trite, I wish to assert that neither is right or wrong, for consumption is not the site of social division, inequity and poverty nor the focus of affluent, conspicuous and rapturous style cultures; rather it is both and all of these, though not necessarily equally, and its significance in either respect varies from time to time and from culture to culture. As a result, a heavy emphasis on the importance of consumption as an aesthetic practice is exclusionary and as partial a picture as an equally strong hammering out of its connections to the economic mode of production and this is the focus of the second chapter.

Suggested further reading

There are no substitutes for primary texts here, see:

Adorno, T. and Horkheimer, M. (1973) *Dialectic of Enlightenment*. London: Allen Lane.
Buck-Morss, S. (1989) *Dialectics of Seeing*. Cambridge, MA: MIT Press.
Frisby, D. and Featherstone, M. (eds) (1997) *Simmel on Culture*. London: Sage.
Marx, K. (1975) *Early Writings*. Harmondsworth: Penguin.
Veblen, T. (1934) *The Theory of the Leisure Class*. New York: The Modern Library.

See also:

Gabriel, Y. and Lang, T. (1995) *The Unmanageable Consumer*. London: Sage.

2
FROM HERE TO MODERNITY – CONTEMPORARY THEORIES OF CONSUMER SOCIETY

Over recent decades, interest in consumption issues has increased consistently and, more particularly, many theorists have sought to incorporate its importance into wider analyses of contemporary society. Some of this discussion has focused on the question of the connections of consumption to wider developments in postmodernity, and this is considered critically in Chapter 8. Although often equally difficult to separate, following my discussion of earlier perspectives on consumer society in Chapter 1, it is my intention to consider the development of more contemporary theories and concepts around consumption in this chapter, paying particular attention to key theoreticians in the area over the past few decades. In addition, although distinctions are often artificial, the focus of this chapter is primarily on the themes of modernity rather than postmodernity.

More particularly, I wish to look in detail at three aspects of contemporary theory in relation to consumer society, namely questions of its history and origins, applications of differing conceptions of culture, capital and control, and recent adaptations of the notion of a political economy. As a result, the chapter has three central sections: first, an analysis of some primary attempts to assess the history and origins of consumer society; second, a discussion of the significance of culture, capital and social control to questions of consumption; and third, a consideration of various more contemporary attempts to re-evaluate class analysis in particular and, more widely, map the contemporary terrain of society in the light of a continued interest in a political economy. Following this, in the final section, I will address the theme of modernity more directly and consider its significance in relation to the study of consumer society.

The origins of consumer society

It is perhaps immediately apparent that consumption has played an increasingly central part in societal developments since the Second World War, particularly in the form of social practices, from sport to home computing, and the expansion of shopping itself into a popular leisure activity *en masse*. These developments have simultaneously gained more political connotations in the expansion of privatization to include public services such as health and education, often set against a context of wider economic deregulation (see Cahill 1994; Keat *et al.* 1994; Sulkunen *et al.* 1997). In particular, what also comes from this discussion is a strong sense of consumption's wider importance economically or politically, on top of its more specific significance as a social practice. It is perhaps not surprising, then, that many contemporary theorists have attached much importance to consumption, often linking it to altogether wider and grander theories of society.

This does start to raise some serious issues, though, for the critical consideration of the role of consumption in contemporary society, most particularly difficulties in discussing the importance of consumption *per se* as separate or distinct from the wider set of developments which it is thought to express. This separation is, of course, at least partly artificial, yet it opens an important question of definition, particularly when trying to unpack what is perceived to relate directly to consumption and what is not, producing an almost constant sense of conceptual overlap. This is most apparent when discussing contemporary theories of consumer society directly and in detail. Interestingly, though, some slightly earlier studies of consumer society have chosen to take the longer and historical view of its development and impact, and it is to this question of the origins of consumption that I now turn.

The origins of consumer society are, of course, the products of historical interpretation and, in the final instance, unknown. What is more, the most recent tendency to see consumer society in primarily more stylistic and contemporary terms has, in some senses, increased the difficulty in understanding its history. However, three comparatively early studies of consumer society have provided some insights into the issues involved and provoked some discussion concerning the complexity of its origins.

The first and most famous of these is Neil McKendrick, John Brewer and J.H. Plumb's *The Birth of a Consumer Society* which, although often labelled as a full-blown history of consumption, is actually a collection of essays by three historians at the University of Cambridge (McKendrick *et al.*

1982). The key driving force of their analysis is economic, yet, like Ben Fine and Ellen Leopold a decade later, they are deeply critical of classical economic theory and the accounts of the development of consumption provided through utilitarianism in particular (Fine and Leopold 1993). McKendrick himself highlights the centrality of the increased acceptance and practice of commercialism as primary in the formation of consumer society. Consequently, he provides a critique of supply-driven economic theory as much as an alternative framework of demand-driven consumption practices. This starts to set up a conflict concerning the extent to which consumer society is supply-led, as in the productivist-oriented or Marxist model, or demand-driven, which often forms an implicit assumption within more cultural analyses of consumption (see also Chapter 8).

What McKendrick illustrates well, however, is the conflation of underlying economic expansion and deregulation leading to greater entrepreneurial opportunity coupled with a marked shift in attitudes, from prudence, restraint and the cultivation of inheritance through to display, extravagance and the valuing of newness. These shifts were themselves marked by the sharp break between the cultures of Stuart and Georgian England in the eighteenth century. As a result, it was the linking of changes in attitudes and expectations *in conjunction with* increased economic prosperity and openness that defined and formed the new consumer society. This is also exemplified in a range of essays by all three authors on issues such as the rise of Wedgwood's potteries, the commercialization of the arts and leisure, and the expansion of fashion and style in concept and practice.

Some parallels in perspective or interpretation are easily drawn here with Colin Campbell's slightly later study of consumption in *The Romantic Ethic and the Spirit of Modern Consumerism* (Campbell 1987). Here he primarily argues, in a line of reasoning based strongly on Weber's study of Protestantism, that the nature of consumption and its attendant meanings have fundamentally altered over time and space (Weber 1930). The emphasis is placed similarly on a shift in social attitudes and, in particular, he asserts that while in developing or traditional societies consumption is centred essentially on the satisfaction of the senses and human needs; under conditions of modernity or in Western society the nature and meaning of consumption change to a concept centred more on romantic wish-fulfilment or daydreaming. Campbell is therefore strongly critical of more materially determinist analyses of consumption, such as those associated with Marxism, seeing the desire for commodities as the product of a hedonistic longing for escapist experiences or alternative pleasures as opposed to status or simple monetary aspiration. Apart from the difficulty in sustaining this distinction in its entirety when some consumption practices such as wearing silk, driving a fast car or taking exotic holidays are to all intents and purposes as sensual experiences as they are romantic, whereas other forms of consumption such as shopping for staple products often lack any such sense of fantasy, the underlying and unilinear sense of sociological *logic* to Campbell's argument feeds directly into a wider study of modernity that I will return to later in this chapter.

Although McKendrick and Campbell have, to varying degrees, both emphasized the eighteenth century as the turning point in the development of consumer society, Grant McCracken, in taking a different and more politically driven perspective, takes the sixteenth century and Elizabethan England as his starting point in his work *Culture and Consumption* (McCracken 1988). The primary focus of his analysis is the rise of court society and its attendant cultivation of competitive style cultures among the lower aristocracy. In particular, it is the end of the patina system, in which families would increase their status and wealth through processes of inheritance, often extending across multiple generations, plus the formation of an overall culture of immediate gratification and newness which are crucial in McCracken's analysis. This was then coupled with the increasing ineffectiveness of sumptuary laws governing consumption practices, which then further underpinned the development of consumer society. Sumptuary laws, as attempts to regulate the conspicuous display of affluence and status, were always ineffective because of the very dynamics of cultural relativism, but the rise of fashion as style and dress alike speeded up the processes of mutation to the point of confusion (see also Chapter 1). Thus McCracken highlights the importance of politics as well as economics in the development of consumer society.

In summary to this section, what we are presented with is a complex picture of interplay of politics, economics, social conditions and attitudes as central in the development and formation of consumer society. Importantly, all of these analyses use England as the site for their more empirical investigations and as evidence for their more theoretical assertions. It is worth comparing their ideas, then, with those of Veblen, Simmel and Benjamin, which I discussed critically in Chapter 1. These authors have taken more North American or wider European focuses for their studies but have a similar tendency to see the interplay of culture and economics as of greater significance than any one factor alone. In addition, what remains open to question is the point at which consumer society is perceived to have, as it were, 'taken off' into its modern form. McCracken takes this starting point to be considerably earlier than do either McKendrick or Campbell, but all of these authors' analyses pre-date those connected with Marxism, let alone those associated with postmodernity.

More importantly, and constantly mentioned and drawn upon, though rarely made explicit, in all of these analyses are the factors of mass production, individualism and the rise of the city as central in the development of consumer society. These factors are often explicated separately in Marxist theory, the wider study of modernity and Simmel's work respectively, yet are rarely pulled into a wider study of consumption. In addition, this also depends on a wider theme of the interrelationship of the cultural and economic as well as questions of social and political control. Therefore, it is to these factors, as well as others, that I now turn.

Culture, capital and control

In this section, I wish to consider the interlinked concepts of capital, culture and control as central to two of the most influential contemporary theorists of consumer society, namely Pierre Bourdieu and Zygmunt Bauman. Although very different in many ways, what unites these theorists is a concern with consumption as a cultural site of social stratification through which the wider economic and political tensions of contemporary capitalism are played out to a somewhat uncertain end.

The work of French social scientist Pierre Bourdieu ranks as some of the most important in the sociology of consumption. This is due in part to his wider significance as a sociologist, particularly in the fields of education, methodology and social theory. He has also sometimes been lumped together with some of his more postmodern of poststructural contemporaries in France, such as Baudrillard, Jameson or Lyotard. This is, however, something of a misnomer as his minutely detailed and tabulated observation of the habits and lifestyles of the French, paying particular attention to factors such as dress, hairstyles and dining out, provides an excellent example of consumption's importance in forming and maintaining personal or group status or identities that echoes Weber's concerns more than any of those associated with postmodernity. More importantly, it also remains an empirically driven analysis which also differentiates it from studies of postmodernity which have a tendency towards more directly theoretical analysis. Similarly, his work has much in common with that of Simmel, whose work is considered in detail in Chapter 1, particularly in his keen concern to pay an equal level of attention to subjective as well as objective realities. In addition, he also shares Simmel's concern with the inextricably bound up interplay of the individual and the social. More particularly, he is also vigorously opposed to ungrounded theorizing lacking in empirical foundation. Consequently, his study of consumption is often as concerned with practice as it is with theory, while practice *per se* is also a key theoretical concern (Bourdieu 1989).

In addition, Bourdieu's importance to the sociology of consumption is linked more directly to his provision of one of the most thorough empirical investigations into consumption as a social practice in his study *Distinction: A Social Critique of the Judgement of Taste* (Bourdieu 1984). His central argument concerns the recognition of taste, often simply considered as personal and idiosyncratic, as social and patterned, which he summed up in the phrase: 'Taste classifies, and it classifies the classifier' (Bourdieu 1984: 6).

Moreover, taste is seen as precisely the mechanism through which individual distinction operates alongside a wider question of social conformity. Interestingly, this often leads him to a reinvention of models of class and stratification rather than a more poststructural analysis of the complexities of culture and identity. This in turn leads him to an elaborate, detailed and somewhat tiresome documentation of the lifestyles of the Parisians, tabulating in minute detail their uses of everything from hair stylists to restaurants and from their reading of fashion manuals to their selection of educational institutions. His conceptualization of a paper chase of social position that this then sets up also echoes Simmel's earlier analysis of imitation and differentiation cited previously, although he stresses differently the importance of 'cultural intermediaries' in sustaining the process.

Cultural intermediaries are defined as style experts, image consultants and editorialists who advise the middle classes on the niceties of taste and the correctness of certain styles, activities or ways of living. Allied to this is Bourdieu's development of the highly influential concept of 'cultural capital' which, in particular, sees middle-class knowledge and expertise, from correctness in matters of taste and style at dinner to issues of access and control across a wide range of institutional contexts including schools and universities, as well as the middle-classes' role in making contacts and networking, as a key mechanism in the maintenance of social status and position.

In addition, a key question concerns the relationship of cultural capital to economic capital, or monetary wealth. These two factors are clearly strongly interlinked, as in the case of education where private schooling is paid for precisely to foster the skills of cultural capital – from knowing one's wines and how to dress for formal dinners to having the right accent and personal contacts. Interestingly, though, a more poststructural spin comes into play here through the example of the new service or information classes whose position is often perilously predicated precisely on their knowhow or cultural rather than economic capital. There is some parallel here with the work of theorists of post-industrialism such as Daniel Bell, Scott Lash and John Urry, or Alan Touraine (Touraine 1969; Bell 1974, 1976; Lash and Urry 1987). It is also at this point that the more political role of cultural intermediaries is also apparent in equally supporting or potentially disrupting the wider cultural system. For example, magazine editors are equally influential in defining 'outs' as well as 'ins' of taste and the people that go with them, as in the case of character assassinations of celebrities.

Central in each case are patterns of consumption in sustaining social practices such as the correct places to dine in or play golf, and in terms of commodities such as the right areas to live, clothes to wear or cars to drive. More insidiously, though, this is then seen to impinge on the mechanism of what Bourdieu calls 'symbolic violence'. Symbolic violence is precisely the violence, through factors such as exclusion and derision, of cultural capital through which more traditional and newer class positions are equally maintained and perpetuated at the expense of others. Thus, consumption is connected to the more structural question of gate keeping, where entry to the members' golf club or restaurant is precisely the mechanism through which wider class and economic position is maintained. In addition, symbolic violence is also the violence of the battleground to gain the power to define and control, as arbiter, taste itself. Therefore, despite the apparent invocation of totalitarian control here, Bourdieu's position is rarely so one-sided, seeing more importantly a significant struggle concerning the question of distinction itself, in defining the 'ins' and 'outs' of culture, that is near dialectical. It is at this point that Bourdieu's conceptualization of the relationships of culture, capital and control is markedly different to that of Bauman, to which I now turn.

Zygmunt Bauman, along with Baudrillard and Bourdieu, has become increasingly labelled as *the* theorist of consumption, mostly because of his various insights into its meaning and practice. Nevertheless, such labelling remains problematic on two counts: first, because Bauman has yet to provide a full-blown theory of consumption as opposed to observations of it in relation to other concerns; and second, the status of his ideas extends over and beyond that of consumption into questions of the overall social and theoretical postmodern predicament. His writings on consumption start late on in *Legislators and Interpreters*, a critique of intellectual life not entirely dissimilar to Lyotard's study of *The Postmodern Condition*. They are extended most controversially in his philosophical study of *Freedom*, and are spelt out very plainly in *Thinking Sociologically*, all of which are seriously criticized by Alan Warde, and his most recent ideas on consumption and social divisions in *Work, Consumerism and the New Poor* are considered in detail in Chapter 4 (Lyotard 1984; Bauman 1987, 1988, 1990, 1998; Warde 1994).

Warde argues that Bauman puts consumption 'at the very centre of the operation of the social world today' (Warde 1994: 58). Considering Bauman's lack of any full study of the importance of consumption, this seems to be something of an over-statement. Perhaps the most important point to make here is that Bauman initially seeks to redress the productivist emphasis of much of social theory by making consumption a central example in many of his writings on wider topics. In particular, consumption becomes primary in his analysis of the relationship of the individual and the social as a means of creating individual identity and social cohesion alike and, in addition, most controversially as a cause of social division.

As a consequence, Bauman sees consumption as an essentially individual and apolitical activity that simultaneously divides society into what he calls 'the seduced', or financially secure and consequently socially incorporated on the one hand, and what he calls 'the repressed', or state dependent and socially excluded on the other. Thus, the initial individualization of consumption practices as a consequence also leads to the formation of social groups and social divisions according to processes of inclusion and exclusion (see also Chapter 4).

This is further enhanced through the operation of group dynamics in the construction of 'neo-tribes' or lifestyle cliques centrally defined by their relationship to consumption practices and identities. Warde is critical of this distinction as overly centred on an essentially false separation of market and state in an analysis that overall places too much emphasis on consumption as individualism. What remains of clear significance here is Bauman's implicitly dystopian vision of consumer society (see also Chapter 8).

This sense of dystopia becomes something nearer to nihilism in his analysis of consumption's importance in *Freedom* (1988). For Bauman, freedom is essentially a relational construct rather than a quality or commodity one does or does not have or possess. There are clear parallels here with Foucault's equally relational sense of power, but the political implications of his analysis lead towards stronger analogies with the nihilism of the Frankfurt School considered critically in Chapter 1 (Foucault 1978). Consumption, he points out, has the unusual capacity to resolve individual and social conflicts in perpetuating socially approved individualism and strengthening the relationship of individual and market where the signifying function of goods is precisely their utility function. The difficulty given the overall usefulness of the situation is political, and consumption, in individualizing and commodifying the social, and in turning every difficulty into something one can throw money at or otherwise chastise oneself for not having the resources for, ultimately *de*politicizes society and acts as a form of social control: 'The strength of the consumer-based social system, its remarkable capacity to command support or at least to incapacitate dissent, is solidly grounded in its success in denigrating, marginalizing or rendering invisible all alternatives to itself except blatant bureaucratic domination' (Bauman 1988: 93). The spectre of bureaucratic domination is communism and the freedom of the market becomes the ultimate 'illusion' of capitalism.

A similar argument is hammered out more directly in *Thinking Sociologically* (Bauman 1990). Here Bauman's attention is drawn more towards advertising and the construction of the consumer, as advertising is seen to simultaneously stimulate and assuage anxiety in provoking needs and providing product solutions. Consumption, in turn, makes life a series of individualized hurdles often solved one-to-one on the advice of experts, paralleling the role of Bourdieu's cultural intermediaries considered earlier, and solved simply at the level of an individual's skill, know-how and purchasing power. For example, noise-creating transport policies are reduced to individual purchases of secondary window glazing. The social glue holding it all together in Bauman's world remains what he calls 'neo-tribalism', which boils down to style cultures that are, in turn, nothing more than 'styles of consumption' (Bauman 1988: 207). A problematic and added sting in this tale is the insatiability of limitless consumption, where the freedom of the market becomes the ultimate *un*freedom, where nothing is ever enough and the price mechanism maintains the boundaries of exclusion and hierarchy according to what can and cannot be afforded.

It is difficult not to find Bauman's conclusions at least a little gloomy, when even the pleasures and desires of consumption become its perfect weapon in maintaining social control, and one cannot help sympathizing with Warde's sense of a simplicity of motive in his analysis. The strongest criticism, though, is that which is also invoked in the work of the Frankfurt School, where the consumer is the epitome of the passive victim, a dupe to capitalist exploitation and the lures of the market alike. Equally, however, one cannot discard such ideas in the wake of assertions of cultural autonomy, nor at the same time hear echoes of earlier and conflicting discourses of the consumer outlined in Chapter 1. Consequently, Bourdieu's sense of *struggle from within* an overall system of stratification has become in Bauman's world something nearer to *domination from without*. At this point we are returned, then, to the themes and variants of Marxism and the political economy.

Mapping the contemporary terrain: a return to the political economy of consumer society?

The concept of a political economy, most classically explored in relation to Marxist theory, has developed some unpopular connotations in recent decades. This is due mostly to three central criticisms of such approaches: first, the heavy emphasis placed on economic determinism in the case of Marxism has led more widely to some significant critique of a lack of individuality, agency or even subjectivity in such perspectives; second, the often colossal importance placed on social class itself has often come in for criticism as undermining questions of race, gender or sexuality frequently tied to a wider sense of political (in)correctness; and third, the concept and practice of a political economy and its attendant theory have come under fire for their outmoded simplicity or lack of sophistication in a world where personal identities and societal systems alike are seen as increasingly fragmented, disrupted and uncertain. In addition, one significant factor in this discussion is that consumption itself is often perceived as the apparent underdog and second fiddle to the great god of production in analyses of political economy.

Not surprisingly, then, recent years have seen increasingly significant endeavours to redress these criticisms and, not least, to address the question of a political economy of consumption. In this next section, then, I wish to consider some of these more recent developments and attempts to deal with the importance of consumerism. More particularly, although more difficult to locate, I wish to focus attention on the work of Ben Fine and Ellen

Leopold, Alan Warde and Rosemary Crompton, and some of the studies of Daniel Miller and Colin Campbell.

As economists, Ben Fine and Ellen Leopold are deeply critical of classical economic theory in their major study of consumer society, *The World of Consumption* (1993). In particular, they are critical of economically utilitarian perspectives on consumption which, they point out, underdevelop the relationship of production and consumption in an often simplistic analysis overly focused on the rise of consumers themselves and consumerist movements as opposed to consumer society. More social psychological and cultural analyses are criticized similarly for their dependence on many unfounded assumptions concerning the consumer and confused definitions of the phenomenon in question. Thus, *The World of Consumption* is perhaps as much a critique of prevailing perspectives as it is an attempt to develop an alternative framework. Nevertheless, an alternative perspective is strongly posited, centred on a model of systems of provision:

> We posit an approach to consumption should always be based on the recognition of distinct systems of provision across commodities, and argue that such an approach needs to be acknowledged theoretically to emphasise the integrity of separate systems of provision and to encourage recognition of the important differences between them.
>
> (Fine and Leopold 1993: 5)

This approach is posited to produce an analysis which, in particular, offers greater specialization and avoids some of the pitfalls of overgeneralization that are often present in studies of consumption. In addition, they point out that it also leads to a greater sense of the interaction of production and consumption that is often omitted in more general perspectives and, perhaps most importantly, it also starts to undermine the sense of stasis often present in many contemporary analyses of consumption as it lends itself more readily to the detailed historical study of differing practices in the consumption of goods across space and time. Most importantly, this is summed up in the development of what they call a more 'vertical' approach to consumption, stressing the importance of individual systems of provision in linking production and consumption, as opposed to the more common 'horizontal' approach which seeks to map general patterns of consumption at any one point in time and space. On top of this, these points are then illustrated through their studies of two very differing systems of provision, namely food and fashion.

These are clearly important points to make and a significant line of analysis is developed which is worth considering further. Their most fundamental point concerning the often sloppy definitions and implicit assumptions often present in the increasing plethora of contemporary studies of consumption is easy to endorse, as is their more underlying critique of the neglect of the connections between production and consumption. In addition, though, it is a little open to question whether the systems of provision model adopted actually overcomes some of these difficulties, or if it adds some of its own making. Although it is clearly true that the consumption, or indeed production, of packets of crisps is not easily equated with the demand for, or supply of, Armani suits, there remains some connection, or at least clustering, in patterns of development and practice across quite different goods and their respective systems of provision. This is precisely the point traded on in marketing and advertising, which now routinely equate reading of the left-wing press with high levels of filter-coffee drinking and so on, and which is also given an altogether more nefarious twist in the work of Pierre Bourdieu considered earlier.

In particular, a distinction in systems of provision for luxury goods from more staple ones, or perhaps perishable from non-perishable commodities, may well be workable but often implies a simultaneous importance to various developments affecting a variety of commodities at any one time. The systems of provision involved in fashion or clothing, cars or many electrical goods, demonstrate significant similarities, as they are all increasingly invested with a strong sense of sign value as opposed to use value, involve similar motives in marketing or purchase centred on the desire to replace often perfectly functional existing products and, in particular, are caught up in increasingly international and fast-paced modes of production, with some underlying sense of technological transformation. For example, young, designer-suit-wearing men are precisely the same men for whom fast cars and electronic gizmos are important and, what is more, marketers and producers also know this, therefore often creating parallels in the systems of provision of otherwise quite different commodities. Thus, although Fine and Leopold are apt to point out that the consumption of different goods or services often requires different explanations, to reduce this to an analysis of individual systems of provision potentially misses many wider or underlying points.

Perhaps most importantly, it is also the sense in which certain developments cut across the differing dimensions already mentioned that warrants and maintains much, in particular more postmodern, attention. In contemporary Western societies, even washing detergents are increasingly caught up in a world of sign values, from purity to ecology, that even cut across international variations, and Sony personal stereos are plugged all too similarly in the ears of Turks and Indians as they are in those of North Americans. Consequently, the question then centres on the more localized patterns of consumption of globalized commodities (Howes 1996).

As a result, Fine and Leopold's analysis provides a powerful critique of many contemporary studies of consumption and leads ultimately to a plea for a simultaneously more dynamic and more situated sense of the consumption and indeed the production of goods and services. Moreover, it lends support to the development of more historical, empirical and economically aware studies of consumer practice and commodities alike and undermines some of the more unfounded assumptions often implicit in many cultural or post-modern analyses. This starts to lead, quite unintentionally, to an increased sense of a stand-off, where culturalist critics of consumption vigorously defend their sense of agency and non-determination on the one hand while political economists assert their sense of injustice and historical specificity on the other. Underpinning this, often implicitly, is the constant re-evaluation of the significance of inequality and stratification and, in particular, social class, in analyses of consumption. This point is put most explicitly in the work of Alan Warde and Rosemary Crompton.

Alan Warde, in his article 'Consumption, Identity Formation and Uncer-tainty', is deeply critical of some of the foremost contemporary theories of consumer society and in particular of their claims to consumption's import-ance in the formation of identity (Warde 1994). Importantly, he highlights the work of Beck, Giddens and Lash and, most problematically, Bauman, whose own ideas as well as Warde's critique of them were considered in the earlier section. In addition, he also questions severely Beck's notion that con-temporary society is essentially premised on anxiety or uncertainty or that consumption provides some sort of resolution to such conflicts (Beck *et al.* 1994). In particular, he highlights the role of advertising in inducing rather than resolving questions of identity and anxiety, and points out that many other factors – from economic insecurity to demographic upheaval – are per-haps more causal of such anxieties. These are points easily accepted and not perhaps so refuted in the work of many contemporary theorists (see also Chapter 3). The important point, perhaps easily overstated, is that con-sumption still provides *one* of the means through which interpersonal states of anxiety are alleviated, as shopping in some senses remains semi-auton-omous of other factors and offers some form of escape from home and work alike.

Warde's critique of these assertions is to question the notion of any rise in anxiety and to point out that shopping as a cultural practice is essentially polyvalent in its personal importance. The latter point is not in dispute and is raised critically in Chapter 5, where the multiple meanings of shopping are considered and the neglect of some of these in much contemporary theory of consumption is significant. The former point, however, is perhaps not easily reduced to clinical rates of depression or neurosis and is equally illustrated in rising rates of take-up of alternative health, therapy and counselling practices.

Another angle to this question, however, is raised in Warde's assertions that consumption still remains a social practice involving convention, ritual and interpersonal contact. This is clearly correct but is equally open to interpretation as evidence for consumption's social as opposed to economic importance and indeed its significance for the formation and maintenance of interpersonal identities. The underlying issue here, then, is not so much whether consumption impacts on identity, as it evidently does very readily, but rather the degree to which this is socially patterned or individually psychic and, as a result, the force of Warde's analysis is to question the notion of consumption as a reflection of hyper-individualism and not, ironically, to question its significance for the formation of identities. As a result, Warde's work acts as a counter-*weight* to some of the more grandiose claims of the most grandiose theorists, rather than a counter-*attack*.

Clearly under scrutiny in Alan Warde's analysis is the idea that if consumption is not the linchpin in the formation of identity, then class is and, conversely, vice versa. This is addressed directly in the work of Rosemary Crompton who writes:

> In brief, some sociologists have argued that, in contemporary societies, 'consumption processes' are in the process of becoming, or have become, more important than production (or 'class') processes in shaping social identities and explaining social behaviour, and that as a consequence the consumer has become a more suitable case for sociological treatment than the producer.
>
> (Crompton 1996: 113)

She makes the very clear and incontrovertible point that class inequalities still persist, and arguably do more so rather than less so in contemporary society. Much of her argument is also driven by a critique of Saunders' highly influential analysis of consumption classes, where he asserts that consumption is overtaking production as the primary source of social stratification and develops the notion of 'consumption classes' to illustrate precisely this phenomenon (Saunders 1987). In addition, though, Crompton also raises the question of consumption's importance in potentially undermining class consciousness and concludes that although divisions do still clearly exist they are increasingly experienced at an individual rather than a collective level. This line of analysis raises several significant issues, not least the ironic sense in which it increasingly links, rather than conflicts, with that of many contemporary poststructural theorists, who cite equally not so much the end of social divisions, or even the end of social class, as much as a decline of class consciousness and the rise of individualism and pluralism in identities (see also Chapter 8).

In addition, Crompton's analysis also raises the very wide question of the connections of consumption to, or its importance in the maintenance of, social divisions. This is a question I primarily address in Chapter 4, but at this point I wish to query some of the assumptions implicit in these analyses. Most importantly, although social class is a useful heuristic tool for social scientists, it has never simply meant occupation or linked itself unequivocally, in practice at least, to work or production, and has often invoked wider social or cultural questions of wealth, status or prestige. To assume, then, that an analysis of consumption is *not* an analysis of class is a misnomer, or, more importantly, to assert that an analysis of consumption must *necessarily* exclude a consideration of production is clearly incorrect.

Significantly, however, what Crompton perhaps inadvertently highlights is the tendency towards the over-separation of the study of production and the analysis of consumption, when the reality is that they are all too clearly connected and, in particular, all too ironically, invoke questions of social class. For example, the young, male, trainee manager is often required to adopt certain patterns of consumption: namely, the wearing of suits and ties, the playing of approved sports, and dining out on appropriate occasions. Similarly, opposite prescriptions may well apply to positions antagonistic to the one mentioned, for example in manufacturing where the frequenting of pubs or playing of football may well be seen as more appropriate. Paul Du Gay in particular has also highlighted how the consumerist ethos has increasingly infiltrated the workplace and how the separation of consumption and production is increasingly redundant, if indeed it was ever very valid (Du Gay 1996). Ultimately, then, production provides the means of consumption, and vice versa, not least in terms of its affordability.

Similar themes emerge in the work of Daniel Miller and Colin Campbell, both of whom to some degree tend to oppose more culturalist or postmodern perspectives on consumption. Miller, in his self-confessedly prescriptive and polemical introduction to *Acknowledging Consumption*, pulls apart what he perceives as some of the central assumptions of much contemporary theory of consumption (Miller 1995). His critique of postmodernism, and many contemporary perspectives on consumption alike, is, however, primarily anthropological following his earlier drawing of parallels of Western consumer society with many other supposedly less consumerist cultures. At the same time, he has also sought to rigorously re-evaluate the theory of objectification and value under the umbrella of the now widely adopted concept of 'material culture', where commodities and their consumption are caught up in the interactive processes of social relations (Miller 1987).

As a result, he is concerned centrally with the relationships of consumers to commodities, and his starting point is that consumption does not, as some postmodernists would apparently advocate, lead to a worldwide homogeneity of commodities and culture as a result of the often very culturally specific and highly localized use of commodities and the consumption practices that surround them. The common stereotype of cans of Coca-Cola in Africa is a prime example of the so-called 'cultural homogenization' thesis. This is an important point to make, yet one which is equally not out of keeping with other postmodern interpretations which highlight precisely the same sense of dialectical dichotomy in the globally led but locally interpolated economy (Featherstone 1991; Howes 1996; Sulkunen *et al.* 1997).

Similarly, Miller's second assertion that consumption does not so much oppose sociality as much as create its own forms of social practice certainly undermines some of the more extreme claims to hyper-individualism in ways we have already seen in relation to the ideas of Alan Warde, yet does not exactly damn the entire canon of contemporary or postmodern theory. His third claim that consumption does not lead to a loss of authenticity is more controversial, however, and undermines the more extreme forms of sign-driven, fragmentary and anarchic contemporary theory, particularly associated with the ideas of Baudrillard, although the extent to which this specifically relates to consumption remains open to question. His final assertion that the rise of consumption does not in fact lead to the formation of particular social identities, as this assumes and confuses a certain character of consumer society with the actual practice of consumerism, provides an added critique of some contemporary notions of hyper-individualism. In sum, Miller then proposes a need for a new narrative of social relations that grounds the study of consumption in an essentially Marxist sense of materialism.

Colin Campbell makes a similar distinction between economically materialist and more cultural or postmodern studies of consumption (Campbell 1995). In addition, in common with Fine and Leopold, he also highlights differences in the necessary explanations of the consumption of perishable goods versus intangible services or more material, status goods. Most importantly, he undermines any simple equation of consumption with social meaning, as this confuses action with meaning, meaning with message, and mixes the sending and receiving of messages due to a teleological tendency to read meanings into consumption practices essentially after the effect is felt or perceived. For example, to assume that a well-dressed person is necessarily intending to send a message of 'Look at me, I'm high status' is simplistic and assumes that the meaning for the person concerned and those around them is not something completely different such as 'I wish I didn't have to wear this', or 'How nice', or 'What a complete plonker'. The clear difficulty raised here is the significance of consumption as a form of communication and, indeed, the academic neglect of the meanings of consumption for consumers themselves often due to the lack of more empirical study. It is not entirely clear, however, whether he sees consumption as, in essence, meaning*less*, or whether its meanings are simply more complex and open to interpretation. The former assertion would seem without foundation whereas the latter is indeed salient. Underlying much of this discussion is a wish to resurrect the significance of the study of modernity from the ashes of more postmodern analysis and it is to this issue that I turn more directly in the next section.

Consumer society and modernity

It is the primary purpose of the final section of this chapter to consider and critically evaluate the relationship of the development of consumer society to modernity, as opposed to postmodernity which is considered more fully in Chapter 8. This immediately raises a monumental difficulty of definition. Definitions of modernity are as notoriously difficult as those of postmodernity, and often explained in terms of what modernity is not, namely traditional society, similarly to the way in which postmodernity is frequently defined as not modernity. In addition, it is also worth making it apparent that any simple separation of postmodernity from modernity, or postmodern theory from modern theory, is increasingly tendentious and artificial, although I hope still ultimately useful heuristically. More significantly, despite the roars of disapproval concerning the diffuse foci and slippery slopes of the theory of postmodernity, perspectives on modernity offer us no respite or comfort from such conceptual anxieties, precisely due to the relational way in which so much of the theory has developed.

To try to anchor this discussion a little, therefore, the following is offered as a summary of some of the main empirical and theoretical points relating to modernity. First, economically, modernity is for the most part associated with the rise of industrial capitalism in the West and, in particular, the development of mass production techniques such as Fordism and Taylorism. More importantly, capitalism is then seen to construct the prevailing forms of social stratification in modern societies around ownership and control, exploitation, and particularly the importance of social class. At the same time this also fundamentally depends on the 'West' setting itself up in relation to the 'Rest' of the developing world (Hall 1992). More socially, these developments are then juxtaposed with the overall demarcation of home and work into private and public realms and the simultaneous rise in individualism following a shift in emphasis from ascription to achievement and the formation of a sense of self not solely dependent on family, community or tradition, at least not entirely. This sense of increased autonomy is also facilitated through the rise of the city. At the same time, and in conjunction with the Enlightenment and the rise of science, the development of modernity then leads politically to an emphasis on individual rights, equality and, to varying degrees, freedom. The most important point to emerge from this admittedly drastically simplistic analysis for our discussion is the rather murky, and for the most part merely implicit or lurking, consideration of the importance of consumption as opposed to production. In addition, this then accounts for the often automatic connection of consumption with postmodernity rather than modernity, a point I will consider in detail in Chapter 8.

This connection of understandings or explanations of consumption with the theory of postmodernity is something Don Slater almost wholly refutes on the following grounds:

> The issues and concepts central to thinking about consumer culture are the same ones that have been central to modern intellectual life in

general since the Enlightenment. Neither consumer culture as a social experience nor the issues through which that experience has been addressed are new or even recent: consumer culture is a motif threaded through the texture of modernity, a motif that recapitulates the pre-occupations and characteristic styles of thought of the modern west.

(Slater 1997b: 1)

This leads him to an essentially twofold analysis of the development of theories of consumer culture on the one hand, and the nature of consumer culture on the other. Interestingly, his use of the term consumer culture is, for the most part, centred on a somewhat Williamesque definition of culture as a way of life, as opposed to the more postmodern and contemporary sense of its relationship to style and art.

Slater then formulates and illustrates a series of propositions that I will outline as follows. First, he asserts that consumer culture is a culture of consumption or part and parcel of the entire contemporary Western way of living as opposed to an isolated or distinct practice. Second, its development and sustenance is wholly dependent on the rise of market society and fundamentally connected to an underlying mechanism of commercialization. The importance of consumption's connections with commercial culture lead to the third assertion of its apparent universality and, through association, its impersonality as the consumer is in a sense anyone, anywhere, in any position. This leads to the fourth claim that consumer culture constructs freedom around notions of individuality and privacy rather than collectivity. For this to succeed, Slater invokes the fifth point that consumer culture crucially depends on the construction of unlimited needs, wants and desires. As a result, and contrary to some of the ideas raised in the preceding section, Slater sticks to the notion that consumption plays an important part in the formation of identities. Lastly, he asserts that consumer culture is simultaneously a mechanism in the exercise of power and inequality.

As a result of this, Slater provides a very theoretically erudite and near philosophical analysis of the development of contemporary understandings of consumer culture. In particular, from this perspective it is also difficult to dispute his underlying and often very strong assertion that consumer culture is still most fully understood within the framework of the theory of modernity, and it is a convincing indictment of any simplistic equation of consumption with postmodernism. Much of this is explained, though, through postmodernity theory's own connections with, rather than separations from, the ideas of modernity, and the difficulty then lies in defining what exactly still *is* new and different concerning contemporary consumption practices when the theoretical tools for their explanation remain in some senses the same as they always were. What confuses the issue further is Slater's own highly scholarly and discursive deconstruction of the entire conceptual context of consumer culture, which starts to slide over a consideration of consumption as a social practice. There is a clear danger here, then, of muddling developments, or not, in theoretical explanations of the phenomenon of consumption with developments, or not, in consumption *per se*. Despite this, Slater provides one of the most important attempts to document the relationship of consumer society to modernity directly and in its entirety, as most theorists, as we have seen already in earlier sections, tend to focus on slightly smaller parts of the picture.

Perhaps more importantly, and as we have already seen in the first section of this chapter, consumer society is not necessarily defined in relation to modernity at all and may pre-date it and relate equally to a far more cultural series of pre-industrial developments. The role of modern Western industrial society is not necessarily to create consumption itself, then, but rather to facilitate the development of consumer society *en masse*. Consumption as a social practice, particularly in the anthropological sense, is perhaps as old as human society itself. Nevertheless, the modern industrial revolution remains vitally important in several respects: first, it facilitated mass consumption of mass-produced commodities; second, it separated to some extent at least consumption from production, primarily through the separation of home and work; and third, it effectively commodified the process of consumption more directly, precisely through the developing importance of money *per se*. Despite this, many other aspects of consumer society – from its role in stratification systems of social cohesion and division to its importance in the changing nature of subject–object relationships, and from its connections to commercial culture to its wider psychological significance – are equally not easily restricted to any singular or narrow notion of modernity. In sum, then, although modernity – however defined – may well prove fundamental in the formation of our contemporary and culturally specific concepts and practices of consumption, the importance of consumption *per se* in the widest sense is not so easily explained or simply related to modernity in terms either of theory or experience. Modernity may well then stand as one of the most significant pointers in the development of consumer society, perhaps even at the very core of its importance, yet precisely because of its centrality it does not stand alone while other perspectives continue to overcrowd it at the periphery.

Conclusions: from here to modernity

Following the preceding analysis of contemporary theory in relation to consumer society, it is necessary to summarize some of the main themes and issues that have arisen during this discussion.

First, there is clearly a sense in which consumption is commonly perceived to have increased in its importance as part of wider explanations of contemporary society. This is due primarily to a common perception of the importance of certain empirical factors, including the rise of consumption as a leisure activity, its increasing aesthetic significance, and its value in relation to the maintenance of individual identities and social practices alike, although the exact extent to which these factors impact on consumer society clearly varies. The controversy here, however, increasingly centres on a division in understanding or interpretation through the parameters of postmodernity on the one hand or modernity on the other. On closer inspection, however, this distinction seems at least partially artificial, as the factors illustrated as central in relation to one mode of understanding are not necessarily dissimilar to those used in the other. For example, neither school of thought would argue that consumption is unimportant to society as a whole nor that its value is solely one of utility. More controversially, it is difficult to see how even the most extreme theorist of postmodernity would assert that consumer society is not essentially still capitalist society or in some senses still socially divisive and exploitative, although the extent to which this is then seen to centre on matters of social class or underlying economic mechanisms remains a contested point. This sense of conflict, then, is centred ultimately more on a question of emphasis and interpretation rather than right or wrong, fact and fiction, which is often conceptualized, incorrectly, as some kind of modern versus postmodern controversy. These are points I will explore more fully in Chapter 8.

Second, and conversely, I wish to assert that the core of this conflict lies more in the varying perception of the relationship of the cultural and the economic. For some more cultural critics of consumption its importance is perceived as at least partially autonomous from economic factors; whereas for other theorists of political economy cultural practices are an outcome of economic mechanisms. More importantly, though, this distinction is also open to misinterpretation as few cultural theorists would not acknowledge some underlying economic precedent, if not determination, of consumption practices.

Third, this sense of conflict surrounding the significance of cultural and economic factors tends to feed into often heated disputes concerning the importance of consumption in forming or maintaining identities. The key question here is not, as Warde has asserted, whether consumption does or does not impact on identity, but whether that identity is seen in more individualized and psychic terms or as more of a socially patterned phenomenon. For some, particularly more traditional theorists consumption remains a primarily social activity; whereas for other, more cultural critics it is clearly interconnected with questions of intense individuality. As we have seen already, Bourdieu's work represents an attempt to implode this dualism through an empirically rigorous and grounded analysis (Bourdieu 1984).

This connects with the fourth area of thematic concern, namely that of consumption's relationship to wider mechanisms of power and inequality. Interestingly, there is once again a strong sense of similarity in the ideas of apparently opposed theorists on this point, as many even extreme post-modern theorists imply at least an element of social control in their analyses of consumer practice. Of primary importance here is the role of social divisions in relation to consumption, and the work of Bauman is particularly significant here. Contrary to popular perception, none of these theorists necessarily sees consumer society as intrinsically positive or progressive and, in fact, its development is often seen in profoundly dystopian or nihilistic terms, epitomized by the gloomy prognoses of Baudrillard which will be considered in more detail in Chapter 8.

This leads me to the fifth and final point of discussion, and one that some writers have already signposted, namely the neglect of a consideration of consumers themselves in many of these, for the most part very sweeping, analyses. The consumer is mostly seen either as a socially controlled victim or as an irrational, pleasure-seeking hedonist. In neither case is the multiplicity or complexity of their actual views or experiences considered seriously. As a result, in Chapter 3 and Chapter 4 our focus must necessarily shift from a consideration of consumer society to an understanding of the meanings surrounding the construction of consumers themselves.

Suggested further reading

Doing justice to mapping the contemporary terrain is nearly impossible, but the following are perhaps particularly useful:

Bauman, Z. (1990) *Thinking Sociologically*. Oxford: Blackwell – easy access to some of his key ideas but his other work remains germane.

Bourdieu, P. (1984) *Distinction*. London: Routledge & Kegan Paul – tiresome to read but it remains indispensable as an empirical study of consumption practices.

Edgell, S., Hetherington, K. and Warde, A. (eds) (1996) *Consumption Matters*. Oxford: Blackwell – useful 'nuts and bolts' collection including work of Rosemary Crompton and Alan Warde.

Fine, B. and Leopold, E. (1993) *The World of Consumption*. London: Routledge – thorough and rigorous economic/social history with detailed case studies of fashion and food.

Slater, D. (1997) *Consumer Culture and Modernity*. Cambridge: Polity – erudite unpacking of theory of consumer culture, particularly from more Marxist and classical perspectives.

3
MARKETING, ADVERTISING AND THE CONSTRUCTION OF THE CONTEMPORARY CONSUMER

Marketing and advertising, as key developments in the twentieth century, seem to epitomize the contemporary nature of consumer society and are of clear importance in this respect. Perhaps surprisingly, historically little academic attention was drawn, at least directly, to advertising or marketing, and particularly their sociological significance to the study of consumer society more widely. The difficulty here is perhaps twofold. In the first instance, the study of advertising and marketing is clearly located most strongly in the fields of commerce and, most recently, media studies rather than the more traditional notion of social science. Second, most of the debates about advertising have been heavily concerned with, and some might say bogged down in, an increasingly sterile question of advertising's influence or not on its television recipients in particular. As some commentators have already pointed out, answers to this question have tended to end in a state of impasse, primarily due to the difficulty of truly providing any empirical evidence one way or another. For example, a rise in sales following an advertising campaign does not necessarily prove that the advertising was the causal link, as opposed to an increase in consumer confidence or a decrease in competition, changes in attitudes or demography, and so on (Leiss *et al.* 1986).

More recently, this situation has started to change, primarily in relation to the rise of cultural studies, which have sought to derive some empirical support for their assertions from the worlds of advertising and marketing, and various attempts at reapplying Marxist notions of commodity fetishism in understanding the contemporary role of advertising. As a result, the more directly sociological literature on advertising and marketing is now vast (Packard 1957; Ewen 1976; Goffman 1976; Leiss 1976; Williamson 1978; Jhally 1987; Wernick 1991; Goldman 1992; Bowlby 1993; Schudson 1993; Nava *et al.* 1997).

Yet perhaps it is the role of advertising and marketing in informing our common-sense understanding or perception of the consumer, and indeed consumer society, that is most central here. Consequently, this chapter has three central sections: first, a consideration of marketing and its construction of contemporary notions of the consumer; second, a more specific analysis of the key functions of advertising and the contentious issue of its effects on its audience; and third, a short and summative analysis of advertising taking the empirical example of cars. In conclusion, I will assert that the importance of marketing and advertising remains complex and contradictory and, furthermore, that its future study needs to address more fully the question of social divisions along with the clear variations in its forms and mechanisms.

Markets and marketing

> Marketing is about trying to incorporate the customer into the production process in order better to satisfy them and thereby increase your chances of making a profit.
>
> (Lury 1994: 94)

This quote from Adam Lury tends to highlight certain important, and perhaps conflicting, aspects of marketing theory and practice. In particular, marketing is apparently more directly centred on the needs of the customer according to a central philosophy of making what will sell rather than simply selling what one makes regardless. In addition, this starts to tip the scales of a more economic analysis of consumer society in favour of a demand-led rather than supply-driven perspective (see Chapter 1). However, at the same time the justification for this view, and particularly its implementation into practice, is the pursuit of profit. Importantly, then, the motive in the case of marketing and selling alike remains the same, namely to make as much money as one can through whatever means one can, although in the case of marketing the means seems to justify the end more effectively. The only difference, and this is still significant, is that the perceived needs of the customer are further incorporated into the process. Perhaps ultimately, then, marketing forms the ideal model for consumer society in producing endless profits while keeping the customer satisfied. One hardly need add that the reality is scarcely so simple.

Marketing is simultaneously seemingly a new phenomenon and one that is difficult to clearly differentiate from older forms of selling. As already outlined, it is traditionally defined according to the increasing attention paid to the needs of customers prior to promotion, or even production, of the commodities in question. Historically, it is also asserted that a marketing orientation of making what will sell has, of necessity, taken over from a sales orientation of selling what is already made, as customers are increasingly knowing and markets for commodities themselves are more competitive. Neither perspective, apparently, is concerned with a production orientation, as this is seen to have disappeared with the industrial revolution (Chartered Institute of Marketing 1993; Randall 1993; Lury 1994). However, as we have seen in previous chapters, it is often difficult to separate such interdependent elements quite so clearly, particularly in contemporary society. The difficulty also concerns the degree of emphasis still placed on the profit motive, or, to put it another way, is marketing simply more effective selling?

Marketers, who often market marketing itself as much as the commodities or services, tend to highlight the centrality of marketers' concerns with consumers' needs *prior* to development and promotion of products, the importance of marketing *research*, and the *investigative* nature of its practice. On top of this, marketing is commonly seen to have quite a strong *managerial* function in creating strategies for market *development* and company profiles. Perhaps more importantly, marketing is still generally perceived as a more complex and more multidimensional phenomenon than selling, which involves issues of the promotion, advertising and presentation of products or services as well as the factors of pricing and placing traditionally associated with selling.

An important point to make here, though, is that the effects of the economy on marketing are immense and, in times of recession or slump in particular, marketing departments are often the first to suffer cuts and market research often ranks as a very low priority despite its potential importance in predicting promotional outcomes. This seems to imply that the underlying rationale of most companies remains one of production and sales, with marketing primarily used merely as an aid to more effective sales and profit development. Marketing is then promptly dropped when excess moneys dry up (Lury 1994).

Perhaps conversely, where marketing does seem to apply increasingly is at the upper levels of commerce, where a competitive edge, often amounting to little more than an image change in selling the same products or services as competitors, is often crucial. In particular, the more far-reaching potential of marketing in terms of truly tailoring production according to consumption remains underdeveloped and perhaps even actively undermined. In addition, as a consequence, marketing also tends to remain marginalized or outside of mainstream corporate practice and production alike, particularly in the wake of the increased tendency for companies to contract out their marketing functions. Post-Fordist, temporary or insecure working practices have, in a sense, ironically perhaps hit their own proselytizers hardest.

Importantly, then, the fortunes of marketing have varied historically. Marketing arose in its modern form primarily after the Second World War, following its development in the United States, where, to all intents and purposes, it originated. The 1960s and 1970s in the UK saw marketing develop primarily alongside more traditional forms of selling and as a concern for large corporations developing and expanding increasingly complex and diverse lines of products. Small and even medium-sized companies were essentially excluded, as they lacked sufficient funds to invest in marketing, as opposed to direct selling, which was still often seen as more direct and cost effective.

However, it was in the 1980s that the face of marketing started to alter rapidly and every company from major to minor sought the expertise of marketers in making production and sales more effective. It is this rather mythic sense of marketing taking over everything in its path that tends to fuel contemporary concerns over its influence. In particular, it was the expansion not only of marketing departments but rather entire marketing organizations that seemed at least to spearhead developments in the 1980s. Allied to this, concerns were raised in relation to marketing's apparent spillage into politics following the highly successful Saatchi and Saatchi advertising campaigns for the re-election of the Conservative Party in the UK. Underlying all of this was the wider deregulation of financial services and the City of London, and it was the service industries, most infamously including the utilities, that now sought marketing expertise. At its peak, apparently no one and nothing was exempt from the influence of marketing and its expertise in everything from company manifestos to product promotions (Cahill 1994; Keat *et al.* 1994; Sulkunen *et al.* 1997).

However, marketing was, and still is, easily confused with wider questions of image management and promotion as well as the use of the media industries socially, politically and financially. Marketing was often hit hard following the worldwide financial crash of 1989 and its attendant recession, with many particularly small to medium-sized companies forced to close marketing departments; and the pressures placed on marketers in large corporations to produce results increased immensely, particularly in the wake of increased use of independent consultancies. As a consequence, it was often the marketing consultancy, not marketing itself, as a low-cost and insecure operation, that remains the lasting success of the 1980s.

At this point, one might well ask, what exactly is it that marketers do for companies or consumers alike. A key factor in common-sense perceptions of marketing is market research. Market research is technically distinct from market*ing* research in terms of scope, as the former simply applies to specific products or services whereas the latter relates to the construction of an entire series of marketing matrices offsetting pricing strategies against advertising techniques in providing an overall company profile. As a consequence, the primary and continuing concept and methodology of marketing is the marketing mix, otherwise known as 'the four p's' of product, price, promotion and place. Product refers quite clearly to the product in question, its design, nature, specification and market salience; while price primarily refers to the means of price setting and whether other incentives such as price cuts or discounts are used. Promotion applies to all forms of promotional activity, from advertising to personal selling, packaging and public relations; while place is in a sense a misnomer for distribution or the management of supply and wholesale in an increasingly complex international arena on various levels. Effective marketing, therefore, rests on successful 'mixing' of these four sets of factors, often in the context of the marketing environment.

The marketing environment is in turn defined in shorthand terms as PEST or Political (government legislation, trade regulations and social policy), Economic (boom/slump, interest and exchange rates, inflation, income and employment), Social (attitudes, lifestyles, demography, gender, ethnicity and environmental concerns) and Technological (computing, new product development, information technology) factors. In addition, a fifth category of Ecological factors is often incorporated into these models, as environmental concerns have started to have an impact at all levels, from company decisions to consumer perceptions of the product (see also Chapter 4). Despite the apparent contradictions of mass consumption and environmental concerns, ecological factors are increasingly used to sell products, particularly in relation to toiletries and fashion, as seen, for example, in the marketing campaigns of the Body Shop or Benetton. These PEST(E) factors and the marketing mix are then cross-referenced to produce a more refined analysis of a company or product's market position. Despite the apparent importance of market research in terms of predicting outcomes, then, it remains a minor cog in a far greater wheel.

In addition, as time has passed, marketing practices have increased in their complexity. Particularly importantly, the development of more psychographic, as opposed to demographic, marketing techniques have led to the now somewhat infamous formation of lifestyle categories, where groups and individuals' patterns of consumption are marked out according to far more vague and mixed factors such as attitudes, domestic practices and leisure activities, as opposed to the traditional demographic factors of age, sex, class, area, occupation and so on. For example, McCann-Erikson, one of the most important lifestyle scales, separates 'Avant-Guardians', who are well educated and self-righteous, from 'Self-Admirers', who are young, intolerant and concerned with appearances, from 'Pontificators', who are older, traditional and concerned with keeping order. The tendency towards stereotyping is clear, yet the apparent success of these scales in allowing companies to target groups and individuals more effectively and promote products through far more sophisticated techniques is equally evident (see, for example, Armstrong 1996). In addition, contemporary advertising now almost completely depends on such categories, which has, in turn, fuelled a series of concerns over its influence, as we shall see shortly (Williamson 1978; Leiss *et al.* 1986; Jhally 1987; Goldman 1992; Kellner 1995).

Significantly, what is often at stake here is a question of product personality, an almost anthropomorphic transformation of a product into a type of person where, for example, BMWs become loaded with associations of success, sexiness, virility and even masculinity, while smaller Renaults are endlessly sold as French, flirtatious and feminine. The more insidious issue here is the commodification of personality that ensues: you are the car you drive and, therefore, without the car you are not 'you', a contentious question to which I wish to return later in this chapter.

Of immediate importance to our discussion, however, is the question of the extent to which these developments in marketing are economically driven or linked to wider and more cultural perspectives surrounding the consumer, and indeed consumption more widely. As I have already outlined, many of the restrictions placed on the role of marketing in creating more effective profits, as opposed to developing a stronger understanding of the relationship of products and consumers, and its clear limitations in terms of interventions in the production process are set economically according to the climate of expectations, confidence and monetary fortunes.

However, marketing is also clearly linked more culturally to prevailing conceptions of the consumer. In *Shopping with Freud*, Rachel Bowlby's highly influential study of notions of the consumer in psychoanalysis, literature and marketing alike, she argues strongly that the development of marketing was founded, and in turn impacted, on perceptions of the consumer that were essentially psychoanalytic (Bowlby 1993). She asserts: 'The marketing concern to discover what might persuade people to make purchases was intimately bound up, both institutionally and intellectually, with the contemporary psychoanalytical focus on the conscious and unconscious determinants of choices in life and love' (Bowlby 1993: 5).

This leads, slightly ironically, to a highly schizophrenic or polarized perception of the consumer as a rational and calculating bargain hunter on the one hand – what she calls the 'classical consumer', and on the other as an irrational, uncontrolled and unconsciously driven pleasure seeker – what she terms the 'romantic consumer'. These two perspectives and their constitutive elements are, of course, mutually reinforcing and two codependent sides of the same coin. In addition, if one then applies this to contemporary marketing practice, one may see each equally in operation as marketers struggle to outwit the increasingly sophisticated and all-knowing classicist while pandering with endless seduction routines to the day-dreaming romantic. Ultimately, of course, this illustrates the entire discursive framework surrounding the consumer and consumer society alike, as I have already outlined in Chapter 1.

In addition, though, it is marketing's role in constructing, or more simply perpetuating, certain conceptions of the consumer which remains critical to our current investigation. While it is perhaps inappropriate to accuse marketing, or even advertising, of maliciously intending to misrepresent the power and whims of the modern consumer, it remains central in shaping our conceptions of ourselves, past and present. In particular, it is the presentation of the consumer as an apparently free-floating citizen, whether rational and calculating or romantic and day-dreaming, that tends to undermine, and furthermore disguise, the more structural and economic strings at work in the consciousness of consumers. Questions of income, access or even more social and interpersonal constraints that come from within households as well as outside them are often left out of marketers' equations in predicting outcomes and promotions. Most importantly, it is the relentless individualizing of the modern consumer that remains most insidious as notions of collective resistance or participation are consistently undermined. These are serious matters to which I will return later in this and the next chapter.

What is perhaps immediately important here is the extent to which marketing has both exploited, and found itself at the mercy of, these same notions and discourses of consumption. As contracted workers, marketers are required to present their ideas and results in an arena where their expertise is open to the whims and preferences of major company managers; or, in short, marketing and marketers are increasingly caught up in the same processes of all-encompassing consumption. To put it more simply, marketing is now a market in itself. Of consequence in this is the question of power and control and for answers to this we need look no further than the nucleus of marketing itself, advertising.

The study of advertising: interpretation and ideology

> The simplest way to define modern advertising – the beginnings of which took place in the second half of the nineteenth century – is to say that is an *active* strategy of selling and marketing . . . [and] . . . The active character of the strategy implies an intentionality which is about more than selling goods: the idea is first and foremost to stimulate demand and thereby to sell as much as possible.
>
> (Falk 1997: 65, original emphasis)

As Pasi Falk implies, perhaps the starting place for the study of advertising lies in its definition. Often perceived as either the epitome of immoral and exploitative capitalism or seen merely as a mediascape of pleasure and interpretation, what advertising actually *is* often remains unclear. Of particular concern here is the often strong sense of equation of definition and intention or, to put it more simply, advertising is what it *does*. The difficulty with this is that what advertising does is often open to strongly conflicting interpretations as the modern opiate of the masses or the site of consumer hopscotch.

A much missed, although clearly important, addendum to this concerns the type or form of advertising in question. Textual advertising in terms of words used in advertisements to sell commodities in newspapers is clearly not easily equated with the highly suggestive world of glossy photography in magazines, which is again different from the increasingly notorious technoscapes of television. In addition to these, one might include direct mailing and leafleting or window displays and roadside hoardings. To crudely equate either the nature or the functions of all of these widely different forms of modern advertising, which range from the mundane to the surreal, seems mistaken but is often overlooked.

What is perhaps more clear are the underlying preconditions for all forms of modern advertising which, as Falk indicates, seem to depend on three factors: first, the formation of mass markets for mass consumption; second, the dependence of this in turn on mass production to stimulate and supply demand; and third, the rise of the mass media, defined in the widest sense to include all aspects of the image and communication industries. In addition, these preconditions also start to highlight the nature and form of advertising itself and most fundamentally its importance as mass communication. Apart from the odd glaring exception such as the advertising campaigns for Levi's 501 jeans in the 1980s, advertising is not *necessarily* particularly effective in stimulating sales of commodities or services, with the exception of detailed product listings. Also, unlike personal selling or perhaps marketing more generally, in terms of the so-called AIDA model of marketing – which stands for the processes through which Awareness leads to Interest, which stimulates Desire and turns into Action or sale – advertising is located firmly at the top in providing maximum awareness with the minimum of impact on sales (Schudson 1993). What it does do, perhaps very effectively, however, is define products or services in terms of their image, style or association and, most importantly, it promotes a knowledge of the product or service *en masse*, particularly through television, in a way that no other sales medium can parallel. What happens after that in terms of its intention, impact or importance remains entirely open to interpretation, as we shall see shortly.

As a result, in the first instance, advertising tends to shift the emphasis from the customer in the shop or on the doorstep to the wider concept of the more 'virtual', or unknown, consumer. This is important, for what it demonstrates is the process of, in some senses, quite literally disembodying the roles of buyer and seller and, by association, consumption itself. Significantly, then, this allows the act of consumption to float less attached to interpersonal interaction, at least until point of sale. Ultimately, this also taps into wider questions of the dissociation of products and services from their representations under conditions of postmodernity (see Chapter 8).

Falk, in particular, also asserts that, as time has gone on, advertising has indeed increasingly lost its attachment to what it is advertising, in terms of an increasing shift of emphasis from facts and specifications to meanings and associations. In addition, he cites the notorious and inflammatory example of the recent Benetton campaigns – which have included photographs of blood-strewn babies, dying AIDS sufferers and Bosnian army fatigues – as evidence of increasingly autonomous signification in advertising, as little or nothing in the adverts themselves actually shows the clothes themselves or other Benetton products. For Falk, then, *all* advertising is increasingly experiential as opposed to product centred, and overwhelmingly more and more visual as opposed to textual (Falk 1994, 1997).

Falk's argument tends to spearhead a wider concern with the historical development of advertising, studied most concretely in the work of Sut Jhally, Stephen Kline and William Leiss (Leiss 1976; Leiss *et al.* 1986; Jhally 1987). The most fundamental assertion underlying all of their work is the increasing commodification of human needs under conditions of Western capitalism. This is explored most fully in Leiss's work *The Limits to Satisfaction*, which explores the historical development of commodified needs and its attendant consequences (Leiss 1976). Leiss's contention is that the shift from traditional to modern forms of society has entailed an increase in human needs in conjunction with their increasingly direct attachment to the values of materialism and commodities and, furthermore, that the contemporary predicament is one that is out of control: 'There is no apparent end to the escalation of demand and no assurance that a sense of contentment or well-being will be found in the higher reaches of material abundance' (Leiss 1976: 7).

The underlying logic of this development is the geometric progression of needs in direct accordance with the proliferation of commodities through the processes of fragmentation and diversification of commodities and needs alike. For Leiss, then, needs are seen to multiply and separate in a precise correlation with the production and expansion of goods and services. His overall prognosis is somewhat pessimistic and exasperated, as: 'The point is that in this process individuals become confused about their wants in relation to the means that are supposed to satisfy them' (Leiss 1976: 21). This seems to inform an analysis of an underlying logic of consumption where human needs or desires and the world of commodities are caught up in a mutually perpetuating programme of escalation. Interestingly, there are some parallels here with Simmel's positing of a notion of the 'overstimulation' of human psychology in the modern city (see Chapter 1).

The specific role of advertising in this process is analysed more directly in the collaborative work of Leiss, Kline and Jhally in *Social Communication in Advertising* (Leiss *et al.* 1986). Although this is partly a textbook critique of prevailing literatures on advertising, it leads to a fairly grandiose theory of the role of advertising as part of the history of Western capitalism, the fundamental starting point for which is outlined as follows:

Advertising is not just a business expenditure undertaken in the hope of moving some merchandise off the store shelves, but is rather an integral part of modern culture. Its creations appropriate and transform a vast range of symbols and ideas; its unsurpassed communicative powers recycle cultural models and references back through the networks of social interactions. This venture is unified by the discourse through and about objects, which bonds together images of persons, products and well-being.

(Leiss *et al.* 1986: 7)

The importance attached to advertising is clearly immense and the underlying thrust of their analysis is anthropological, centred on the argument that advertising has, in a sense, ended up as the new totemic system in a society that has otherwise lost its sense of more traditional, and spiritual, meaning. Consequently, advertising not only gives meaning to goods and commodities, but also to the people who purchase and use them and, on top of this, it plays an important role in the maintenance and formation of social order through creating easily recognized coded systems of meaning.

There are several immediate difficulties to raise here. First, the thesis of secularization, although easily supported in general terms, is not necessarily complete, and the rise of alternative religions gives further credence to the notion that even if there is a significant loss of spiritual meaning in contemporary Western society in Christian terms, this is not necessarily reclaimed through advertising or even consumerism. Second, and perhaps more importantly, the assertion that advertising is automatically an effective communicator of social values, or indeed more mundane matters of the importance of its own products, is open to interpretation and, as we shall see shortly, often severely challenged through the downright uninterest of the audience. Third, in traditional societies, the world of commodities is often far from meaningless and is frequently integral to social or spiritual value systems (see Chapter 2). The point of difference, and indeed alienation, as explicated more fully in variants of Marxist theory, is the *separation* of subjects and objects that then becomes 'reconnected' in capitalist society through the processes of commodity fetishism (see Chapter 1). A similar point also applies to Jhally's own more personal work on the role of advertising, which posits the argument that advertising has become a modern-day religion (Jhally 1987). Much of this debate centres not so much on the role of advertising *per se*, but on the impact of television watching which, in North American society in particular, is perceived to have reached epidemic proportions. As a result, there are clear dangers of oversimplification of a more complex series of cultural and historical developments.

However, Leiss, Kline and Jhally also produce a more detailed empirical analysis of the development of modern forms of advertising, which are seen to have moved through four successive stages. The first of these is located in the years immediately prior to and after the turn of the century, when advertising operated primarily through newspapers and magazines. This stage is seen to illustrate a more *rational* or information-based form of advertising, centred on an overall strategy of *utility* or use value within a cultural frame for commodities identified as *idolatry*. The second stage, from about 1920 to 1940, is seen to become increasingly *non-rational* and *symbolic*, using radio as its key mechanism in an era of advertising through a culture of *iconography*. The third and fourth stages, which occupy the 1950s to 1960s and 1970s to 1980s respectively, are centred on the development of advertising through television and are seen to move from a *behaviourist* strategy centred on *personalization* to a market *segmentation* strategy centred on the use of *lifestyle* categories. This in turn represents a shift from *narcissism* to *totemism* in terms of the overall cultural frame of reference surrounding commodities. Underlying this are three key developments: first, the recognition of consumption as a legitimate form of self-realization; second, the increasing valuing of the consumer's psychology over the product's utility value within the strategies of marketing and advertising; and third, advances in the development of media technologies. Ultimately, this is then seen to influence the entire social value system, which is seen to increasingly approximate the mechanisms of advertising. Advertising thus becomes the mere tip of the iceberg of a sea change towards modern consumer culture.

Although accepting that advances in technology and the media industries more generally have led to a rise in more visual forms of advertising, I dispute whether this has in fact led to some kind of 'annihilation' of earlier forms. More particularly, the mode of advertising seems to vary enormously from product to product and service to service. Most electrical goods, for example, are still advertised for the most part in textual simplicity in newspapers, proclaiming their price over everything else; while cars seem located in a schizophrenic stratosphere, ranging from surreal television advertising aimed primarily at the new car market to tedious lists of cut price deals in the secondhand and classified sections of local journals; and the advertising of perfumes seems almost entirely locked into the alluring world of glossy magazines, the gift market and Christmas.

In addition, the advertising of different products, even within the same mode of address, varies enormously, from the increasingly archaic attempts to sell washing powder to surreal adverts for car tyres. For example, a recent Pirelli tyre advert features an athletic woman seemingly running across an entire southwestern state of the United States effectively 'glued' to everything from water tunnels to mountains; while the 'Daz doorstep challenge', where housewives are invited to show the television camera which powder washes their whites whiter almost teeters on self-parody. My argument, then, is that there is some significant variation in differing forms of advertising, older and newer, which also opens up the question of a need for more multiple interpretation, not so much *within* forms of advertising as *across* them. What this also leads to is a need for a more sophisticated analysis of advertising's functions and effects than is often currently invoked in an increasingly polarized dispute which I now wish to investigate.

Advertising as ideology

The earliest and most influential perspectives on advertising have one factor in common, namely a perception of advertising as strongly ideological. Advertising is seen, in essence, to 'sell' either the product or service or, most pervasively, a consumerist lifestyle or perspective. Vance Packard's *The Hidden Persuaders* forms a primary example of this viewpoint and, as its title implies, is severely critical of advertising's role in apparently duping the consumer and controlling the minds of the general population (Packard 1957). In addition, linked to this was the more implicit and insidious idea that the consumer society of the 1950s was increasingly rendering the population as a whole politically passive as well. Packard's assertions were centred on a potent pot-pourri of fears and anxieties concerning the increasing popularity of behavioural psychology in advertising on the one hand, and the perceived threat to individual consciousness from multinational conglomerations and commerce on the other. He cites numerous examples of the implementation of psychological techniques in the advertising strategies of large and commercially successful companies and there is some parallel here with the safety campaigns of Ralph Nader discussed in Chapter 4.

In particular, it was the twin spectre of subliminal control and overt provocation of anxiety that caught Packard's attention. The most sensational example of this process was the discovery that some companies were piloting an advertising technique involving showing a product or service on screen for one frame per second, thus rendering the selling invisible but subliminally potentially very effective. As is perhaps already apparent, this was in some ways a peculiarly North American cocktail of paranoia, with a shot of the Cold War thrown in to make up the measure. Importantly, though, it also paralleled the more sophisticated critique of mass culture and control exposed in the work of the Frankfurt School which also informs the work of Goldman, which I will consider shortly (see also Chapter 1). As it stands then, the extremes of this perspective often seem outdated yet make the vitally important point that whatever advertising's function is, it is neither culturally nor politically neutral.

A more sophisticated and somewhat later perspective was developed in the work of Stuart Ewen in *Captains of Consciousness* (1976). Ewen's perspective was essentially historical and, for him, the rise of advertising in the 1920s and 1930s was critical as cause and effect alike in the construction of contemporary capitalism. In particular, he makes the connection of mass production and scientific Taylorism on the one hand with the rise of consumerism on the other. For Ewen, then, consumerism, and most particularly advertising as its primary cultural constituent, forms a major social control mechanism in motivating and manipulating the affluent factory worker. Members of the working class are increasingly seen to fall victim to the power of advertising in constructing their identities as consumers. More importantly, Ewen argues, this formed a primary mechanism in controlling any escalation in worker unrest on the Fordist factory floor. As a result, corporate capitalism now controlled its workforce from within rather than without as, Ewen asserts, advertisers and corporatists developed a mutually reinforcing relationship. As a result the 'captains of industry' or commerce were equally the 'captains of consciousness'.

The relationship between advertising and corporatism was perhaps never quite so simple, and Ewen's perspective was criticized later for underestimating its complexity, yet it remains a perceptive and historically well-documented account of their conflation. Although centred on the United States, this is not many miles empirically from the work of Galbraith, or even Goldthorpe and Lockwood's studies of worker instrumentalism and materialism in the UK (Galbraith 1958; Lockwood 1958; Goldthorpe *et al.* 1968a, 1968b, 1969).

A more recent analysis of advertising's ideological significance is given in the work of Robert Goldman in *Reading Ads Socially* (Goldman 1992). Goldman's analysis is centred on an application of critical theory to the relationship of ideology through what he calls the 'commodity form'. The commodity form is essentially the mechanism through which advertising creates meaning and ideology. Consequently, how it operates is related precisely and directly to its effects. Advertisements are seen, in the first instance, to structure wider social meanings so that they produce commodity sign value. To put it more simply, any advertisement takes a human value or emotion – from maternal love to happiness – and turns it into a metaphor or symbol that can then be commodified. Second, as the underlying commodity form or mechanisms of advertising are already known to them, the audience are themselves drawn into a cycle of producing, rather than merely reading, commodity sign values. Goldman uses the example of perfume advertising, and there is some parallel here with the work of Williamson on whom he draws significantly and whose work I will consider shortly. However, although Williamson is primarily concerned with the varied semiotics of advertising and their ideological consequences, Goldman is effectively quite determined to grind any such variance down into one singular logic of argument.

As a result, Goldman's analysis develops a third dimension, namely that of the changing forms of advertising over time, for which he takes three primary examples: the incorporation of feminism into commodity culture, the success of the Levi's 501 advertising campaign in the 1980s, and the movement towards greater reflexivity in advertising epitomized in the later advertisements by Reebok. Goldman's problematic argument here is that all of these examples simply demonstrate the way in which advertising can, in effect, turn anything and everything towards its own ends. Consequently, he asserts: 'Advertisers have tried to harness the ideological currency of feminism, re-routing feminist critique for the purpose of extending commodity relations' (Goldman 1992: 108). Thus, in an interesting play on Marx's theory of commodity fetishism, he sees advertisements that play on women's increased independence or sexual autonomy, or alternatively their anxiety and stress in playing the role of 'superwoman', as illustrative of a 'commodity feminism' where control over such factors as one's appearance is equated with control over one's life and future.

Of linked significance is the question of increased reflexivity in advertising. According to Goldman, whose analysis is more or less wholly centred on the United States, during the 1980s advertisers were aware of the scepticism of their audience who, faced with an escalating array of styles of advertising and advertisements, were growing more cynical. Advertising companies sought to incorporate this sense of scepticism into the advertising itself. Reflexive advertising was therefore characterized as increasingly pared down and dependent on the audience to make sense of it. The famous advertising campaigns for Calvin Klein's 'Obsession' fragrance range, using monochromatic and near silent yet highly sexually charged images, are seen to epitomize this appeal to an increasingly dissenting audience. In addition, the Levi's 501 jeans advertisements of the 1980s are equally seen to reinvolve, and therefore recommodify, the alternative values of the audience through incorporating a mixture of myth and authenticity through the associations of street culture and soul music. The advertisements also used a device he calls the 'knowing wink', where the audience is drawn in to interact with the actors in the advertisement. Moreover, then: '*Levi's* showed how advertisers could absorb criticism of advertising by turning criticism to become a part of their meta-message' (Goldman 1992: 174, original italics).

A similar principle of pastiche and parody is seen to be applied in the Reebok campaign which plays on a series of apparently bizarre applications of the product, including scenes of pensioners square dancing in red sneakers or a ballerina vacuuming a rug on the grass outside while practising her *plié*. In all cases, the examples are used to fuel Goldman's condemnation of postmodernism and to reassert his argument that '. . . the motor of hegemonic ideology now lies in the very openness of the ads as texts' (Goldman 1992: 198).

Such perspectives have since come in for significant criticism on several grounds. First, and most immediately, for their apparent simplicity, particularly in relation to questions of intention or function. Although some companies may well use advertising to varying degrees as a kind of self-promoting propaganda, not all do or necessarily even could. Second, an equally clear consideration concerns the one-sidedness of the equation in rendering the consumer completely passive and little allowance is made for resistance or opposition. Third, then, the power relationship of advertisers and consumers is seen to heavily and perhaps disproportionately favour the advertiser. Fourth, this leads to the situation where if the consumer falls for the values of advertising at whatever level they are accused of false consciousness. What this creates, then, is the ultimate no-win situation for the consumer in consumer society. Consequently, there is therefore a tendency to see meaning as residing *within* the advertisement rather than as coming from *without* and it is this factor in particular, along with the other criticisms, that has since informed the opposing perspective of advertising as interpretation.

Advertising as interpretation

> The more general argument that we put forward here is that advertising is crucial to our sense of the present, whatever its relation to products advertised and their consumption, and that while advertising should be studied in parallel with consumption, it must also be studied in relation to *interpretation*.
>
> (Nava *et al.* 1997: 4, original emphasis)

The starting point for a more interpretivist perspective on advertising is, for the most part, a certain scepticism concerning its power and influence. This is put most forcefully in the work of Michael Schudson who, in his work *Advertising: The Uneasy Persuasion*, presents a detailed account of the limits of advertising and the impact that it may or may not have on society as a whole and, in particular, the individual consumer (Schudson 1993). More particularly, there are several levels to his analysis: first, he asserts that advertising is not sales driven and for the most part *cannot* lead directly to sales, and its role instead is primarily an informative one as what he calls an 'awareness institution'; second, he posits that advertising is often more important to the commercial world in terms of selling products or services and companies to each other than it is to the ordinary consumer; and third, he argues strongly that consumers do not particularly fall for the ploys of advertisers and: 'Advertisements ordinarily work their wonders, to the extent that they work at all, on an inattentive public' (Schudson 1993: 3).

Nevertheless, he does *not* assert that advertising is simply insignificant. In particular, he documents with some sensitivity the differences in vulnerability to advertising across global society, arguing that the poorest, least educated, most isolated and generally disadvantaged are at far greater risk of seduction from the allures of advertising. Also, in common with Leiss and Jhally, he takes a somewhat anthropological slant on the rise of modern consumerism and is concerned that advertising only truly sends one message: 'It glorifies the pleasures and freedom of consumer choice. It defends the virtues of private life and material ambition. It idealizes the consumer and consuming. It holds implicitly or explicitly that freedom, fulfilment and personal transformation lie in the world of goods' (Schudson 1993: xix). The net result of this is to provide a fairly severe critique of an overly propagandist interpretation of advertising, as outlined in the works of Ewen or Packard, while remaining sensitive to the wider impact of advertising as a phenomenon and as part of consumer culture.

As such, it is not entirely dissimilar from what is perhaps the most eminent example of advertising as interpretation, namely Judith Williamson's *Decoding Advertisements* (1978). As a journalist and cultural critic, Williamson crucially invoked the use of semiotics as part of a wider study of the varying context of advertising itself through a series of textual interpretations. In particular, this removed any immediate and simplistic sense of advertising's *message* and problematized its *meaning* within wider developments in commerce or consumption, focusing on advertisements as complex texts open to interpretation.

Consequently, the work has two halves, the first focusing on how advertisements work and the second focusing on the wider context, or 'referent systems' of meaning, within which they work. Her initial assertion is that advertising itself has no meaning other than that which develops through the processes of how we interpret them: 'We can only understand what advertisements mean by finding out *how* they mean, and analysing the way in which they work' (Williamson 1978: 17, original emphasis). This Williamson does with some flair and with considerable detail, particularly in relation to magazine advertisements of commodities aimed at women.

The primary example of these processes is an early magazine advertisement for the perfume Chanel No. 5. A picture of the coffret of perfume itself is juxtaposed simply and directly with a photograph of Catherine Deneuve as the epitome of a particularly French form of feminine sophistication and stylishness. This example, which for Williamson is 'paradigmatic', is seen to illustrate several important points: first, that the advert itself has no meaning and that its message relies entirely on its audience to fill in the gaps and make the connections; second, that these processes of connection work only in relation to a wider referent system of meaning which exists outside the advertisement, in this case the association of all perfumes with feminine sexuality and the wider understanding of cultural and media icons such as Deneuve; and third, that this then forms part of a wider process of transference, equation and generation of meaning *within* the advert itself. Thus, the association of feminine sophistication is transferred from Deneuve to Chanel No. 5, and this is then directly equated with the perfume so that purchasing it is seen to generate the association quite independently of the advert. The end result is that purchasing and using Chanel No. 5 give its wearer precisely those qualities that she sees in the advertisement and that the advertisement transfers, with her help, on to the product. Consequently, advertisements and their consumers seem locked into a cycle of production of one another.

This is, of course, the perspective that underpins much contemporary work on popular culture, which attempts to read advertising through empirical examples rather than focus on its theoretical or political ramifications out of context (Nava *et al.* 1997). Nevertheless, Williamson's perspective is not easily equated with the work of contemporary cultural critics, for the other side of her analysis is a decidedly more political critique of the ideology of advertising. The underlying theoretical and political thrust of her analysis is, therefore, Marxism and not poststructuralism and she remains deeply concerned at the way in which advertising removes meaning only to place it on the product as part and parcel of the wider processes of commodity fetishism.

A key example of this is her reappropriation of Levi-Strauss's notion of 'cooking', which she applies to the advertising of food and nature. For Williamson, nature is precisely 'cooked' to become culture, devoid of its rawness, which is in turn endlessly 'produced' through the discourses of science in advertising, which in turn play on notions of nature in a highly artificial way. In short, 'nature' is destroyed and turned into 'the natural' as a device of advertising. This is particularly the case with beauty and body products, and those associated with food or cooking, all of which play heavily on notions of freshness, vitality and health. Furthermore, given the lack of a specific temporal location in most advertising, such advertisements are also seen as mythic and timeless. This leads Williamson into some hazy notions of advertising's role as a quasi-religion, but her underlying analysis remains ideological, seeing advertising as insidiously self-defensive and self-perpetuating: 'Thus, ideologies cannot be known and undone, so much as engaged with – in a sort of running battle, almost a race since the rate at which all their forms, especially advertising, reabsorb critical material, is alarmingly fast' (Williamson 1978: 178).

Nevertheless, in Williamson's case, the advertisements are still essentially interpreted as realist texts rather than as interpretive constructions or, to put it more simply, the emphasis is firmly placed on the decoding rather than the encoding of advertisements. More academically, others have since started to develop a sense of the theoretical and empirical ramifications of this perspective in producing more conceptual frameworks centred on the importance of reception itself in the production of texts and their significance, or ethnographic studies of their incorporation and interpretation into the practice of everyday life (see, for example, Hall 1980; Williams 1980; McRobbie and Nava 1984).

This starts to lead to a sense of contradiction in the analysis of advertising. If advertisements are understood wholly as interpretivist texts dependent entirely on their audience for their (varied) interpretation, then this is difficult to reconcile with an analysis of advertising as having an overall ideological function. A key issue here is that an analysis of advertise*ments* does not necessarily equate with an analysis of advertis*ing*. Although there is a strong tendency for an analysis of advertisements to shift towards a more interpretivist perspective, particularly more recently, the role of advertising itself is seen almost unanimously as ideological. However, this can also work the other way around.

A prime example of this process is the now-classic analysis of advertising given in Goffman's work on *Gender Advertisements* (Goffman 1976). Famed for his development of a dramaturgical sociology of human interaction as socially governed and near theatrical in its playing out of equally conspicuous and often hidden roles, Goffman's analysis of advertising is fundamentally driven by a wider analysis of the significance of gendered rituals of display through which the sexes communicate and interact with one another as men and women who play and display themselves *as* men and women. Moreover, this is welded to a simple though thorough content analysis of more than 500 advertisements randomly collected from magazines.

The advertisements are used to demonstrate a series of 'genderisms' or patterned displays of gender roles. There are roughly six of these and they are clearly interlinked. First, in an analysis of *relative size*, Goffman notes that men are mostly represented as taller or larger than women, except when men are clearly playing a subordinate role as in the case of servants or service workers. Second, in *the feminine touch* he asserts that women's hands are comparatively more important than men's and are shown in positions where they are touching or caressing themselves, another part of the woman, or a man. Similarly, and third, in *function ranking*, men are shown as taking charge or in a more active or assertive light in many situations, whereas women are represented as spectating or more passive. Fourth, in pictures of *the family*, men are shown as taller or overarching their wives and children who sit or stand alongside but underneath them in a typical display of patriarchal paternalism. Fifth, in the *ritualization of subordination*, men are most often shown to stand firm while women kneel, lie, curve in some way or simply smile. Finally, in *licensed withdrawal*, women are shown as more removed from the immediate situation, watching, often powerless, or showing greater emotional distress.

The underlying effect in all cases is to reinforce the passivity of women and activity of men as a gender ideal and, furthermore, to sometimes infanticize women and to strongly associate them with the dependency of children. In addition, although dated, this also fuels wider feminist accusations of sexism in advertising and the representations of women more widely (see Chapter 6). The extraordinary irony here, however, is that Goffman entirely fails to draw on this more ideological dimension and alludes instead to a vague notion of the innocence of advertising. He concludes: 'If anything, advertisers conventionalize our conventions, stylize what is already a stylization, make frivolous use of what is already something consistently cut off from contextual controls. Their hype is hyper-ritualization' (Goffman 1976: 84). Thus, the ideology of the advertisements themselves is missed in a stingless analysis of the role of advertising.

Others have also pointed to the changing position of advertising as an increasingly insecure and free-floating practice that depends on very competitive securing of short-term company contracts (Wernick 1991; Lury 1996; Nava *et al.* 1997). In conjunction with this, as already outlined, advertising and marketing have never connected directly with wider corporate decisions or production methods and have tended to practise within their own limits, primarily as a consultancy and not as a corporation, fuelling speculations concerning perceptions of the role of advertisers as, more accurately, 'cultural intermediaries' rather than propaganda merchants (Bourdieu 1984). Most importantly, then, this starts to open up the precariousness of advertising's position as an ideology and an institution alike.

The clear difficulty here, however, is that such an overly reflexive or interpretivist stance can lead to an intense relativism where, in a sense, 'anything goes'. In addition, it can also lapse into the particular strain of uncritical populism exemplified by the work of Fowles:

> Beyond an objective examination of the two leading contemporary symbol domains, this book intends to endorse consumers (who are, after all, exactly like you and me, no better and no worse, only replicated numerously beyond our spheres of empathy) and to validate the individual consumer's personal interpretations both of advertising messages and of advertising's companion and matrix, popular culture.
>
> (Fowles 1996: xv)

Apart from the point that some interpretations clearly are not valid, the severe difficulty here is the sense of almost total divorce of advertising from wider questions concerning politics, the economy or even consumption itself. As a consequence, although the emphasis has tended to shift slightly from the study of advertis*ing* to the analysis of advertise*ments*, it seems that we have returned to square one, where the consumer is either rendered the passive dupe of some capitalist conspiracy or the free-floating, unconstrained and pleasure-seeking interpreter. As neither is truly accurate, is there any way out of this academic impasse?

One potential solution comes in the work of Andrew Wernick who, with some scholarly flair, seeks to re-evaluate the cultural legacy of the Frankfurt School and the limits of poststructuralist theory alike in *Promotional Culture* (Wernick 1991). His starting point is to define advertising in terms of promotion, which in turn equates it with a wider sense of generality and a simultaneously more compound and dynamic series of processes alike. As a consequence, advertising is argued to apply to all products and services on all levels and includes state as well as private institutions and, most significantly of all, involves its individual practitioners as much as the ill-defined consumers they seek to persuade. In addition, as a result of this: 'It is defined not by what it says but what it does, with respect to which its stylist and semantic contents are purely secondary, and derived' (Wernick 1991: 184).

Wernick also argues that promotional mechanisms were integral to the working of the capitalist system from the start of the industrial revolution in a complex intertwining of the processes of production and promotion, where the 'commodity sign', defined in postmodern terms and derived from the work of Baudrillard, and the 'promotional sign', defined essentially as the commercial representation of the commodity, are completely interlinked (see also Chapter 8). In addition, this also connects the processes of production and consumption, where the same process of signification impacts on the processes of design and representation alike. For example, the design of a car is seen to reflect its semiotic value as much as the design itself impacts on its semiotics in an entirely continuous and circular process. In this sense, then, advertising is neither the demon propagandist nor the open space of interpretation so much as part and parcel of a wider process of promotion which is fundamentally integral to the very functioning of the modern capitalist system. In sum, what this then adds up to is an entire promotional *culture* which affects higher education as much as it does fast cars. Consequently: 'As a determinate element, then, of the economy whose cultural disturbances it promotionally mediates, advertising operates as a kind of cultural gyroscope' (Wernick 1991: 45).

The clear difficulty with an otherwise persuasive perspective is that, in incorporating the consumer and producer alike in the analysis, promotional culture acts as the ultimate 'super system', or centrifuge, or what Wernick himself calls a 'promotional vortex', into which everything gets sucked with or against its will. In particular, this then renders both the consumer and the producer as a commodity through the additional commodification of self, where 'being is reduced to having, desire to lack' (Wernick 1991: 35). Plenty of examples of such processes are provided in relation to the increasing incorporation of men as well as women into the pernicious signification of advertising, the reincorporation of advances in technology in the case of cars, and even the construction of a promotional politics where the same processes are used to promote Polish Solidarity and Thatcherism. The likely consequence of these processes, then, is that the amalgam of Marxism and poststructuralism seems merely to lead to the ultimate Orwellian nightmare:

It is as if we are in a hall of mirrors. Each promotional message refers us to a commodity which is itself the site of another promotion. And so on, in an endless dance whose only point is to circulate the circulation of something else. To be caught up as a cultural consumer in the vortex of promotional signs is not only to be continually reminded of the myriad things and experiences we lack. It is to be engulfed, semiotically in a great, swirling stream of signifiers whose only meaning, in the end, is the circulatory process which it anticipates, represents, and impels.

(Wernick 1991: 121)

All of this also raises the question of whether this is the full story concerning advertising. To address this, it is worth looking at the example at the apex of conspicuous capitalism: the car.

Reinventing the wheel: signification, advertising and cars

Car imagery, like the rest of the manufactured signage of advanced capitalist culture, is reaching the stage where its signifying gestures refer us only, in the end, to the universe of symbols from which they are drawn.

(Wernick 1991: 89)

Does the advertising of cars, indeed, merely and simply reinvent the wheel over and over again in its own self-referential circle? Wernick's answer to this question is, one suspects, in the affirmative. However, I wish to reconsider this assertion in the light of what I perceive to be the often paradoxical and contradictory nature of advertising of cars and, in addition, it is my intention in this final section to summarize and re-evaluate some of the controversies surrounding advertising and advertisements.

In the first instance, there are perhaps some parallels in the historical developments of advertising and the car. In particular, cars and advertising crucially took off through technological advances and productive expansion in the 1920s and 1930s to then turn into significant factors in the postwar construction of a consumer society in the 1950s and 1960s. Similarly, it is now equally difficult to conceive of the world without either cars or their advertising. In addition, they are also strongly associated with the capitalist values of financial success, independence and personal freedom. On top of this, and as we have already seen, these are precisely the values that advertising is often predicated upon and promotes. In this sense, cars and their drivers, and indeed advertising, are perhaps now set up as the new social pariahs of the environmentally conscious third millennium.

More particularly, the motorist and the car owner have recently come in for heavy criticism as environmentally destructive and sometimes raving mad, as in the recent sensationalist cases of so-called road rage. Although cars are increasingly a necessity for many people because of the declining fortunes of alternative forms of transport coupled with the need to travel further to work, school or to maintain social or familial contacts, the motorist – and particularly the young, single motorist – is often stigmatized as some kind of greedy corporatist and for precisely the same reasons that the car is valued: independence, status and personal success.

What this presents us with is an increasingly paradoxical picture concerning the car. As peak-hour traffic congestion turns into a way of life, as the costs of owning a car escalate, and as the counter-cultural attack on cars and their owners increases, the car's social significance as a lexicon of individual status and freedom simultaneously multiplies in a peculiar geometric progression to the point where the modern car and its driver have gained almost mythic proportions. Fuelling this, along with the petrol, is advertising.

Advertising, particularly in its glossy magazine or televised format, routinely tends to perpetuate the mythic dimensions of modern driving: namely, that driving a certain car will create freedom, independence or personal success for its driver. The additional paradox is that the increasingly dismal reality of car ownership as a tiresome, uninspiring and costly necessity is exploited in advertising as cars are presented racing across open roads, almost jumping or skipping around cities, thwarting crime and rendering their drivers relaxed, safe and joyful. Consequently, particularly in its televised format, what car advertising constantly perpetuates is a fantasy or an ideal of car driving, often overriding the detailed significance of the car itself. As a result, there is a sense in which car advertising illustrates precisely the shifts towards greater visual content and lifestyle fantasy that Leiss and his colleagues illustrate (Leiss *et al.* 1986).

Moreover, however, the history of car advertising has also consistently played on these themes, which have, in some senses, changed little over time. As Wernick notes, these have included three key and interlinked factors: first, the car's incorporation and control of technology and, through extension, the driver's control of that same system through the skill of driving itself; second, the car's invocation of status, starting as the privilege of the upper classes and spreading to include the identities of the population as a whole; and third, the car's connection with the family or family roles, where the father as driver, mother as passenger and children as rear-seat occupants, or irritants, has increasingly found itself usurped in favour of lone or women drivers, although children remain firmly seated in the rear (Wernick 1991).

Central in the construction of more recent car advertising, however, is the more free-floating question of identity, which has increasingly led to the construction of cars as the ultimate example of what marketers call 'product personality'. Indeed, the latest advertisements for the Renault Mégane features the car actually talking to its owner. This is, though, also a wider and not so new phenomenon, as cars have historically taken on human characteristics: headlights as eyes, badges as noses, and radiator grilles as teeth or mouths, let alone the infamous Herbie movies or the phallic connotations of rounded rear-ends and long front-ends epitomized by the E-type Jaguar.

More seriously, contemporary car advertising increasingly tends to create lifestyle categories for its owners which, in particular, are strongly gendered. Smaller cars are routinely targeted at young, independent women and larger, executive cars are still used to connote successful masculinity. Family presentations now seem entirely restricted to the newest class of vehicle, the people carrier. In particular, this gendered dimension taps into wider cultural concerns relating to socialization as the toy car is as strongly culturally equated with the play activities of little boys as the Barbie doll is with those of little girls. Car magazines, meanwhile, overwhelm their specifically male readership with the details of ride, handling and performance, producing endless test statistics under the auspices of some kind of scientific analysis and perpetuating a hopeless sense of aspirationalism in printing glossy pictures of hyper-expensive sports cars. Significantly, though, it is the car's equation with self that constitutes a greater sense of concern here as the car is seen as acting like a kind of third skin working almost like another layer of clothing, where that fast little French car feels like a little French dress and the executive's Audi merely adds to the Armani suit. This is precisely the commodification of personality that concerns writers as diverse as Goldman and Leiss or Ewen and Williamson, as well as Wernick (Ewen 1976; Leiss 1976; Williamson 1978; Wernick 1991; Goldman 1992).

An additional factor here, particularly in the more television-driven advertising of cars, is the question of nationality. Upmarket German vehicles are routinely associated with German engineering typified in the Audi 'vorsprung Durch technik' campaigns, incorporating a kind of Germanic gobbledegook; while BMWs as the 'ultimate driving experience' have almost become the Aryan race of vehicles. Similarly, small French cars are endlessly paraded as typically French, feminine and flirtatious, of which the story of Nicole, Papa and her Renault Clio forms the primary example; and Italian cars are presented as Latinate lovers on wheels, frisky and fast, as in the case of Fiat's 'Spirito di Punto'. Meanwhile, 'Relax, it's a Rover' vehicles are still sold according to a sense of refined Englishness – and the list goes on, and on and on.

The irony is that the cars themselves, located as they are within the same central advances in technology, are increasingly similar – hence the claim that people can't tell them apart. Importantly, though, this leads to the most central paradox of car advertising and car design. As roads clog up and speed cameras are imposed, the cars are designed to go faster and faster and are sold precisely according to the same technological advances, and many even very modestly sized engines will far exceed national speed limits. On top of this, the further spectre of death or accidents on the roads is raised yet, ironically, manufacturers relentlessly add to the safety of cars with everything from air bags to impact bars just so that you can go faster, and faster, without worrying.

There is something slightly sinister in this sense of impulse to test all human limits, fuelling an increasingly postmodern sense of *fin de siècle* implosion (see Chapter 8). More importantly, though, it also feeds into the psychology and indeed psychoanalysis of car driving, and particularly its exotic equation of sex and death, as fast driving is routinely equated with sexuality, particularly male sexuality: doing it faster allegedly requires greater skill, and yet equally invokes connotations of risk taking and death. This equation of sex and death in relation to cars and driving was recently the focus of much attention in relation to David Cronenberg's direction of the film *Crash*, itself based on J. G. Ballard's book that tells the story of a group of young people who are increasingly and quite literally sexually turned on through experiencing car accidents. The equally violent level of controversy surrounding the movie's release and the attempts to censor it provided some testimony to the social and cultural anxiety still surrounding the car and sexuality.

This leads to the question of the connection of advertising to the construction of identity more widely. It is routinely asserted that cars act as extensions of personality and this is a factor clearly exploited in car advertising, as we have already seen. However, what is also very clear, although often missing in many analyses, are the *limits* of advertising in impacting on personality or identity. Although affluent and style-conscious young men looking to extend their egos *may* enjoy driving their glamorous vehicles, others perhaps couldn't care less, can't afford it or refute it outright. Also of significance here is the variation in advertising itself. Fast, flashy or new cars may well have repeated viewings on prime-time television; the rest do not and consequently have none of the associations, positively or negatively.

What, then, are we to make of this often highly contradictory situation? Three factors stand out as of particular significance: first, the increasing sense of equation of luxury cars or commodities with not only status but a *compote* of product personality and lifestyle associations; second, the escalating sense of social division that extends from the advertising of cars, where not only are lifestyle categories constructed but the gulf between new versus old car owners itself widens; and third, and most importantly, the sense in which car advertising, through its appeal to the ideals of freedom and independence, is increasingly devoid of any connection to lived reality or experience.

This final factor in particular also affects the consumption of cars as commodities and their advertising alike. Although some people may well enter the increasingly surreal world of television advertising for cars, many others, particularly those excluded or uninterested, may find the situation increasingly ridiculous. As a result, the advertising of cars not only operates more independently of its commodities, it also perhaps acts semi-autonomously of its audience of consumers as well, who may regard the advertising as a self-contained entity for amusement in itself, like mini-movie entertainment, and may well divorce it entirely from any purchasing decision. Schudson's detailed list of restrictions surrounding the influence of advertising is particularly significant here (Schudson 1993). In this sense, then, car advertising represents the power and control of producer and consumer alike, caught up in a constant and circular process of trying to keep one step ahead of one another.

A primary example of these processes at work was the recent, and much acclaimed, advertising campaign for the new Volkswagen Passat. Despite the 'yuppie and whiz' associations of the Golf GTI in the 1980s, Volkswagen cars have tended to rank as quite mundane in the status stakes, at least relative to their German competitors Audi and BMW. The new Passat, which car enthusiasts rapidly hailed as an outstanding technical success, was advertised in the press and television alike as an object of perfection 'born out of obsession by laboratoires Volkswagen' while white-coated scientists flapped around the vehicle in its 'laboratory'. The double reference here to both Calvin Klein's fragrance 'Obsession' – the advertising for which epitomized 1980s minimalism and lifestyle surrealism *par excellence*, in turn giving the likes of Baudrillard and the Krokers enough 'textual excrement' to send them into 'hyper spew' for decades – on the one hand; and the slightly kooky French scientific pretentiousness of Laboratoires Garnier skin products on the other, rendered Volkswagen and the Passat itself as at once technically superior and super-stylish as well as self deprecating and clever (see also Chapter 8).

The advert also highlighted a new development in advertising – namely, reflexivity. The trick here was that such self-referential advertising, which is increasing in its popularity as a genre *per se*, makes the viewer or reader, also the potential consumer, feel equally involved or clever in getting the joke. Consequently, the skill of advertising in playing the trump card with its own reflexive status seems merely to confirm Goldman's surmise that the game of cat and mouse with consumers and advertisers is, quite simply, never over (Goldman 1992). However, the consumer is perhaps neither the victim or dupe of some capitalist conspiracy nor merely a pleasure-seeking and frivolous individualist, but a fellow conspirer in the world of advertising, sniggering one minute and taking it all too seriously the next. As we have already seen, much depends on the type of advertising involved and the social or demographic position of the audience. As a consequence, consumer, producer and advertiser alike are perhaps caught up in the mutual perpetuation of their own relationships, but the importance of advertising is not necessarily so easily explained away and for this we need to return to the central themes of this chapter.

Conclusions: marketing, advertising and the construction of the contemporary consumer

In many respects, advertising, and marketing more widely, seems to stand at the apex of developments in consumer society throughout the twentieth century. Consequently, the importance attached to them as institutions and in relation to their impact on society is often immense. In some senses at least, this attention may seem a little misplaced.

In the first instance, it is often juxtaposed with the increasingly precarious state of marketing and advertising as commercial concerns that are as likely to fall victim to entrepreneurial competitiveness as they are to exploit whatever power they have over their rivals or their audience. As we have seen, advertising and marketing alike have also come in for significant criticism as manipulators of consumer consciousness or exploitative profit motivators. However, this is then often offset against the increasingly insecure and reflexive states of advertising and marketing as practices and the consumers' own thwarting, intentionally or unintentionally, of attempts to control them.

More academically, many theorists have also sought to question the extent to which advertising or marketing truly influence, in any one-way sense, the consciousness of the modern consumer, who is seen equally to reinterpret and redirect, or even reinvent, that with which he or she is presented. Despite this, the importance of advertising as an ideology where the supposed freedom of the consumer to choose, which is often allied to a wider notion of consumer democracy, also perpetuates the commodification of social values *per se* through the production of product solutions to the problems that advertising itself manufactures. Moreover, this tends to lead to a sense of impasse academically, where advertising is *either* a matter of ideology *or* a matter of interpretation. One solution of sorts to this contradiction is to start to separate the analysis of advertis*ing*, which does retain a varied although overall ideological function, from individual advertise*ments*, which are clearly wide open to multiple interpretation and may miss their mark as often as they make it. As we have seen, marketing and advertising also vary significantly in the techniques they use and the products and services to which they apply. In the end, then, despite the all too apparent trend towards equating advertising and marketing with personality and lifestyle, there is no real uniformity in intention or effect.

Ironically, despite the endless construction and deconstruction of discourses around the consumer as either a powerless victim or an empowered hedonist, a dupe operating under false consciousness or an active agent engaged in the production of consumption, there is often little attempt to document academically exactly who the audience is or precisely what it thinks. What is perhaps increasingly clear is the escalating sense in which advertising and marketing are more specifically, and indeed divisively, targeted towards certain status groups and market segments. As a consequence, it is this sense of rising divisiveness in consumer society that informs our analysis in the next chapter.

Suggested further reading

Goldman, R. (1992) *Reading Ads Socially*. London: Routledge – part textbook and part polemic, this includes some useful empirical examples of more recent developments in advertising including feminism and postmodernism.

Randall, G. (1993) *Principles of Marketing*. London: Routledge – textbook marketed at marketers but germane to sociologists.

Schudson, M. (1993) *Advertising: The Uneasy Persuasion*. London: Routledge – the most convincing counterweight to the advertising as ideology thesis.

Wernick, A. (1991) *Promotional Culture*. London: Sage – arguably the most full-blooded exploration of the relationship of marketing and advertising to contemporary consumer society.

Williamson, J. (1978) *Decoding Advertisements*. London: Marion Boyars – old but hardly out of date, this remains seminal to the formation of more cultural critiques of advertising and a highly original blend of Marxism and interpretivist sociology.

4
NEVER-NEVER LAND – SOCIAL POLICY, SOCIAL DIVISIONS AND CONSUMER SOCIETY

Social policy has not traditionally, to say the least, had a history of association with the world of consumer society, and yet it takes little consideration to realize that there are many and varied connections of social policy to the experience of shopping, control of expenditure and the politics of consumption – to name only some areas of concern. Some immediate examples include taxation and the regulation of credit and debt, protective legislation in relation to trades and descriptions, or the handling of shoplifting. More widely, one might extend the list to include town planning, transport policies or even international monetary exchange. At the same time, some groups such as environmentalists or those disenchanted with consumer society more generally have sought to challenge their perceived oppression in consumer society. In addition, such developments have often happened in tandem with wider economic and political shifts in the ideology of consumer welfare and social policy. More importantly, it is now pointed out that, as consumption increases in its importance as one aspect of society, so social, economic and even judicial policy is developed to shape its outcomes (Cahill 1994; Keat *et al.* 1994; Sulkunen *et al.* 1997).

As a consequence, this chapter falls essentially into two halves: first, a consideration of the economic and historical context of consumer welfare and social policy which, most importantly, sets up the parameters for the succeeding discussion of social policy as it applies to or affects consumer experience or practice; and second, conversely, a discussion of the significance or impact of consumer practices or activism for or on social policy, leading in turn to a concluding discussion of the position of social policy in relation to consumer society, highlighting in particular its significance in the construction and/or eradication of social divisions. In doing so, this chapter attempts to formulate a complex and somewhat underresearched series of connections concerning consumption, social policy and social divisions and, as a result, is intentionally exploratory and sometimes provocative as opposed to definitive.

'Crisis, what crisis?': contextualizing consumer welfare

It is important to realize that the relationship of social policy and consumer welfare, although not always explicit or apparent, is also clearly dynamic and has changed over time. Most importantly, the relationship of social and economic policy to consumer welfare has come under critical scrutiny more recently, particularly in the wake of the so-called 'crisis' of the welfare state. The UK in particular was set up as a model of a social welfare state to the rest of the Western world, following what is commonly now known as the 'post-war consensus' where the main political parties were perceived as entering a state of agreement concerning welfare. This perception also centred on the setting up of a triumvirate of welfare initiatives in the 1940s in the form of compulsory, state-funded education to secondary level, National Insurance as a primary means of funding for sickness or unemployment and, most importantly, the National Health Service.

All of these developments, and the series of policy reforms that went with them, emerged in the wake of the Beveridge Report of 1942, which, put simply, sought to establish three basic principles of social welfare: first, the *universal* right to welfare assistance and services, including health and education; second, the provision of a *safety net* for those who fell on hard times for whatever reasons; and third, the setting of a *basic minimum* standard of living, as set by levels of absolute poverty and rates of benefit (Beveridge 1942). The immediate and problematic issue that one needs to be clear about here is that it is not the policies that are in question or at stake, but the *principles* that are perceived to lie behind them that are now often so hotly contested in national and international political arenas. Put crudely, the so-called 'crisis' of the welfare state is centred not only on the economic and demographic changes that have emerged since the Second World War, including the OPEC oil crisis and its attendant worldwide recession, the ageing of the population and increasing burden of dependency on those in work, and an overall culture of rising expectations leading to a constant escalation in demand, but on an *ideological challenge* to the very foundations of social welfare (Mishra 1981, 1984; Williams 1989; George and Wilding 1994).

This ideological challenge has come most strongly from neo-liberalism, an umbrella term to describe various schools of political and economic thought that have sought to undermine the foundations of liberalism on which our common-sense understanding of social welfare has come to depend and that were promoted most loudly by proponents of the New Right and particularly Thatcherism and Reaganomics in the 1980s. This challenge has taken several forms: first, an undermining of the basic principles of state welfare as encouraging dependency and therefore leading to an erosion in both the level and range of benefits available universally; second, a perception of the state and the public sector as bureaucratic and costly, thereby creating a need for greater competition, accountability and ultimately, in some cases, privatization; and third, a strong emphasis on the state's perceived interference in the workings of the free market, and the need for wider economic deregulation and generation of wealth.

From the perspective of economics, this also marked a shift from Keynesianism – associated with John Maynard Keynes' advocacy of government intervention in the market to control competing tendencies of inflation on the one hand and unemployment on the other, with the intentional and planned financing of deficits – to monetarism, which advocated freedom for the market itself to foster growth and prosperity. This perspective had an equally long history of more academic association in the work of Friedrich von Hayek and Milton Friedman and Adam Smith (Smith 1838; Hayek 1944; Friedman 1948, 1968). Put most simply, this has also led to an increasingly polarized sense of conflict concerning the state *or* the market as the provider of individual and national prosperity alike, when in reality the state *and* the market clearly often interrelate if not totally interlock.

Academic and sociological responses to these developments are wide-ranging to say the least. For Len Doyal and Ian Gough, this situation has led to a need to reassert a sense of basic human needs in the face of wider academic as well as political onslaught that has come from a mostly constructionist framework, which has sought to culturally locate the concept of need itself (Doyal and Gough 1991). The key difficulty that they raise is the sense in which cultural relativism may lead to a situation where 'needs' in their entirety are seen as social constructions, with the potential political consequence of undermining *any* notion of a right to a minimum standard of living. However, for theorists such as Jürgen Habermas the decline of a consensus around social welfare has illustrated a far wider crisis in terms of the legitimation of the state and social policy, which is itself located in the wake of a wider decline in civil society that he traces back to the eighteenth century (Outhwaite 1996). The state is seen to become both the victim and the vehicle for modern media-driven 'publicity', as distinct from an earlier notion of 'public' or civic debate and discussion (Habermas 1976). A growing sociology of money, combined with an increased emphasis on globalization, has also sought to illustrate the increasingly turbulent and uncertain position of both the national and international money markets and their attendant nation states (Zukin and DiMaggio 1990; Dodd 1994; Lash and Urry 1994). This has also sparked some more grounded cultural histories of recent changes in attitudes towards money and markets, the state and welfare alike (Zelizer 1983; Leyshon and Thrift 1997; McDowell 1997).

Many of these theories do not consider consumer society *directly*, but incorporate an analysis of consumption as part of a far wider narrative. However, although it is clearly not within the scope of this work to analyse all of these theories fully, there is a need to attempt to relate such ideas, and their attendant empirical developments, to the analysis of consumption and consumer society more directly. One link in the academic chain of events comes in the work of Claus Offe, who sees the contemporary crisis of the welfare state as indicative of the working out of a wider series of inner tensions that also parallel those of Habermas alluded to earlier. For Offe, the position of the welfare state is essentially contradictory as it is located within a capitalist system that requires it to maintain economic production, leading to an inherent tendency towards self-regulation and limitation. At the same time, the state seeks to uphold an ideal of amelioration of the nefarious consequences of the same capitalist system, leading to an equally inherent tendency towards costly intervention. This tends to result in an overall state of paralysis in the face of internal conflict (Offe 1984, 1985).

Furthermore, the state has several even more self-destructive tendencies: first, to overspend and create fiscal crisis; second, to have failures in planning for the future because of the unintended consequences of its own precedents; and third, to lead to an overall crisis of legitimation whereby mass loyalty is both uncertain and/or unlikely. Consequently, the welfare state has a tendency to self-destruct, but, more positively, at the same time, its internal and external struggles tend to lead more widely to the generation of alternatives in which the role of pressure groups and reform movements within and outside the mainstream political system are particularly important. For example, the Green Party in Offe's native Germany has a strong history of influence over more mainstream political processes and decision making.

Offe also applies some of these principles to consumption directly, if somewhat prescriptively. In the first instance, he notes that only in advanced Western or capitalist societies that have undergone a process of 'differentiation' – whether of production from consumption, or the separation of home and work, or the spheres of public and private – has the notion of consuming or the consumer any true significance. When this occurs three groups are set up in competition with each other. These are the manufacturers and suppliers of commodities and services, the state and other legislative groups that seek to regulate production, and the consumers and their attendant organizations. The important point he also notes here is that these groups are not equal and: 'Within the field of consumer policy, in short, the interested party is weak and the strong party is disinterested' (Offe 1984: 224). To put it simply, then, consumers have little power and manufacturers and the state alike have little interest in supporting them.

Politically, it therefore remains to empower consumers and/or reintegrate the spheres of production and consumption. The former is problematic because of difficulties in mobilizing consumers, who are a very hetero-geneous group, but the odds are more favourable if consumer safety is at stake, the consumption patterns involved are more 'basic' or homogeneous, there are obvious pay-offs in consumers participating, a visible monopoly is opposed, or a wider issue of collective identity is invoked. The activities of Ralph Nader, considered later, provide a good example. The strategy of reintegration really only works through the centralization of the adminis-tration of production and consumption together, the (re)formation of house-hold production methods, or the incorporation of consumer interests directly into production, such as through the application of market research. The difficulty of Offe's work on consumption is that it remains primarily prescriptive, if not utopian, in intent and there is a need to address the ques-tion of social policy and consumerism more pragmatically, which I take up in the next section.

In addition, it is perhaps helpful to try to summarize some of the changes in the ideologies surrounding social policy and their impact on consumer practice and consumer welfare more directly. First of all, there is clearly a strong sense in which the ideology of neo-liberalism compounds a more basic notion of consumer sovereignty primarily through the promotion of *choice* as a key value of contemporary society and as an important mechan-ism in social amelioration. In addition, the key justification for cuts in social welfare is precisely that the individual and not the state is most well placed to decide what is the most favoured option for them. More importantly, and second, this links directly to the *privatization* of state institutions such as health and education so that these services, and perhaps even the state itself, are then increasingly part of the competitive world of the consumer market-place. The consequences of privatization are perhaps not entirely certain and yet it seems equally important to realize that such developments have the potential at least to undermine the very principles of universality and the safety net that have underpinned social welfare in the UK in particular since the Second World War. Consequently, and third, this starts to add to the sense of increased *social divisiveness* surrounding, and indeed inherent within, consumer society. To put it most simply, one pays for the right to choose in terms of the undermining of universal state provision for the very poorest, who either cannot afford, do not know how, or have only very limited options to choose at all. It is the purpose of the rest of this chapter to try to unpack the importance of this ideology of consumer sovereignty and its significance in terms of social divisions through a more pragmatic analysis of social policy and consumer practices in the UK.

Social policy and consumer practices

The ensuing discussion is focused on developments in the UK and may not necessarily apply in detail to other societies. Nevertheless, the underlying principles of the following considerations are relatively easily located across a wide variety of advanced Western cultures. More particularly, some points of comparison are easily made in advance. In the first instance, the UK is relatively unusual in the vociferousness of its consumer movements and the strength of its protectionist legislation compared with the relaxed attitudes and practices prevalent in some other, usually southern, parts of Europe. In many respects, the development of consumerism in the UK has paralleled more that of the United States, where the postwar expansion of consumption went in tandem with an increase in consumer activism, particularly under the auspices of Naderism – considered critically in the next section of this chapter.

However, the comparative power of consumer movements in the UK and US is itself open to question as neither society has developed more than an essentially *ad hoc* series of protectionist measures in relation to consumption. In addition, the primary impact of government legislation on consumption has tended to come in the form of more *economic* policies concerning interest and exchange rates or taxation of income. Put most simply, interest rates and taxation are used according to a fairly simple logic of controlling spending, as raising or lowering rates of income tax, interest rates on lending or saving, or monitoring the value of a given currency is used to undermine or enhance consumer confidence and discretionary income. The additional complication here, however, is that as money markets of every kind, production and manufacturing, and indeed patterns of consumption in themselves have become increasingly subject to wider processes of globalization, as well as inflation more generally, any *direct* sense of control of consumer expenditure has become increasingly undermined. Conversely, this in turn has reinforced a wider concern with the underlying *lack* of support for consumers in the face of a particularly piecemeal series of developments in more directly *social* or ameliorative policy.

In order to anchor this discussion a little, it is suggested that social policy, as applied to consumer practice, has three primary areas of impact: first, on pricing through taxation and related costs; second, on spending through taxation of income and supplementary provision of credit; and third, on crime, primarily in relation to the two concerns of shoplifting and debt collection. Allied concerns also include trades descriptions and the regulation of advertising, the growing awareness of shopping addiction as a social problem, and the impact of consumer campaign groups. These factors are considered in detail in later sections of this chapter.

Social policy and pricing

The primary aspect of social policy affecting pricing in the UK is VAT, or Value Added Tax. Similar tax measures are operated in other nations, often in the form of sales taxes placed on goods directly or at point of sale, and the commentary here is relevant internationally, at least in general terms. VAT is technically an indirect tax, that is one which is paid indirectly through the purchase of goods and not directly from personal income, and also a tax that is widely seen as regressive or non-distributing of income and wealth, as the poorest pay most as a proportion of their income. This is an important point to make, as one of the justifications for constant increases in the rate of VAT is the perception of its application to luxury or inessential goods only.

The difficulties with this point of view are twofold: first, VAT is applied to many goods and services that we would now consider rudimentary, if not necessities, such as many electrical goods or, in particular, adult clothing; and second, the distinction of the essential from the inessential is socially and personally relative. For example, an array of expensive fashions or perfumes is perhaps extravagant for a nurse, yet clearly of perceived necessity for many of those working in advertising, image or media industries.

The rate of VAT is currently set at 17.5 per cent in the UK, more than twice what it was when the Conservative government came to power in 1979. More to the point, the recent furore over VAT on fuel highlighted the changing perception of the tax as an increasingly anachronistic, inappropriate and socially divisive lining of central government's purses that hits the poorest and most socially disadvantaged hardest and does little to provide the services that these groups need. In addition, the recent re-election of the Labour Party shows few signs, as yet at least, of any reversal in taxation strategy.

Additional tax duties are levied on alcohol, tobacco and some imported fashion goods perhaps more fairly, although with the same degree of moral censure often implicit in the policy. The recent dropping of the sale of duty-free goods at airports according to European legislation may also illustrate the European Union's tendency to further *dis*empower consumers in the process of setting up a free market. As some commentators have pointed out, and as highlighted earlier, the free market is not in itself necessarily supportive of consumer rights, and what is at stake here is often a far more ideological notion of consumer sovereignty which in turn tends to extend out of utilitarian economic theory (Winward 1994).

This is, in part, not a new series of processes or developments. For example, sumptuary laws, although often ineffective, were used to control the perceived extravagance of the middle classes, particularly in the wake of Puritanism in pre-modern, mercantile capitalism (McCracken 1988). It is, perhaps, more precise, then, to see some continuity in this, as the current use of VAT in the UK is applied to goods perceived as somehow luxury, including stationery, information technology, electrical goods, alcohol, adult clothes, cigarettes and tobacco, cars and petrol. The recent controversy concerning VAT on the utilities and other proposed areas, including children's clothes and the press, was raised precisely in relation to the perceived necessity of these goods.

It could be argued, however, that in an increasingly consumer-led society – and one that enjoys a consistently higher, if unequal, standard of living – these distinctions are becoming redundant (Cahill 1994). In particular, as most of the population now owns at least one car and uses it increasingly as a necessity to get to work, continual and relentless increases on fuel, road tax and car prices are rapidly losing any degree of justification and governments have consistently had to turn to environmental as opposed to economic justifications. Likewise, increasing concern over international price differentials for some commodities looks set to increase political controversy concerning price setting. The US in particular is now well known to undercut many European prices, and cars are taxed particularly heavily in the UK. Equally, taxes placed on alcohol and tobacco derive as much ideological support from health and morality campaigns as they do from any sense of economic fairness, as the population as a whole has relatively easy and frequent access to alcohol and cigarettes alike.

It is immediately clear, then, that social policy as applied to consumption is far from neutral, value free or insignificant. It is, perhaps, a growing and increasingly controversial area of concern that strikes at the very core of our values and morals, as well as our sense of equality and freedom. This raises an important issue concerning the juxtaposition of civil or individual rights to freedom against wider questions of social costs or protection from exploitation, and these questions are considered in the final sections of this chapter.

Social policy and spending

The traditional impact of social policy on spending comes, once again, in the form of taxation – although this time directly through income tax. The impact of income tax on spending is, at first sight, commonsensical and clear: the more one is taxed, the less one can spend, and vice versa, in an apparently direct inverse correlation of taxation and spending. The immediate difficulty of this equation is that the factors affecting spending are far more complex, involving other aspects of income and monetary worth such as personal wealth, employment position, demography, interest rates affecting housing and savings, exchange rates affecting travel and the value of a given currency, inflation, economic growth and recession, and not least the psychology of spending or the much-discussed 'feelgood factor'.

Income tax is technically a progressive tax in the sense that it is proportional and the poorest pay less or least. This progressive factor has, however, suffered serious regressive effects in the UK in the form of massive cuts in the top rates of income tax, which are now less than 60 per cent of what they were 20 years ago, and lower basic rates of income tax are compensated for through rises in VAT. In addition, economic recession traditionally hits areas such as expenditure on luxury or fashion goods hardest as a result of their price and income elasticity or dependence. One would assume, then, incorrectly, that spending on such goods has fallen significantly, when in fact it has tended to increase.

A key factor in this increase is the rise of multiple means of payment and, in particular, credit. The use of credit in the 1980s accelerated to unprecedented levels through the opening of a whole series of financial services and money markets and, in particular, the development of store cards or in-store credit. At its peak, it is estimated that more than one-third of all purchases in the UK were made on plastic (Cahill 1994). Of particular importance in this were department stores, electrical stores and high-street fashion outlets, which developed a dazzling array of credit options. It is now the case that many major high-street retailers offer and actively promote their own credit cards, frequently offering discounts, competitions and other offers with which to tempt the unsuspecting customer, often at point of sale. Many of these developments, including the expansion of shopping malls and supermarkets covered in Chapter 5, are imported from the US, where they are, in a sense, 'nothing new'; while the development of these practices in other parts of Europe, particularly southern Europe, is far more limited.

Optimistic though many of these developments may seem in providing customers with more options to choose from in terms of an array of products and means of purchasing them, the underlying reality is often less rosy. At the centre of the increasing controversy surrounding such developments is the potentially phenomenal rise in debt. The problem of debt is starkly illustrated by one striking statistic relating to the amount of outstanding credit: *exclusive* of mortgages and inclusive of inflation, outstanding credit rose more than 35 per cent, from £54.4 billion in 1987 to £73.5 billion in 1996 in the UK alone (Office for National Statistics 1998). Studies conducted by the National Consumer Council and the Policy Studies Institute similarly illustrate concern over rising levels of credit and advocate greater governmental regulation as well as gearing of credit to current income levels rather than records of prior defaults on payments (National Consumer Council 1990; Berthoud and Kempson 1992).

More widely, there is now a growing literature concerning credit and debt and their effects in the UK, all of which tends to highlight certain central concerns. First, although credit levels expanded exponentially during the 1980s as a result of wider patterns of economic deregulation, access to credit, including financial services and store cards, did not expand equally across the population. In particular, affluent and financially secure groups, including early middle-aged groups in the South-east of the UK, were the primary beneficiaries of the expansion of multiple means of credit. Conversely, these options were increasingly closed to poorer groups, who were in turn often more reliant on other forms of state, as opposed to private, credit, or legalized money-lending agencies. The poorest of all, such as lone parents, were often forced into a world of illegal money lending, or 'loan sharks', although the violence and intimidation associated with these were often exaggerated and the key difficulty was often ignorance in understanding interest rates rather than anything else. As a result, the provision of, and access to, credit was, and remains, deeply socially divisive.

Second, the overall rise in levels of credit, in conjunction with the undermining of state welfare for the very poorest, and particularly the privatization of council housing, has added to severe levels of poverty and a growing disparity in the positions of rich and poor. Third, this raises a further issue of poverty which is not solved simply through the expansion of credit but through an improvement in minimum levels of income. In addition, more moral judgements, which perceive debt as resulting simply from personal extravagance and use of credit cards, are seen as stereotypes rather than as statements of fact. The vast majority of debt was related to housing and was caused by changes in personal circumstance or never having enough money in the first place or, more simply, poverty (Ford 1988, 1991; Rowlingson 1994; Rowlingson and Kempson 1994).

There is, though, perhaps a wider and as yet less investigated issue concerning the easy availability of credit combined with the very high numbers of incentives in every form, from advertising and discounts to interest-free accounts, which has perhaps facilitated, if not caused, considerable numbers of people to get into serious debt. The individual is often blamed for their apparent stupidity in not seeing the long-term problems coming. However, the responsibility does not necessarily lie with the retailers or credit companies, whose non-stop luring in of customers is understandable, but with the lack of government-led regulation of accountability. Today, it is perfectly possible to wander from shop to shop opening a credit account in each one subject only to a confirmatory phone call to ascertain credit status, promptly gaining the facility to spend vast sums in total, and in addition to any credit cards one may already have, and then to open an equally vast array of mail order accounts entitling one to yet more spending. The only thing stopping this process, therefore, is the willpower of the individual; that is, until the monthly statements start to land on the doormat. The primary issue here, then, is the comparative *lack* of social policy that is applied to credit, whether in terms of its governmental provision, as the vast majority is provided commercially, or questions of access and regulation. This in turn informs a wider discussion of social divisions.

Also, as I have already highlighted, access to credit in many ways also now forms one of the main forms of social division in contemporary society and taps into our deepest concerns with civil liberties on the one hand, and the ethics of personal and social responsibility on the other. Generally speaking, anyone with a relatively secure, though not necessarily permanent, income from full-time work who falls within the limits of socially appropriate consumption in having a permanent home address and a perceived capacity to pay in terms of income not spent on housing or other loans, and who has no record of serious credit default, can generally gain credit from anywhere at any time. Those not in full-time employment, without a fixed address or with records of credit default cannot.

Records of credit default essentially work retrospectively, that is they are set in place once the consumer is already in serious arrears. In addition, computerized records are increasingly kept on an individual's credit status, often through readings of the use of the cards themselves, and are used to regulate future transactions, access to facilities and to target promotional activities. This quite clearly divides the affluent and working population from the unemployed, casually or part-time employed, low-paid, students, minors, the elderly, the ill, homeless or temporary residents and lone parents. This second cluster of groups, although potentially the poorest payers, are often the most in need of at least minimal credit. This also accounts for the tendency of such groups to fall into the trap of using private money lenders, who often use extortionate rates of interest and occasionally threatening tactics to operate effectively. The additional difficulty here is that the lowest rates of interest often correlate with the strictest conditions in terms of collateral and access, often not forthcoming for the most disadvantaged. As a consequence, as access to credit has increased, so has default on credit payments.

These difficulties and pitfalls concerning consumption and credit are gradually gaining recognition as social and not merely individual or idiosyncratic issues. Nevertheless, to truly redress the situation would in all likelihood require a curtailing of some forms of individual freedom and access to spending as one pleases, or perhaps the use of more vociferous forms of means-testing in controlling credit levels. However, each of these measures remains potentially more divisive and deeply unpopular, perhaps understandably, with both the public and governments alike. Difficulties concerning access to credit, credit default and escalating poverty continue to increase, though, with some even more deleterious consequences.

Social policy and consumer crime

Consumer crime essentially takes two forms: first, shoplifting or theft; and second, credit default leading to criminal prosecution. The production and promotion of goods and services are also subject to certain forms of legislative regulation and protection and this is considered in the next section.

Shoplifting is an indictable crime as well as a partially recognized mental illness in the form of kleptomania. These two elements of crime and illness account for the often contradictory reaction to shoplifting; namely the perception of it as a costly social problem and also seeing it as an individual and psychological phenomenon. The former perspective has proved most influential in justifying incorporation of shoplifting costs into price policies. There is a tendency to exaggerate its significance here, as is the case with industrial action when there are points to score on all sides in doing so, although the effect on the consumer is often neglected. The second perspective has often fuelled populist feminist rhetoric concerning the psychological effects of isolation and housewifery. Frankly, neither of these perspectives is entirely correct, as much shoplifting is staff created. This is hardly surprising, given the increasing prevalence of high-tech security and surveillance devices in many high-street stores which severely restrict the customer's, rather than the staff's, opportunities for theft. However, concern is also raised as to the deeply stigmatizing effects of the system of prosecution for shoplifting on those customers who either make mistakes or who *are* in some way psychologically ill or simply depressed.

This is linked to similar issues concerning so-called shopaholicism or shopping addiction, where customers shop to fulfil deep-seated psychological or social needs in a similar way to numerous other forms of addiction such as alcoholism or drug dependency. There is a certain popular psychological foundation to such allegations, as well as a strong North American influence in the highlighting of its social effects and this is discussed in detail in Chapter 5. Of significance to the present discussion, though, is the lack, once again, of any full or developed social policy to protect the interests of consumers or retailers alike. As a consequence, frustrated shopkeepers may take Draconian action against sometimes minor or confused cases of shoplifting; and so-called professional shoplifters may otherwise exploit the easy warranty or returns policies of many major chain stores. Shopaholics are themselves increasingly indirectly facilitated through the development of the same returns policies in the newly developing practice of 'un-shopping' or returning goods in order to fuel further spending on alternatives and go shopping all over again.

The second factor of credit default is often dealt with in a highly individualized way, rather than socially regulated. In the UK, credit default is generally dealt with on a case-by-case basis and by debt counsellors such as those employed by the Citizens' Advice Bureau who seek to advise and assist those in trouble by drawing up lists of outgoing and incoming moneys, and sharing out all income unused on essentials to all creditors on a proportional format. It is important to point out that most creditors will freeze interest and accept some form of reduced monthly payment, provided payments are kept up without default and credit facilities are cut. The difficulties tend to concern banks and similar major or institutional money lenders who are frequently hostile to freezing interest rates, require added securities and are more likely to threaten and harass the customer into paying up, particularly if levels of credit are high. If creditors do refuse to freeze interest or continue to make excessive demands on the customer, there are few courses of action that the consumer can take, and few sources of support.

One recent development is the formation of Credit Unions in the UK, which are essentially local authority agencies that act as co-operatives and provide credit on lower interest terms. The main difficulty for the poorest here is that one has to pay in first and pay-outs are not immediate. The problem remains, then, the slippery slope of any form of credit, as it is exceedingly difficult to clear deficits when they accrue to often very high levels without significant income injections, increased cash flow or circumstantial support. Credit in fact forms the ultimate poverty trap, as once difficulties set in there is a strong tendency to spiral downwards into poverty. Ultimately, when all else fails the final recourse is repossession of all forms of property, and bankruptcy.

The Consumer Credit Act of 1974, the Trades Descriptions Act of 1968 and the later Consumer Protection Act of 1987 all seek to provide the consumer with some protection from psychological or simply financial exploitation in the name of profit, whether in terms of hard sells, misrepresentation of goods or poor after-sales service. The difficulty lies, though, in the fact that making a claim often lies entirely in the hands of the individual, who must take on increasingly monopolized retail giants. The credit default register or 'blacklist' is compiled according to serious allegations of non-payment or refusal of payment on the part of the customer, and it is up to the company or creditor concerned to report the customer. The customer is not necessarily informed directly of their situation and access to information is severely restricted. In addition, the essentially judicial mechanism is set up according to a logic of 'won't pay' rather than 'can't pay'. As highlighted earlier, this is rarely the case. Although an individual can apply to clear their name, they will need to clear all outstanding debts and are required to show evidence of a significantly improved financial position in terms of employment, for example, and, for the vast majority of those who fall on to the register, this is wholly unattainable. Unemployment, along with the break-up of a personal or family relationship and the illness or death of an economically active party, in fact form the main causes of serious debt. This, in turn, raises issues concerning credit, debt and poverty as *symptoms* rather than *causes* of major social and economic problems.

In conclusion to this discussion of social policy and consumption practices, primarily in the UK, consumer society is often presented as the epitome of opportunity for all or, to put it simply and literally, as an 'open shop'. From the preceding analysis, this is quite clearly empirically limited if not entirely mythical. Consumer society does indeed present many opportunities for pleasure, self-expression and self-fulfilment for those who can afford it and for those who have access to it. It is particularly apparent, then, that when we are talking of the opiate pleasures of consumption, we are primarily referring to a fairly select group of affluent consumers well located in economic and geographical terms, with the transport, time and money to shop for luxury goods. In particular, this then excludes many or all of the elderly, the poor, the unemployed, those without their own transport, single parents, the infirm or those with minimal discretionary income. These groups are equally likely to neither afford nor have full access to the opportunities and pleasures of consumer society. Alternatively, their affordance of such luxuries may depend on access to credit which remains a high risk to them financially, with potentially wider psychological or social costs in the form of the stigma that still surrounds those who get into debt.

Consequently, what all of this tends to add up to is the reconstruction of new social divisions often centred on older, traditional divisions of class, race, age and gender. Zygmunt Bauman's work, *Work, Consumerism and the New Poor*, is more than germane here (Bauman 1998). At the crux of his analysis is the now well-tried and well-tested notion of relative poverty. Poverty in consumer society is defined precisely as a lack of opportunity or access to consume. At the same time, it is juxtaposed with the Protestant work ethic, which still attaches a stigma to the poor, whose poverty is seen quite simply as their own fault. The key factor in defining and ranking poor and rich in consumer society is according to their position as consumers or 'non-consumers', or alternatively as 'the seduced' and 'the repressed' (see also Chapter 2). This would seem to wholly contravene the more traditional sociological perspective that one's identity and status depend on one's occupation, or role in production. However, in invoking Offe's notion of 'de-coupling' income *entitlement* from income *earned*, the poverty of consumer society is for Bauman only overcome in overthrowing the work ethic as much as the ideology of consumerism, which is itself also centred on the same values of individual freedom, meritocracy and choice. These are very large political and ideological issues to which I wish to return later in this chapter.

In addition, the decidedly piecemeal state of social policy in taxing the poorest hardest, creating difficulties in gaining credit for those on low incomes, stigmatizing shoplifters and offering every incentive to everyone else, often adds to the sense of the same social division. This is an insidious situation and one that tends to lack critical academic or more political attention, with some exceptions (Cahill 1994; John 1994; Keat *et al.* 1994). Such a situation is partially explained as the outcome of the expansion of post-structural theory and cultural studies around consumption, which seek to separate consumption from economic determination and assert instead its semi-autonomous state as a semi-autonomous sphere of activity or culture (see, for example, Featherstone 1991; Lury 1996; Mort 1996). Although such approaches clearly highlight the significance of cultural phenomena for those incorporated in its parameters, this equally tends to exclude consideration of the rest and reinforces academically the same sense of divisiveness. Thus, although there is clearly a need for the insights of such studies, there is also clearly a need to redress the emphasis.

It is also partially explained as a result of the continued, and perhaps in neo-liberal terms expanded, ideology of consumer sovereignty. In consumer society, the consumer *per se* must at least *seem* to be free to enjoy its pleasures and rewards. As a result, any attempt to interfere with these processes of personal choice from an apparently free market of competitively produced goods runs counter to the values at the very core of advanced Western capitalism. The paradox here is that consumers are in reality not at all free to choose, as they are constrained by the ties and knots of not only income and social divisions but the political and ideological policies of taxation and economic regulation that surround them. More fundamentally, they do not control the production of the commodities they 'choose' from. The problem encountered in taking such an alternative perspective, however, is that it has a tendency to render the consumer a passive victim of consumer society, as opposed to an active, if constrained, part of it. As a consequence, the second half of this chapter focuses directly on the influence of consumer activism and practice on social policy, and consumer society more widely.

Consumer practices and social policy

Given the inequities clearly present in consumer society, it is perhaps not entirely unexpected that there is some element of consumer resistance. What is surprising is that this has, historically, suffered from academic neglect, with a few exceptions (de Certeau 1984; Fiske 1989a, 1989b; Maffesoli 1989; Cahill 1994; John 1994; Gabriel and Lang 1995). This is, at least in part, explained as a legacy of structuralist and Marxist explanations of consumer society, which have tended to dominate academic discourse until recently with the rise of cultural studies and poststructural theory. As outlined in Chapter 1, early Marxist theory and particularly the work of the Frankfurt School has tended to construct the consumer as a passive victim of consumer society, its pleasures merely acting as the ultimate opiate to the exploited masses. More recent poststructural theory, in attacking such thinking and stressing the activity of the affluent Western consumer in particular, has, ironically, often still omitted any consideration of the importance of opposition from oppressed groups or those more intentionally distancing themselves from consumer society, a point I consider more fully in Chapter 5.

The strongest assertions of consumer activity, as opposed to passivity, have come from some cultural critics, particularly the work of Michel de Certeau (de Certeau 1984). De Certeau's work is primarily concerned with a philosophical and cultural analysis of *The Practice of Everyday Life* or, more precisely, the activity of using. Consequently, consumption is defined not in terms of commodities, but in terms of the consumer's using of products and services. The overall analogy is one of reading, and a linguistic parallel is drawn up through which, as in language, consumers 'make do' with an appropriated linguistic system, within which they 'write' their own sentences and 'poach' their own texts. Also, although 'weak', through a variety of 'trajectories', unconscious 'strategies' and 'tactical raids', ranging from misappropriation of commodities to using shopping malls as social centres, they are seen to assert their *active practice* as consumers.

Although written in a wilfully opaque style, de Certeau's work has been considerably influential in the rise of more culturally driven studies of consumption, epitomized by the work of John Fiske who, in *Reading the Popular*, asserts: 'Shopping is the crisis of consumerism: it is where the art and tricks of the weak can inflict most damage on, and exert most power over, the strategic interests of the powerful' (Fiske 1989a: 14). Shopping malls are seen as social arenas in which youth culture is constructed through 'hanging around' or 'window shopping', activities that are seen as purposeful and active as opposed to aimless and passive; while women are armed with a consumer weaponry of knowhow and skills that make them particularly good 'shopping guerrillas' (Fiske 1989a). Style wars, jeans ripping and shoplifting are equally seen as active, as: 'Every act of consumption is an act of cultural production, for consumption is always the production of meaning' (Fiske 1989b: 35). There are strong parallels here with identity politics more widely, and particularly the feminist work of Rachel Bowlby, Mary Douglas or Mica Nava, whose discursive and cultural analysis seeks to reveal the essential *activity* of women as shoppers, which is considered more fully in Chapter 6. What remains palpably lacking, however, is any awareness of the social divisions that variously constrain and control the activities of consumers, without necessarily rendering them passive dupes in the process.

Consequently, in this section, I wish to consider the significance of consumers themselves, whether collectively or individually, in resisting the expectations often placed on them, reinventing the significance of consumption practices or commodities, or in attempting to intervene in the production, retailing or selling of goods and services at some level. As a result, there are three interlinked sections or considerations: first, moves towards various forms of consumer protection from misinformation, poor quality or exploitation in the selling of goods and services; second, a consideration of attempts to empower consumers in various ways, whether through information or intervention; and third, drives towards increased consumer activism, whether in the form of crime, alternative consumption patterns or simply opting out.

Consumer protection

Consumer protection primarily refers to state-driven and legislative developments that have sought to protect consumers, often at the point of sale. For example, in the UK this has included the Consumer Credit Act of 1974, which allowed the consumer a period of time to change his or her mind after signing and which required a clear indication of the costs and annual percentage rate of interest; and the Trades Description Act of 1968, which sought to regulate the advertising, packaging and information surrounding goods and services. The Consumer Protection Act of 1987 in the UK sought to tighten up previous restrictions and, in particular, impose further restraints in relation to personal selling and financial services in the wake of wider economic deregulation. In addition, such legislation is generally endorsed more privately at the level of consumer groups such as the Consumers' Association in the UK or the activities of Ralph Nader in the US (Tench 1994).

However, several points arise as immediately important in relation to this discussion of consumer protection. In the first instance, none of these developments, at the level of the state or privately, actually questions the practice of consumption *per se*, as they merely seek to outlaw the most extreme examples of its exploitative aspects. This, in particular, is an important point of contrast with consumer activism, which I will consider shortly. More importantly, it is still also open to question exactly how effective, as opposed to simply palliative, these developments are, and their function, at least in practice, is not entirely clear cut or as simple as it seems. For example, the Consumer Credit Act in the UK hardly questions the foundations of credit and could well act more as its facilitator. Critics have also pointed to the lack of clarity or confusion concerning interest rates and its reliance on the judicial system. More significantly, the underlying ethos of consumer protectionism is the empowerment of consumers in making the correct purchasing decision and not to question the values of the commodities or services themselves or to undermine their practice of consumption. In addition, unintentionally perhaps, it thus acts as a form of more effective selling or promotion. This is particularly apparent in the heavy emphasis often placed on (good) *value* for money. Most importantly of all perhaps for this discussion, these are not necessarily initiatives that have come from consumers themselves, at least directly, but more from a wider enforcement of fair trade, although there is a clear sense of the more generic influence of consumer resistance.

Consumer empowerment

Although in some senses consumer protection *is* consumer empowerment, consumer empowerment refers more specifically to attempts to empower consumers, particularly at the level of product information or redress for poor-quality merchandise or inferior services. Moreover, there is often an underlying sense of injustice which related institutions or organizations seek to redress. Examples of these include the work of the Consumers' Association in the UK and some extensions of Naderism in the US. Naderism refers to the influence of Ralph Nader, who pioneered safety campaigns and corporate investigations in the 1960s following his exposé of safety risks associated with the Chevrolet Corvair, a popular car at the time, and setting up of the Center for the Study of Responsive Law and the Project for Corporate Responsibility in 1969. Naderism is also a good example of the attempts of some organizations to challenge monopoly and corporate power and remains popular in the United States, where the championing of individual civil rights and the challenging of corporate power are historically far more central than for some of their European counterparts.

It is worth making it very clear here that there is often a very fine dividing line separating consumer protection from consumer empowerment. What tends to divide them is the strongly sensationalist element that is often involved in consumer protectionism as opposed to empowerment. Consumer protection is often a highly emotive issue that is frequently linked to media-driven disaster or horror stories. Some primary examples include matters of safety, particularly those affecting children's toys, of which media demonstrations of the inflammable teddy bear are a profoundly lurid case in point, and, similarly, demonstrations of the horrors of the pushy salesman with his foot in the door of an elderly, lone and anxiety-ridden pensioner. Some more recent disaster stories have included the selling of time-share apartments in Spain, masks melting on the faces of children at Hallowe'en and exploding oven doors, to name only some. There is indeed a sense in which such information is important, if not empowering, for consumers, but the sensationalist impact of the way much of it is presented in the media is enough to make those with more nervous dispositions hide behind their sofas for cover. This sense of sensationalism often comes from the insidious linking of certain highly emotive elements, namely personal security (the home, a child's toy), vulnerability (being abroad, elderly, alone) and innocence (the child, the unsuspecting consumer) with the status or overall symbolic significance of the goods or services (the teddy bear, the pension, the holiday).

In contrast to this, the work of organizations such as the Consumers' Association offers a less sensationalist and more scientific foundation for consumer information, with the ultimate goal of empowering the consumer in their purchasing decisions. As a consequence, the Consumers' Association invests much time and money in testing products and services, from colour televisions to insurance policies, producing detailed, if not necessarily exhaustive, reports and surveys of products and services, often making full use of volunteer trials and consumers' experiences. At its peak, the

Consumers' Association's *Which?* magazine had a circulation of more than one million in the UK, which is testimony to its popularity and usefulness. It has, however, since suffered criticism for its Middle England middle class-ness and lack of overall representativeness, and has had a decline in fortunes. Some theorists have argued that this is largely due, however, to its individualist ethos in not developing more collective forms of support rather than any lack of representation or hipness (Gabriel and Lang 1995). Others, though, have pointed to the way in which the Consumers' Association's construction of consumer rationality and emphasis on 'use value' rather than 'sign value' has precisely led to its out-of-date and out-of-step quality (Aldridge 1994). For example, in testing jeans, designer versions and Levi's 501s were slung into the laboratory laundry and rated alongside the others, regardless of their significance in the stakes of style.

The Consumers' Association has since, in a sense, perhaps become the ultimate victim of its own individualism in trying to sell itself back to the consumer who, faced with an increasing array of alternatives, has looked elsewhere. The rise of consumer affairs issues on television in the UK, particularly the BBC's prime-time *Watchdog* programme, which comes complete with consumer phone-ins and candid camera, has also put nails in the coffin of the quieter Consumers' Association and similar organizations. Ironically, then, the process of consumer empowerment has itself fallen foul of the processes its seeks to expose as consumers pick and choose their own information. In addition, it also adds to the undermining of any dividing line of empowerment from protection, as although the Consumers' Association was not averse to detailing the odd horror story, its TV legatees thrive on disaster, distress, demonstrations and a hint of militancy – which leads us neatly into the next section.

Consumer activism

Consumer activism refers primarily to those activities and practices that in some way seek to oppose or resist consumption itself, or at least some aspect of it, usually intentionally. It may take many forms, from violent crime to peaceful protest or opting out, of which I wish to outline at least five. However, what these all have in common is a sense of opposition to the perceived prevailing modes of consumption within Western society.

The most blatant or obvious form of consumer activism is rebellion which, most commonly, involves criminal activity. It ranges from the violent and destructive, as in the case of joy-riding, where cars are stolen and driven at high speeds often on housing estates, or ram-raiding where cars are again stolen and driven into store windows or displays whereupon the stock is stolen. A less violent variation is intentional shoplifting. Of clear significance in this is the importance of social class, gender and race, as joy-riding and ram-raiding are primarily, though not exclusively, young, male, white and working-class activities; while the more passive crime, shoplifting, is more commonly associated with women. What stands out for some writers, there-fore, is the central significance of frustration and/or the violations of high-status conspicuous consumption, particularly in the (mis)use of fast, expensive vehicles (Fiske 1989b). What, ironically, is also clear is that such activities do nothing to challenge the prevailing system of values surround-ing consumption. For example, the fast car or shop full of hi-fi electrical ware retains all its former allure if not more. Similarly, shoplifting, whether rational, calculated and intentional or irrational, depressive and anxious, does little to assault the cultural, if not monetary, worth of the commodities in question. In addition, retailers and insurance companies alike often have the last laugh in justifying raising their prices to cover costs.

A slightly less extreme example of similar processes is the alternative use of commodities which many fashions often epitomize. For example, jeans are made into designer accessories, sportswear hits the catwalk, or the suit and tie is turned into mod culture. Of clear significance here is the role of identity politics, a point that many academics were not slow to pick up on following the explosion of new wave and punk cultures in the late 1970s (Hebdige 1979; Frith 1983; McRobbie and Nava 1984). This process of reinscription of significance through alternative uses of the pieces of appear-ance and display has been coined 'bricolage', particularly in the work of Dick Hebdige who similarly posits the concept of 'incorporation', which pri-marily applies to a process of returning to mainstream acceptance through, in particular, corporate 'commodification', as in the case of punk fashions placed on the catwalk in the work of the designer Vivienne Westwood. In addition, in relation to consumption more widely, incorporation is precisely the process of making styles and commodities, and indeed their uses, *cor-porate* which opens up once again a wider question of the limits to consumer resistance, particularly through counter-cultural styles, a question con-sidered in detail in Chapter 7.

A second mode of consumer activism or opposition applies to the use of alternative consumption patterns or, to put it more simply, consuming one commodity or service instead of another according to principle. This clearly applies to all consumption, as we routinely choose one item over another, but it refers here to the *politicization* of this process, as decisions are made not merely according to personal taste but according to certain anti-consumerist criteria. A clear example of this is purchasing or using products from small enterprises or shops, as opposed to large conglomerations, thus supporting such facilities directly and undermining larger organizations. A significant and linked factor in this are ethical and environmental concerns, of which animal rights protests and the green movement are prime examples. Some processes of resistance are also more focused on corporate power, as in the critique of Nestlé's international trading practices, which led to the boycotting of Nescafé and the rise of Café Direct. The non-wearing of fur or animal skins, vegetarianism and a refusal to use cosmetics and similar products tested on animals are also examples of an ethically centred mode of alternative consumption.

More environmental considerations are, however, frequently more controversial, and issues are often raised in relation to the construction of alternative markets of consumerism. In other words, in not purchasing aerosols one simply ends up purchasing roll-on deodorants instead. An added difficulty concerns the effect on producers, many of whom have now taken on elements of environmental concern, of which the manufacture of cars with catalytic converters is one example. One can demonstrate that such measures are a direct response to pressures from environmental groups, particularly at a governmental level. However, one can equally state that such measures are, in turn, turned into a marketing device through which companies may maintain their profits through alternative means. For example, many domestic electrical goods such as washing machines and dishwashers are now sold quite flagrantly according to their economy functions. Ultimately, then, this is a classic question of the structure and action of consumption and supply and demand, or to what extent do consumers or producers dictate what they consume?

A prime case in point is The Body Shop, an environmentally friendly and apparently politically correct enterprise that arose in the 1980s under the directorship of self-proclaimed global feminist Anita Roddick. Serious questions have since been raised concerning both The Body Shop's claims to political correctness in terms of the manufacture or retailing of its products and its clearly very strong sense of marketing initiative. At the same time, it is difficult to see how the enterprise could have succeeded had the demand from consumers not preceded it and continued to support it to the point of its continued worldwide expansion.

A similar sense of consumer opposition comes in the formation of consumer co-operatives, which have, importantly, some historic precedent. The co-operative movement in its modern form is thought to have originated in Rochdale in the northwest of England in the mid-nineteenth century and is now for the most part an international phenomenon (Gabriel and Lang 1995). At its core is a strong ethos of communality, equality and the construction of an exchange system through which even the poorest may take a slice of the mutually baked cake. It is clearly a challenge to the dominant ideology of the individual and middle-class consumer, as much as an alternative undermining of corporate capitalist enterprise. It does not, however, seek to attack the concept or practice of consumption itself, but to widen its scope and facilitate opportunities for its development in poorer communities. Similarly, many such developments were precisely an outcome of wider social division and exclusion from credit services. In this sense, it is ultimately a spoke in the wheel and not a spanner in the works of consumer society.

In contemporary society, however, co-operative consumption has also developed an increasingly counter-cultural ethos, as in the case of LETS (Local Exchange Trading System), where cash and credit are undermined in a system mimicking that of pre-capitalist trade and exchange and totally opposed to modern Western patterns of consumption. For example, as Gabriel and Lang point out, their system is premised on at least five sources of opposition to prevailing consumer practices (Gabriel and Lang 1995). First, the producer and consumer are reconnected in an emphasis on home-made goods and a rejection of all forms of advertising and marketing. Second, they therefore also include those otherwise excluded through lack of credit or cash. Third, this process also crosses many distinctions and divisions drawn out in contemporary consumption according to class, location or individual lifestyle signifiers. Fourth, the entire process of production and consumption is localized. And finally, they avoid nearly all forms of state or private legislation or red tape, including taxation.

Clearly, though, the difficulty in this otherwise rather utopian vision of counter-cultural consumption is one of scale, control and resources. Even with significant levels of skill, individuals or small groups cannot make or produce the entirety of their needs without resort to at least some outside resources, such as utility services, technological invention or raw materials. More importantly, its scope for development is always limited in these respects and, perhaps most significantly of all, only a minority of the population is likely to reject its fashions, dishwashers and colour televisions in favour of cow milking, weaving and communal living. Moreover, there is also a strong connection here with the wider difficulties following various 'crises' in consumer welfare outlined earlier, as those in collectives and co-operatives are sometimes also those most excluded from the expansion of consumer society.

Moreover, though, that same minority remains important. In particular, perhaps the truest strength of opposition to consumer society comes in not consuming at all. This may take the form of boycotting certain products or brands on ethical grounds, as outlined in modes of alternative consumption, but may also go much further in giving up or rejecting the need for a given product or service at all. As a result, if consumer rebellion in the form of ram-raiding electrical stores in BMWs merely reinforces the dominant values of consumer society, the 'real' rebellion comes in the form of walking around glamorous stores, disliking what one sees and leaving empty-handed. In this sense, the ultimate consumer passivity is the epitome of opposition and, ironically, it happens all the time. Every hour of every day, millions of would-be consumers worldwide choose not to buy, or reject the goods or services on offer, for a multitude of rational and irrational reasons that the marketer will never understand. This choice to turn on their heels, put down their telephones, switch off their televisions, close their magazines or throw away their free advertising, think about something else and do something else, is the most practised form of consumer opposition, and is also the truest measure of resistance in consumer society.

In conclusion to this section, then, we are presented with a rather paradoxical picture of the consumer as simultaneously a strongly constrained and yet constantly active constituent of consumer society. More particularly, most of the social policy applied to the empowerment of consumers is, for the most part, piecemeal and ameliorative in merely seeking to provide protection from the worst excesses of exploitation in consumer capitalism. Similarly, much of the more recent interest in consumer activism at the level of alternative practice and identity politics seems limited to localized initiatives or is reincorporated into wider aspects of consumption, as in the case of the marketing of many environmental concerns.

Conversely, though, there is equally a sense in which corporate consumerism is not immune nor in a vacuum in relation to wider consumer concerns and, although maintaining its monetary status, it is still, at the very least, often pressured to develop alternatives to cater for a more politically aware market. More significantly, it is forced to make wholesale alterations to modes of production, technical specifications or product information, frequently at the level of consensus-driven and socially produced national policy. None of this, however, even remotely opposes or undermines the notion of consumption itself, the values it often extols or the commodities associated with it. As a result, this level of resistance still resides with the individual consumer who, ironically, remains powerful in their capacity to adopt or drop commodities or services, often for complex reasons still not fathomed in marketing campaigns. This is precisely de Certeau's concern in seeing consumers as actively and tactically 'making do' with what is, and what is not, on offer to them (de Certeau 1984). The problem remains, though, that some have to 'make do' more than others. What is significant, then, is the fact that individual consumers are not equal nor positioned on a level playing field and it is this sense of connection of consumption practice, policy and social division that informs the final section.

Open shop? Social policy and social divisions

In relation to consumer society, divisions in consumption are essentially premised on two mutually dependent factors, namely economics and access: or to put it more simply, money and transport. On top of this, these factors interlock with wider measures of oppression such as social class, race, gender, sexuality, or simply location, but it is one of the ironies of consumer society that, because of its tendency to individualize issues through the ideology of consumer sovereignty, these wider concerns are reduced to the question of money and access. This discrepancy is at the heart of the contemporary paradox of consumer society as an apparently 'open shop' to anyone with the material, temporal and spatial access. Yet, whether one has these is precisely *not* under one's control nor reducible to individual will.

At the same time, there is some real sense of blurring of boundaries here, or a kind of 'quasi-reality' to consumer democracy. Women, the working classes, racial and ethnic minorities, or gay men and lesbians are not necessarily *ex*cluded from consumer society; while men, the middle classes, white Westerners and heterosexuals are not necessarily *in*cluded in consumer society. There is, then, a very real sense in which the open shop of consumer society really couldn't care less who you are when you cross its threshold, other than for the financial status you walk in with. However, this leads precisely to the trade-off of style and taste that then tends to form a reinstatement of the hidden social divisions of class, race and gender in particular (see Bourdieu 1984).

A key cultural example here comes in the form of the Julia Roberts call-girl character in the Hollywood film *Pretty Woman*, who, armed with wads of dollars, is still barred from shopping in Rodeo Drive because she chews gum, her skirt is too short and her demeanour is all wrong. The dream of consumer sovereignty, which appears shattered at this point, is promptly reinstated when she later returns in an apparent disguise of appropriate decorum and conspicuously turns her nose up at what is on offer. Therefore, her position is precisely predicated on that precarious slope of 'cultural capital', where her 'true' status constantly threatens to crack her 'masquerade' as a wealthy socialite and not a working-class call-girl. In addition, she depends on the support of Richard Gere as a wealthy white (and male) mogul to maintain the charade. Consequently, the film forms a primary example of where the reality of social divisions and the ideology of consumer sovereignty meet head on.

Clearly, participation in consumer society is still fundamentally dependent on the amount of money one has, yet, more complexly, it relates to one's overall financial position, including sources and regularity of income, credit rating and possession of pieces of plastic and accounts. As a result, what is often significant is not necessarily wealth, which may well affect income indirectly, but working capital and uncommitted personal income. Middle-class people on high incomes therefore do not *necessarily* have more money to spend than their lower-paid or working-class counterparts, nor higher credit ratings, for the essential factor in determining spending is discretionary income unspent on housing, essentials or dependants. This clearly explains the constant importance of, and marketing aimed at, affluent young professionals with few financial commitments, and the increasing significance of the so-called 'grey power' of their counterparts at the other end of the age spectrum.

More importantly, discretionary income alone does not determine one's participation in consumer society, as a second factor, access, is also necessary. The question of access refers to several factors: first, transport and whether one owns or drives a private vehicle; second, area or geography, as where one lives determines what one has local or similar access to; and third, physicality, as ill-health, poor vision, frailty or physical impairment all drastically reduce one's capacity to take part in consumer society. For example, then, massive discrepancies exist when comparing young, fit and employed people living in or near major towns or cities with those, even wealthy, people who cannot walk, who are elderly, poor of vision or hearing, or who live rurally or cannot drive, which may well explain the lack of attention to such groups despite their affluence. As a consequence of all of this, consumer society does not eliminate nor undermine pre-existing class, gender or racial divisions; rather it tends to add a series of its own to which they relate. In addition, this is a situation which is rapidly expanding to global dimensions (Lash and Urry 1994).

As we have seen, social policy is for the most part piecemeal in its attempts to deal with these issues, even when any attempt is made. Much depends on initiatives coming from private or commercial enterprises themselves. For example, some supermarkets are now providing transport and help to the elderly or those without cars, and it is often company policy to provide ramps and wheelchair access. These developments and processes remain piecemeal and only partially satisfactory. In particular, despite limited social legislation, such services remain limited in the UK and woefully inadequate in the US and many European countries. Where social policy has traditionally had greater impact is in relation to issues of consumer protection in the form of legislation controlling advertising, selling practices or simply product information. In addition, the media, in providing mass attention to certain issues from thalidomide and cot death to car and toy safety, is often critical in applying national pressure on certain issues.

Perhaps more insidiously, most Western societies impose various forms of highly regressive taxation, from VAT in the UK to sales taxes in the US, all of which hit poorest groups hardest and make no allowances for questions of income or access. Not surprisingly perhaps, little policy exists to control consumption itself, other than interest and exchange rates, which attempt to control spending on an (inter)national level. In the final instance, this is an illustration of consumer society's ultimate dependence on notions of consumer sovereignty and its links with the mechanisms of the market or capitalism *per se*.

The contemporary drift of many more empirical developments in relation to consumer society is equally mixed and not particularly positive. The expansion of shopping malls in the US in particular has developed alongside increasing patterns of surveillance which seek directly to exclude certain groups, particularly those from racial or ethnic minorities. Similarly, the rise of smart tills and EPOS (Electronic Point Of Sale) information that comes from store and credit cards tends to add to this sense of often very undercover monitoring and regulation of consumption patterns. More importantly, the impact of increasingly pervasive and media-driven consumerism on impoverished white groups, often in the face of rising unemployment among the young, has led to an escalating sense of frustration and violence in many, predominantly male, cases. More positively, many more advantaged groups have simultaneously sought to oppose some aspects of consumer society politically in adopting ethical forms of consumption, for example centred on animal rights or environmentalism, or in developing alternative non-corporatist and localized exchange systems where opting out of at least some aspects of consumer society is increasingly an option.

Ultimately, though, the greatest concern resides with those groups who have neither the option to opt out nor the position to participate in sometimes violent forms of politics: depressed and impoverished housewives, men facing unemployment late in life, the rurally isolated and the physically impaired or elderly. Developments in home shopping and delivery services could well improve the lives of some of these groups. Most importantly of all, perhaps, it is contemporary consumer society's increasing tendency to form its own underclass of poverty-stricken and credit rating-less, state-dependent and police-surveillanced 'non-consumers' which constitutes the most cause for concern and is in direst need of redress, for once you have fallen foul of its downward spirals it is almost impossible to climb back up the all-too-greasy poles of consumer society. Bauman's work, outlined earlier, seems seminal here (Bauman 1998).

Conclusion: never-never land

In conclusion to this chapter, rather than presenting a summary of points raised, I wish to provide a single, concluding insight. It is this: in witnessing the expansion of contemporary consumer society to all aspects of life in Western societies, from the privatization of health and education to fast cars and designer fashion, one point remains curiously missed, which is that this expansion has taken place not simply at the expense of plundering the resources of the Third World or developing societies, although this is indeed valid, but more immediately at the cost of excluding, or not including, greater and greater sections of the Western population itself. When thinking of affluent Western society it would seem that we are considering an increasingly limited and narrowly defined group of consumers: young(ish), gainfully employed, located in cities or their surrounding areas, often professional and with relatively few financial or personal commitments. Other important consuming groups do, of course, exist, particularly in terms of supermarket cultures, but the dominance of the aforementioned group characteristics at the expense of the elderly, unemployed, those in rural locations or with low discretionary incomes, as well as the entire credit 'underclass', is a salutary reminder that consumer society is not for everyone.

Moreover, and very importantly, consumer society seems increasingly premised, despite its apparent and paradoxical expansion, on a small core of high-spending consumers. It would seem, then, that, especially in light of the enormous expansion of credit to include populations who could not even hope to afford its luxuries, consumer society is, in effect, walking the plank into never-never land. In addition, this is perhaps what informs the postmodernist's sense of its dystopian implosion, yet for a stronger sense of the empirical importance of this paradox we need to consider the activity at the very core of consumer society, and its most fundamental linchpin: shopping.

Suggested further reading

Bauman, Z. (1998) *Work, Consumerism and the New Poor*. Buckingham: Open University Press – increasingly influential essay on the significance of social divisions in consumption.

Cahill, M. (1994) *The New Social Policy*. Oxford: Blackwell – easy to read and original move forward in the debates about social policy.

John, R. (ed.) (1994) *The Consumer Revolution*. London: Hodder & Stoughton – useful collection from the Consumers' Association.

Offe, C. (1984) *Contradictions of the Welfare State*. London: Hutchinson – important bridge between national consumption issues and the wider political picture.

Sulkunen, P., Holmwood, J., Radner, H. and Schulze, G. (eds) (1997) *Constructing the New Consumer Society*. Basingstoke: Macmillan – eclectic collection that offers more 'postmodern' perspectives on social policy and consumer society.

5
RAPTURE OR TORTURE – THE CONTEMPORARY NATURE OF SHOPPING

Shopping is commonly perceived as the linchpin of consumer society, for the whole concept and development of consumerism seems to depend so completely on its continued practice. Perhaps more importantly, shopping is also often seen as a new and sometimes postmodern phenomenon crucially dependent on the development and expansion of late capitalist consumer society. This is perhaps something of a fallacy, as shopping, in the sense of the sale and purchase of items, has its origins located more concretely in the processes of market trade that extend into the medieval period and pre-industrial capitalism. It is more apt to point out that what commentators on the connections of shopping and postmodernism are often commenting on are the changing formations and nature of the shopping *experience* rather than the nature and development of the shopping *phenomenon.*

Despite the apparent, and not entirely unprecedented, expansion in analyses and studies of consumer society, there remains a paucity of sociological literature on shopping *per se*. This is explained partially as a result of the location of the study of shopping in the fields of commerce and retailing rather than the social sciences; yet it is, more importantly, explained as a consequence of the tendency of the social sciences to simply not take shopping, whether as a historical phenomenon or as a cultural practice, particularly seriously (Miller 1997). When compared with the grand foundations of industrial capitalism and production, consumption tends to run in a poor second in terms of the academic attention and funding it receives. However, the recent increase in more populist interest in consumerism in the media, coupled with its connections to questions of postmodernity, has tended to force the issue of consumption into the centre of academic analysis. At the core of this discussion, on occasion, is shopping (Shields 1992; Bowlby 1993; Falk and Campbell 1997; Humphery 1998; Miller 1998; Miller *et al.* 1998).

Interestingly, as Daniel Miller has demonstrated, the contemporary analysis of shopping shares much in common with its historical precedent, which is centred strongly on the work of Walter Benjamin and his *Passagen-Werk*, or Arcades Project, a mostly historical and partly ethnographic study of the rise of shopping arcades and department stores across Europe. Some related points are reproduced in *Illuminations*, but it has been analysed most extensively by Susan Buck-Morss (Arendt 1973; Buck-Morss 1989; Miller 1997). Although strictly a contemporary of the Frankfurt School, the main thrust of Benjamin's analysis is more sympathetic to the cultural forms and practices of modernity and, in particular, he evokes strongly a sense of the visual and textual landscapes of the modern city. Linked to this also was his analysis of the stroller or *flâneur* as a consumer of the purely visual cultures of the arcades. In addition, Simmel's analysis of the psychological 'overstimulation' of the city and the psychology of money is often evident in more contemporary analyses of shopping (see Chapter 1).

The key difficulty here, however, is that the more culturalist aspects of these analyses have tended to have the unintended consequence of acting as a justification for some of the more extreme claims of contemporary cultural analyses of the shopping mall in particular, as exemplified most strongly in Shields' edited and influential collection of essays on *Lifestyle Shopping*, which focuses on the significance of the spatial dimensions of consumption or 'atrium culture' (Shields 1992). While Benjamin and Simmel clearly questioned the impact of such visual developments in shopping culture, still seeing them as potentially politically exploitative and indicative of wider movements towards growing meaninglessness under conditions of modernity, the Shields collection renders the consumer as an active agent in the construction of their own identity and visual culture alike. Consequently, the heavy emphasis placed on personality and self, often derived from a mixture of poststructural theory and psychoanalysis, has also often fuelled a wider discussion of shopping and identity and, more particularly, its gendered dimensions (Nava 1992, 1997; Wilson 1992; Douglas 1996). In addition, the underlying thrust of these analyses was also to question the passivity of women as consumers, a point that I consider more fully in Chapter 6.

The added, and often significant, difficulty here is that we are consequently presented with a dichotomy of perspectives on shopping and consumption, where the consumer is *either* an enraptured pleasure seeker *or* a relationally constrained actor locked into a series of rituals, when there is, in all likelihood, some evidence to support *both* of these perspectives. More-over, what each perspective still tends to miss is the importance of social div-isions, which ironically also often form the point at which the perspectives come together and complement rather than oppose one another. These are important points to make, and an underlying theme of this work, which I wish to unpack further in this chapter.

This chapter is, then, primarily concerned with the nature and formation of this contemporary and dual notion of the shopping experience. It has, as a consequence, three central sections: first, a consideration of the history and development of the concept and practice of shopping; second, a discussion of the practice of shopping in relation to its spatial environment; and third, a discussion of the often contradictory nature of the contemporary shopping experience in relation to individual as well as social developments.

From markets to malls: the historical development of contemporary shopping

As pointed out previously, shopping has its earliest roots in the development of market trade and mercantile culture. As explained in Marxist theory, the development of a specifically capitalist cash culture did, however, start to transform the nature of the shopping (see Chapter 1). In particular, the shift from a simple exchange of goods to paying for commodities with money tended to create a culture that was often inherently more acquisitive. This was not simply in respect of the profit motive, but rather in relation to the possession of tangible goods in exchange for intangible and earned money. At the centre of this point is, of course, the Marxist concept and practice of surplus value. However, the increasing intangibility of buying, exacerbated by the credit boom, is a point with implication and one to which I shall return shortly.

As Grant McCracken has asserted, a linked and important factor was the decline of the patina system, which for the most part came to an end in the nineteenth century after a long decline (McCracken 1988). The patina system applied to the practice of primarily familial inheritance, where household items in particular were passed on from parents to children, most commonly on marriage. McCracken rejects the simple assumption that this merely represented a growth in material wealth, for what the end of the patina system truly represented was a shift in values attached to commodi-ties and consumption. Most importantly, inherited goods lost much of their personal value in favour of the perceived increase in the worth of newness in itself. The tawdriness associated with many secondhand commodities that continues today is a common example of this development.

However, we are presented with something of a paradox here for, as is well known, wealth remains an inherited rather than an achieved asset, despite the sensationalism sometimes attached to personal success. On top of this, household items in particular are often passed from parents to children, on death if nothing else, and are therefore often still valued in deeply personal ways as a consequence. What is perhaps clear, however, is that what one might call the contemporary valorization of newness has expanded from an elite practice to a mass culture.

The other most important development, though, was the move from mere individual or small-scale production to group and mass production, and with it the separation of ownership and production. This is, of course, also an implicitly Marxist perspective, yet the point remains a simple one: production was increasingly separated from consumption through the expansion of an autonomous ownership and exchange system. Whether this then automatically adds up to a two-class society, exploitation and potential revolution is entirely another matter.

This sense of the increased separation of production and consumption has led to the opening up of a further controversy concerning the extent to which mass consumption was supply led or demand driven. The more orthodox Marxist interpretation is that mass consumption was a necessary justification for mass production and, as a consequence, predominantly supply led. Other commentators, however, have pointed to the pre-existence of mass consumption practices and cultures prior to capitalist expansion, and there is some common-sense truth in this, as the practice of consumerism in terms of the culture of widespread purchasing of commodities or services in particular is clearly not solely dependent on capitalist expansion (McKendrick *et al.* 1982; McCracken 1988; Fine and Leopold 1993).

Conversely, this still leaves open the question of the extent to which capitalism has shaped the form, nature and meaning of contemporary consumption in inculcating an increasingly individualistic and acquisitive ethic. This question is raised directly in the work of Colin Campbell who, in common with others already cited, sees mass consumption as predominantly demand driven and, in particular, premised on the rise of a 'romantic ethic', or fantasy of the consumer as day-dreamer, which in turn shaped the conception and practice of consumption and spurred on the development of a mass consumer culture (Campbell 1987).

None the less, the formation of mass production quite clearly still necessitated mass consumption and with it the means to market and sell. In the first instance, this related to the marketplace itself, set up simply and with minimal personal investment – a practice often still thriving today in relation to novelty, charity or small-scale operations. Mass-scale operations implied something altogether different, though: the outlet, store or specialized premises for the sale of products – in short, the shop. It was hardly surprising, however, that this development should start in the most affluent parts of the city, or where investment and demand were particularly high; or that it should apply initially to the wealthy and middle classes only, while the working classes were still confined to markets as consumers as well as traders; or that the earliest stores should show a certain similarity to the marketplace, whether as corner shops selling every necessity or as department stores encompassing numerous markets in themselves. All of these developments did indeed for the most part take place under the auspices of industrial and financial capitalist expansion in the nineteenth century. Consequently, the high street, or series of specialist shops as we currently know it, is a relatively new invention heavily reliant on capitalist financial expansion, increasing transportation and the development of the city itself (Shields 1992; Falk and Campbell 1997; Humphery 1998).

Of primary underlying importance in all of this is the rise of mass consumption coupled with mass production. The involvement of the working classes as consumers, then, remains as critically important as their involvement in production. This is, of course, one of the most common sources of complaint in relation to more orthodox and some more recent forms of Marxism. The point primarily and often made is that Marxism has tended to neglect the role of consumption as a result of the heavy emphasis placed on the means and/or forces of production alone as the loci of identity, struggle and development in capitalist society. Importantly, and not coincidentally, this has also formed one of the most primary assertions of the theory of postmodernity (see also Chapter 8).

Also a key factor in such discussions is the question of cultural variation and the history of shopping, and the development of mass consumption is interesting in this respect (Humphery 1998). Although many major European cities including Paris, London and Milan played a pivotal role in spearheading many contemporary developments in shopping culture, particularly in relation to the development of arcades, pedestrian zones and department stores; the United States has since tended to dominate the formation of mass consumption and particularly the development of the supermarket and the shopping mall. These formations were equally cultural, historical and economic, dependent on pre-existing and often elite practices in historic cities in the case of Europe, and injections of wealth and enterprise culture along with a predominance of highways and wide open spaces in the United States.

Certain points from this discussion of the history of shopping emerge as significant. First, the great ogre of industrial capitalism and the profit motive is not necessarily causal of the whole development of the shopping phenomenon, and its primary impact has centred on the nature and formation of the shopping experience or, to put it more simply, how and why we shop rather than what we shop for, although this is still a point open to discussion. Second, the increasingly common complaint that shopping is a site of inequity, not only in terms of exploitative costs but in relation to questions of access, is not entirely new, as shopping has a history of inequity and, most importantly, mass consumption has never simply meant mass access. Third, the current concern with the acquisitive and associated cultural value of commodities is also not necessarily new and may have its history in the development of systems of exchange rather than in many later developments. This is, though, a point I wish to pick up on in the next section, for what has, perhaps, altered is not so much shopping itself, but our experience of it and the meanings attached to it, all of which depend heavily on the context in which it is practised.

Consuming the customer: the construction of shopping spaces

Following the preceding discussion of the historical context of shopping, in this section I wish to discuss the significance of developments in the more physical context of shopping or, to put it more simply, the spaces and places in which we shop. This focuses primarily on five shopping contexts: the market, the high street, the supermarket, the department store and the shopping mall, which I shall consider in turn.

As outlined earlier, shopping practice as a simple system of exchange has its origins in early market trading, itself partly developing under the auspices of the Reformation in the sixteenth century. Interestingly, the relationship of religion and shopping still remains controversial, particularly in relation to disputes concerning the selling of goods and services at festival times such as Christmas or Easter, illustrating a triangulation of state, church and market that together form the foundations for the regulation of contemporary consumption. Although the freedom of the market has come to dominate most of the Western world, though certainly not equally or unequivocally, it remains only one element in the formation and contemporary nature of consumer society and remains interwoven with pious and secular restrictions alike. Controversies concerning Sunday trading in the UK in particular have tended to illustrate the legal system's role as mediator in disputes centred on the rights of the free market on the one hand and the moral restrictions of the Anglican Church on the other.

There are also echoes of similar tensions throughout Europe, sometimes on a decidedly 'postmodern' terrain, where tourists trail around stores at all hours on nearly all days while the populations of their host nation simultaneously try to continue cultural traditions to varying degrees. The sight of local residents often fully dressed in dark clothes, engaging in various religious rituals while their tourist counterparts wander nearly naked from café to café and shop to shop in high summer on the Mediterranean is perhaps a prime example of the processes of social division and the tensions of the local and international. Similarly, the popularity of market trading, still prevalent across Southern Europe, is frequently juxtaposed with the growth of upmarket retail outlets aimed at tourists (Sulkunen *et al.* 1997).

The market still thrives in many parts of the most affluent Western societies despite numerous advances in the means to consume, although its form and meaning have developed and perhaps changed. The reasons for the continuing success of the market as a cultural context for the practice of consumption and shopping remain the same across time and space. Markets offer an ease of setting up for their traders and a cultural and social experience for their consumers that remains unmatched in many later developments. More importantly, the market as a mode of contemporary consumption has consistently adapted to prevailing trends, offering increasingly stylized and individualized alternatives to the world of mass retailing on a mass scale, of which London's Covent Garden and similar city markets across Europe are primary examples. Similarly, the downside of markets also remains, namely their dependence on the open air, their potential for exploitation of customers without legislative protection, and openness to some forms of crime, all of which help to explain the rise of a more recent series of alternative sites.

The first of these alternatives was the formation of the high street, primarily in the latter half of the nineteenth century. Its development depended as much on the geographical and cultural histories of cities as on the expansion of mass consumption as an economic complement to mass production (Bowlby 1993; Nava 1996; Falk and Campbell 1997). In addition, and central in its formation, the high street offered several central advantages over the market for traders and customers alike. In particular, the high street offered security and some protection for traders and their goods and, at the same time, put customers and their potential purchases under cover. Moreover, it also facilitated expansion and an increased variety of stock. As a more physical development, however, the high street was wholly dependent on the expansion of cities, city populations and increased capital investment. It also started to exclude the poorest, as increased overheads for shop owners were compensated for by rising prices for the customer. As a result, then, for most of the nineteenth and twentieth centuries, the market and the high street, which were not always spatially distinct, coexisted and developed in tandem in what was essentially an increasingly two-class system of consumption. Ultimately, neither the market nor the high street ever entirely won over the custom of the other and, in the end, each fell victim to a further development, the supermarket.

The development of the supermarket indicated a shift in international fortunes. Whereas the rises and falls of the market and high street were essentially European developments, the takeover of the supermarket was primarily, if not exclusively, premised on certain economic and technological developments spearheaded in the United States. In retrospect, it is convenient to explain the development of the supermarket in terms of its importance and convenience for the customer, but this undermines the extent to which it formed a major economic and cultural initiative in the world of consumption, where it was at least as advantageous to the owner or retailer as it was to the consumer. Particularly important was the rise of retail engineering or store design in the United States, which then spread internationally. Stores were, and to some extent still are, constructed to manipulate the consumer into purchasing in excess of their intentions. The pitching of sweets at children's eye level, forcing customers to walk around entire stores for just a few items, blocking their way with particular commodities, or folding clothing so customers are made to handle the items to see them, are just a few examples of these processes in action (Humphery 1998).

Of primary importance in the development of the supermarket was an alteration in the *way* one shopped. Although in high-street stores of varying sorts, the customer and the retailer were separated by a counter, the supermarket depended on an entirely different form of shopping first practised in major department stores – self-service. Here the customer was invited to peruse and inspect commodities at first hand, and the all-important counter, or separation of customer and retailer, was removed. Not surprisingly perhaps, such a radical development encountered some resistance from customers, who often required some significant cajoling to get them into the stores and further instruction on how to shop in such an environment.

The practice of supermarket shopping also depended on certain technological developments, in particular the invention of the shopping trolley as opposed to the smaller basket, which contained less and was also heavy to carry, and added sophistication in systems of stock control, the check-out, cashiering, pricing, advertising and display, and product information. In addition, this also required a whole new series of increasingly specialized tasks for supermarket staff, who now had to pack shelves, present displays, operate cash registers, price products and keep track of stock, often at very increased speed. Consequently, it also led conversely to the demise of the shopkeeper and personal service, which remains a common complaint particularly with elderly customers. As Kim Humphery notes, it also started to mould the gender relations and divisions of supermarket shopping as men increasingly withdrew from the low-status work of shelf-filling or cashiering into the science of retailing and traditional masculine roles of store management, in turn tending to render the store itself an increasingly feminized environment (Humphery 1998). In addition, it had unintended consequences in creating an opening for a new form of crime, shoplifting, which remains a primary concern of owners of supermarkets and similar self-service stores today.

In sum, this added up to changes in the nature of shopping, the importance of which should not be underestimated. First, it facilitated the creation of impulse consumption, where the customer could pick up items at whim without even the forethought to ask for them; second, it placed far greater emphasis on the relationship of the product and the customer, and tended to cut out the importance of the shopkeeper which, in particular, increased the importance of display, packaging and the role of the manufacturer in the process; third, it also clearly facilitated greater spending and there is little to equivocate here in terms of the role of the profit motive; fourth, the shopping environment itself increased in importance as the customer now spent far longer in one store; and finally, and most critically, it reconstructed the customer as a *consumer* and turned shopping into *consuming*. In sum, in the space of 20 or 30 years since the Second World War, the nature of shopping had changed from entering single stores or market stalls with a list of requirements negotiated with individual shopholders or market traders to the limitless, seamless and sometimes unconscious, if not intensely private or voyeuristic, individualized and stylized activity of consuming.

This change in the nature of shopping and the transformation of shopping from an interaction of customers to one of seamless consuming perhaps has some of its origins in the nineteenth-century development of department stores and their attendant cultures of consumption. As some commentators have documented, the large and grandiose department stores of the mid- to late nineteenth century were in many ways a far cry from many of those in operation today (Buck-Morss 1989; Bowlby 1993; Nava 1996). Centred at the heart of major European cities, department stores such as Selfridges and Harrods in London or Galleria LaFayette in Paris were landmarks in themselves and the centres of upper-middle-class and tourist attraction alike. Often occupying entire sites across one or more city streets, they were primarily upmarket and glamorous worlds aimed at the most affluent middle classes, and particularly wealthy wives who were offered significant and trained personal service, often spending an entire day shopping in different departments for clothing or household goods, and partaking of lunch along the way. What is often significant here is the role of the staff, many of whom were interviewed and trained scrupulously for their often still comparatively poorly paid posts, for which they were also accommodated on site. Interestingly, the role of the personal shopping assistant is staging something of a comeback in the wake of affluent yet frenetically overworked or jet-set consumers, who require guidance and assistance on occasional shopping trips.

Also of critical importance in the development of department stores was the cultivation of the shopping environment itself, often intentionally constructed to encourage its customers to spend massive amounts of time as well as money in enjoying the entire experience of the store and its sights. It is this sense of voyeurism that informed Walter Benjamin's studies of arcade culture at the turn of the century, outlined in Chapter 1, and that is also significant in the analysis of the *flâneur*, or stroller, whose role in shopping was as visual as it was material. As a result, the department store, although focused on a specifically elite population, came to pre-empt the development of the supermarket and, most importantly, the shopping mall.

A partial explanation for the development of the shopping mall also lies in the demands of consumers themselves, tired of little or no transportation, poor parking, traipsing all over town from shop to shop in all weather conditions, and carrying it all home again. The shopping mall therefore offered convenience for some, namely those with the transport, time and money to pay often higher prices to support the increasing overhead costs. Additionally, the development of malls and mall culture once again depended on the influence of the United States in possessing and then utilizing large land sites as well as major capital investments in developing shopping malls as centres of cultural activity. Much attention has consequently focused on shopping malls as particularly postmodern examples of late capitalist culture (Shields 1992).

Prior to entering a discussion of shopping malls and postmodernity, it is perhaps apt to outline the key characteristics of their construction. First, and critically, it is important to point out that the shopping mall is an essentially artificial construction, effectively an architecturally led development that often in no way depends on the prior existence of property or even transport networks, which are frequently constructed in conjunction with the mall itself. Second, and critically linked to the first factor, shopping malls also offer an equally artificially controlled environment where time, space and climate are manipulated if not entirely wiped out in an enclosed and windowless world of lights, mirrors and air-conditioning. In addition, any sense of where one is locally, nationally or even internationally, is lost. This sense of enclosure, however, is often hidden or masked, particularly in some Californian developments where entire city areas are turned into 'mallesque' theme parks. Citywalk in Los Angeles, for example, reconstructs in its entirety a kind of transhistorical Hollywood mediascape which plays on media stereotypes of Los Angeles itself and where any strict sense of entrance and exit is eradicated, fuelling discussion of the connections of shopping malls, hyper-reality and postmodernity. Third, this feeds into a key feature of all malls, namely their immense size, which varies enormously but is rarely small enough to allow sight of all its dimensions at any one time and often sufficiently large to facilitate getting lost. Also, many shopping malls are increasingly multifunctional, including recreational, leisure and entertainment facilities – from cinemas and swimming pools to play areas and restaurant suites; even hotels and miniature churches in some cases, such as the now somewhat infamous West Edmonton mall in Canada. Fourth, and significantly, mall culture is essentially mid- to upmarket culture premised on affluent populations with plenty to spend; while the socially undesirable, including the homeless and, most controversially, unemployed youth are sometimes excluded through increasingly sophisticated security and surveillance techniques. Fifth, and equally significantly, shopping malls are premised and constructed quite contradictorily on individuality and difference while offering the same opportunities and the same outlets with nullifying repetition. This even occurs within malls themselves, as the same shops often occupy more than one position. Sixth, this extends on to an international plane as shopping malls present increasingly similar products and services across the entire developed world while retaining some small element of local culture or experience. Finally, and perhaps most importantly, shopping malls are premised completely on the visual processes of looking, presenting never ending displays and reinventing the social practice of window shopping, elevating it into an apparently seamless and wholly voyeuristic process of visual pleasure seeking.

What all of these points add up to is the sense in which the shopping mall has provided the ultimate point of no return in the postwar construction of the experience of shopping, entirely transforming the functionally specific and social actor of the customer into a more free-floating and directionless consumer:

> Everyday life has been transformed into an extension of consumer capitalism and the person rendered a consumer or spectator in whom the commodified meanings, the symbolic and affective values embedded in the sign system, have been interiorated as representations of reality.
>
> (Langman 1992: 47)

A parallel development to shopping malls, which taps into similar themes, was the expansion of mail order into previously unexposed upmarket areas. Mail order since the Second World War, in the US and UK in particular, had formed one of the central means of gaining credit for clothing and household goods, with few questions asked and often achieved through extensive use of warehouse clearance of cheaper-quality merchandise. Its success was also centred on certain demographic factors and, in particular, the preponderance of working- and lower-middle-class women with time on their hands, little money and a network of other women living in similar positions with whom they could use the catalogues to gain friends.

The difficulty with these early forms of mail order agency catalogue systems was not only the often inferior quality of the goods, or even the 'cheap and nasty' associations that developed around them, but the rise of working women themselves, for whom such purchasing was seen as inappropriate as they had less time, more money and often required more upmarket, stylish goods that were easily ordered, quickly received and did not involve anyone else.

Not surprisingly, then, the solution lay in the development of more upmarket and practically efficient forms of mail order. A trendsetting example in the UK was the *Next Directory*, launched in 1988, which offered a wide range of fashion goods, including children's wear and home furnishings as well as adult clothing, aimed at the style-conscious and affluent 20–35-year-old age group of men and women with upmarket lifestyle aspirations if not necessarily matching income. Importantly, agency or networking for commission-related administrative duties were disposed of and a fast telephone and 48-hour courier delivery service put in their place, while the clumsy catalogue was replaced with a glossy and professionally styled 'directory'.

Of significance in this process was the scaling down of the range of goods on offer, giving a greater sense of exclusivity coupled with a far stronger targeting of specific lifestyle markets. The rise of this kind of niche marketing coincided with a wider series of developments including lifestyle retailing already considered in detail in Chapter 3, but tended also to have its origins in the US where the Sears group, roughly equivalent to Littlewoods in the UK, was forced to drop its bumper catalogue in favour of more specifically targeted brochures or even 'brochettes' advertising sometimes fewer than 10 items, which were already developing elsewhere, particularly in California. Clear parallels also exist with the rising tide of pamphlets and catalogues that clutter magazines, Sunday papers and doorsteps alike. Junk mail in this sense is not so much an unnecessary effluent as an irritating outcome of the growth of niche markets.

Ultimately, then, if anything threatens the future development of out-of-town shopping, it is the move towards mail order and the involvement of various forms of information technology in purchasing goods and services that offer the potential to undermine the entire social practice of shopping. Given the continued importance of shopping as a social or cultural activity, however, such claims may well prove overstated, although the advent of systems removing even the need for shops, let alone their staff, still provides potential ammunition for the annihilation of the customer in favour of an increasingly drifting and 'virtual' consumer. The sum of these developments, then, leads us perhaps not surprisingly to a study of shopping and postmodernity.

I shop therefore I am: postmodernity and the contemporary nature of shopping

> Shopping, even for everyday items, had now almost entirely lost its status as an activity and become simply an experience. It had lost a materiality and become a cultural event.
>
> (Humphery 1998: 114)

Concepts and catchphrases such as 'I shop therefore I am', 'shop till you drop', or even 'the shopping experience' seem new and indicative of a contemporary series of developments. In more academic terms, this is translated into the relationship of shopping and postmodern society, or shopping and late consumer capitalism, also seen as part of the contemporary, cutting edge of society. At the centre of such claims is a series of assertions that I wish to consider in turn. An additional concern, though, relates to the question of whether the whole of these assertions adds up to more than the sum of its parts, a point I also wish to explore later.

The first and key assertion related to the notion of the changing nature of a contemporary shopping experience concerns the idea that shopping is increasingly a leisure activity and not simply a matter of mundane necessity or utility (Shields 1992). This assertion rests on a series of other more empirical points, including the fluidity of income and rising living standards, coupled with a declining working week and increasing leisure time, plus the development of supermarket or self-service stores that specifically allow the customer to peruse and inspect as opposed to simply purchase. These points are of themselves contentious, particularly considering the variety and inequity of individual and group shopping experiences in terms of financial and geographical access, according to class, occupation, sex, race or age, to mention only a few of the potential variations and sources of discrimination and inequity. It is perhaps simplest to point out, then, that shopping is a major and increasing source of leisure only for certain population groups or individuals.

Second, and allied to this, it is also asserted that shopping and consumption are increasingly constitutive of identity, that is to say, people are increasingly defined according to their consumption patterns (Bourdieu 1984; Langman 1992; Bauman 1998). Increasing support for this assertion comes from the marketing of commodities, which is centred more and more on complex notions of personality and lifestyle types, as defined in terms of consumption patterns as opposed to simpler notions of socio-economic groups (see Chapter 3). It is also easy to point out that personality is at least partly constituted or reinforced through commodities, particularly those which are clearly apparent or easily recognized, including clothing, cars and property.

Two more particular difficulties arise here, though, as: first, these ideas or practices are not new and were formulated academically much earlier in terms of concepts such as commodity fetishism, conspicuous consumption and the separation of content and meaning; and second, in the contradictory fact that those with the most leisure time to consume often have the least access or money, such as the unemployed, single parents and the elderly. Particularly contradictorily, it is important to point out that to go shopping does not necessarily mean to go spending and, in this sense, shopping *is* perhaps constructive of identity as it is the practice of looking, desiring and interacting that is critical, or the simple *process* of shopping itself which is significant. This factor is then connected with the earlier nineteenth-century concern with the processes of seeing and being seen, or voyeurism and exhibitionism, that underpinned Walter Benjamin's work on arcades and department stores and Simmel's work on the city (see Chapter 1).

Third, an underlying and central issue concerns the associations and meanings attached to commodities. In particular, many theorists of postmodernity, particularly Baudrillard, have asserted that the symbolic or sign value of commodities has become increasingly significant and is overtaking the validity of their use or utility value (Baudrillard 1988). Very importantly, therefore, it is also asserted that purchases are made according to a series of equally idiosyncratic and socially structured values surrounding the goods and not intrinsic to them. This is partly a matter of taste and partly a matter of status, two points put together simply in the work of Pierre Bourdieu (Bourdieu 1984). The difficulty here is the sense that this is again not necessarily new, as goods have given their owners status since the goods themselves were invented and, in addition, this was also understood academically in terms of a paper chase of social class, where people were caught up in processes of imitation and differentiation (Simmel 1904; Veblen 1934). In addition, though, an added concern is raised as to the allure of advertising and marketing, promotion and packaging, in constructing an essentially artificial significance for the goods affected. The difficulty here concerns the question of the role of the consumer, who is then sometimes seen as a passive dupe operating under false consciousness, a point put most forcefully in the work of the Frankfurt School (see Chapter 3).

This ties in with the fourth point, that the processes of shopping and consumption rest on the invocation of a whole series of unconscious desires, dreams and, ultimately, a psychoanalytic process of unconscious wish-fulfilment. This perspective is put most persuasively by Rachel Bowlby in *Shopping with Freud*, where she analyses the whole transaction of viewing, wanting and purchasing goods, or simply consumption as constructed in psychoanalytic terms (Bowlby 1993). The difficulty here, however, rests on the implication of an empirical assumption, namely the unconscious. Interestingly, as outlined in Chapter 3, Bowlby also shows how psychoanalytic and marketing discourses have increasingly intermingled during the twentieth century. Appealing as this perspective may seem, this is perhaps explained as the outcome of operating within a post-Freudian world framework of concept, understanding and experience.

A fifth and final point is that shopping is primarily now a subjective experience of image processing, association and value interpretation that is as individual and idiosyncratic as it is social and structured. Given the overwhelming variety of goods on offer to fulfil every need there is some credence to the idea that consumer choice is hardly a simple, rational calculation of utility. Similarly, given increasing access to vast arrays of often near-useless or luxury goods, it is easy to assert a growing concern with values, wants and needs that have very little to do with survival. However, there is some concern as to whether the acquisition of commodities ever was simply a matter of utility value and survival, although it is perhaps also important to assert that the matter of the use*less* value of goods has consistently increased over time, particularly as disposable incomes have risen considerably, at least for some population groups. Porsche cars and designer fashion are prime examples of the stupendous excesses that exist in contemporary consumer society and yet, although we may moralize against them, it is precisely their sheer excessiveness that is at the crux of their appeal, for there is little rational justification or cost-conscious sense of quality that explains spending six-figure sums on cars or four figure sums on items of clothing: the only reason for doing so is that it makes you look, and feel, good. In addition, it is this sense of excess which at least partly determines the mark-up on the price.

To pull all of these points apart in turn, though, is perhaps unfair, for if shopping is now primarily a leisure activity, at least for some, and constitutive of identity through a series of socially constructed, subjective and perhaps exploitative experiences then we are indeed considering a whole new and potentially important, if not necessarily 'postmodern', shopping phenomenon. The problem remains, however, the interpretation of this new form of shopping experience which, on closer inspection, seems particularly paradoxical.

So far I have discussed the underlying assumptions and prevailing accounts of primarily postmodern or poststructural theory of the shopping experience. Put at their simplest, these perspectives state most importantly that the contemporary shopping experience is one of expression of personality and that it is an increasing part of the development and perhaps ultimately the dissolution of identity, constitutive of an inner world of psychological desire and need, as well as an increasingly significant factor in the formation of an image- or representation-oriented society. Consequently, although there is some controversy concerning the exact outcome and implications of these developments, there is an implicit assumption that this is the primary or driving logic of contemporary consumer society.

Contrary to this assertion, I wish to stress that this is, in fact, only half of the story as far as the contemporary nature or experience of shopping is concerned and that, as a consequence of this, what we are considering is ultimately a shopping paradox. It is primarily a shopping paradox, for the other half of the story paints a far less rosy and indeed far more ordinary picture. To put it simply, although shopping is a seductive, pleasure-seeking experience for some people some of the time, for many people a lot of the time it is simply a mundane if not tiresome chore that has all the excitement of wiping the floor. Various empirical studies of supermarket shopping in particular lend strong support to such a claim (Humphery 1998; Miller 1998; Miller *et al.* 1998).

Daniel Miller's *A Theory of Shopping*, perhaps more aptly titled 'An Anthropology of Shopping', provides a distinctive perspective on shopping practices as strongly grounded in social relations and ritual (Miller 1998). It is centred on an ethnographic study of 76 UK households in north London, focusing strongly on the roles of women in shopping for provisions. More importantly, these practices are interpreted anthropologically, adapting Bataille's theory of sacrificial ritual in particular, seeing the purchasing of provisions as an illustration of love and the perpetuation of personal relations in the household. Therefore, in spending time shopping for the household, women were often consciously or unconsciously expressing their love for their partners or children and adopting specific rituals of 'sacrifice' in controlling spending and putting others first, or alternatively providing a 'treat' for themselves or others according to a wider and often dialectical discourse of thrift and excess. Given the move towards secularization in Western society and away from conscious sacred rituals, the contemporary importance of love often tied to a wider notion of 'the pure relationship' is seen as stepping in to take its place as a modern ritual of sacrifice and devotion of which shopping for provisions forms an important part (see Giddens 1992).

An allied, and rather more rigorously grounded, study is also provided by Miller and his colleagues in *Shopping, Place and Identity* (Miller *et al.* 1998). This is also centred on an ethnography of shopping practices in north London, although it takes the focus further towards the importance of the sites of shopping themselves, particularly the Brent Cross Shopping Centre and Wood Green Shopping City, two of the earliest malls in the UK. The underlying thrust of the analysis is to counter the overly culturalist and individualized perspectives on shopping often associated with more postmodern forms of theory and cultural studies. This is, in turn, centred on six assertions: first, that shopping is only partially concerned with purchasing and is also understood as part of a wider system of production, marketing and selling as well as a network of social interactions; second, shopping is an everyday activity that is mundane and often not consciously particularly personally significant or reflected on; third, shopping also forms an arena where a series of wider social, moral and personal dilemmas are played out; fourth, shopping also concerns social relations and the family as much as the self or the individual; fifth, that shopping also is crucially located in the world of the goods or commodities and is therefore concerned with production as well as consumption; and sixth, that shopping is also the locus of place and identity. Also highlighted throughout is the significance of social class, age and the fears and difficulties of the elderly, and race and ethnicity as factors that interact with the overall construction of identity in particular localities. This leads to an analysis which illustrates the contradictory, and indeed near dialectical, relations of shopping, place and identity:

> If the identity of the person is in part lodged in the very places themselves, such as shopping centres, then both the autonomy of subject (identity) and object (shopping centre) is refused, and what academic encounter reveals is rather the contradictions which are thrown up by the articulation between person and place within which both person and place are forged.
>
> (Miller *et al.* 1998: 193)

Kim Humphery in *Shelf Life* provides a similar, though more varied and detailed, cultural history of the supermarket in the UK, US and Australia particularly (Humphery 1998). As mentioned earlier, he highlights the importance of retail engineering and gender divisions within a wider frame of international and comparative cultural history as particularly significant elements in a similarly contradictory dialectic of power:

> If the spaces, practices and ideologies of consumer capitalism do have a power to reshape everyday life in their own image, and I would not dismiss this, it is a power which constantly has to be worked at, reframed and reconceptualised; it is a power constantly undermined both by its own logic and by the people it attempts to subject.
>
> (Humphery 1998: 16)

This leads Humphery into an analysis of the discursive dichotomies of shopping concerning its role in individual activity and resistance, levels of choice and manipulation, its tendency towards the perpetuation of self-expression and also conformity, and its involvement in the expression of feelings of pleasure and also guilt, all of which are evoked most strongly in his own ethnographic study of supermarket cultures.

The clear difficulty in all of these empirical studies is, however, the sense in which the contradictions of shopping remain only partially explained. To unpack this further, it is necessary to construct some more general commentary. As I have already outlined, the strongly cultural emphasis in the analysis of shopping has come under fire for its lack of empiricism, particularly in the work of Daniel Miller (Miller 1998; Miller et al. 1998). Miller asserts with some vigour that shopping is as mundane an activity as it is a fantastical one, which, in particular, is strongly socially relational and connected to the ritualized practices of the traditional and modern household alike. The difficulty here is that the fantasy world of the free-floating individual is also lost in such a rigorously grounded and relational analysis. This is of some empirical significance given the increasing importance of single-person households.

An additional dimension to the contradictions of contemporary shopping concerns the categorization of the activity itself which, on closer inspection, is often dualistic in nature. If you ask many people whether they like shopping or what their experience of it is, the common response is to ask what sort of shopping one means, as for many people there is a clear distinction between the credit-card rapture of shopping for clothes and jewellery in glowing shopping malls or taking trips along quaint alleyways for holiday souvenirs and the weekly trudge around a supermarket on a rainy afternoon groaning over the rising prices of staple products and negotiating a cramped car park. For many commentators, this then highlights a distinction concerning shopping practices, where *doing* the shopping, defined as instrumental and centred on the consumption of staple commodities, is separated from *going* shopping, defined as less focused, more visual and loosely connected to luxuries. Similar conceptual distinctions have also included shopping *for* versus shopping *around* (Radner 1995; Falk and Campbell 1997; Miller *et al.* 1998).

At the crux of this distinction is the role of 'just looking', or pleasure-seeking window shopping, supposedly gaining in importance during the twentieth century. A key question centres on assessing exactly what is happening in going window shopping and certain factors stand out as significant here: first, such shopping practice primarily applies to luxury goods, of which fashion forms a primary example, and not so much to staples or the supermarket; second, the expansion of window shopping is connected primarily to the simultaneous development of shopping malls as climate-controlled and glitzy zones providing acres of shop frontage precisely for voyeuristic purposes; and third, it is also an activity increasingly tied up with the investment of self, as the desire to look, to try, or to decide prior to purchase occurs where the risk to self, financial or psychological, is greatest. As a result, it is hardly surprising that stores selling high-status or high-fashion goods are the primary sites of window shopping, and it is partly the development and expansion of some of these goods themselves that explains the paradoxical nature of the contemporary shopping experience. For example, the development of many electrical and technical goods has formed an entire series of markets, and the sheer variety and profusion of everything from shirts to shoes, and from spray cans to shopping powders, dazzles the consumer and forces them into endless perusal and inspection of options.

However, several factors emerge as of importance here: first, the two forms of shopping increasingly overlap as supermarkets themselves turn into spectacles of conspicuous consumption and malls are increasingly perceived as mundane and repetitive arenas of spending; second, the distinction of the 'use value' versus the 'sign value' of commodities, which is seen to underpin the separation in shopping practices, is itself open to interpretation, as conspicuous consumption significantly pre-dates the developments of contemporary shopping cultures; and third, and most importantly, the distinction is more truly centred on the structural question of social divisions as one *does* the shopping precisely according to the limits of one's income, and, for the poorest, the practice of shopping for pleasure is either excluded or simply depressing.

Perhaps most importantly, shopping as a contemporary leisure activity is increasingly riven with social divisions according to access, transport and provision and, most simply, money, and many, particularly the elderly, single parents, the poor, the unemployed, and the physically or mentally impaired do not have the means to partake fully in it. Ultimately, a primary paradox here is that those with the most money to spend, namely those in dual-income full-time working households, have least time; while those with least money, such as the unemployed and the elderly, have hours to kill every day. The difficulty here is that shopping, as an activity in itself, is a relatively free invitation to the isolated, depressed or simply dislocated. Easy access to credit, and the sense of not paying that comes from it, also opens up particular difficulties for the relatively poor and easily led especially, while the poorest of all are simply excluded. As a result, it is hardly access to shopping for the affluent that should concern us, as this is often solved through mail order and now the Internet; rather, the simultaneous tempting and excluding of the lost and impoverished for whom shopping is experienced as a window through which they are invited to look and a door through which they cannot enter.

Although no such measures exist, one suspects strongly that one of the contemporary causes of psychological illness, such as depression, concerns the pressures of living without the means to consume. More importantly, these 'non-consumers' may now precisely provide the foundations for 'the new poor' (Bauman 1998). Some, very limited, evidence for this assertion is provided through the rises in rates of shopping addiction, or shopaholicism, and shoplifting which are often also connected to increases in credit default and debt. Estimates of the extent of these problems vary enormously, often as a result of difficulties in defining the issue and the stigma associated with what remains an often very private activity. For example, Richard Elliott at Oxford University in the UK has recently conducted a study into shopaholicism where he estimates that there are upwards of 700,000 shopaholics in the UK alone, who are mostly women often otherwise living very unfulfilled and isolated lives owing amounts roughly equal to the then national average wage of more than £15,000. Other reports have suggested far higher figures and focus strongly on the psychological effects of shopping in increasing one's sense of self-worth, power or control. Limited evidence is also provided in the examples of voluntary self-help groups including, Lawrence Michael's 'Wallet Watch', which, with only small-scale operations, receives more than 1000 phone calls a year from worried spenders. Reports from the association of Citizens' Advice Bureaux, who provide one of the very few examples of free debt counselling as well as links with government Credit Unions in the UK, also confirm that the problem is expanding and takes up an increasing proportion of all cases and resources. Consequently, although for some people the contemporary shopping experience is one of pleasure and expression, for others it remains the epitome of misery and exploitation, often added to through inept social policy, points explored previously in Chapter 4.

A more complex point concerns the particular nature of the shopping experience for the affluent and pleasure-seeking populations. Some of these groups commonly complain of a lack of variety, at least in the provinces, and a strong sense of limitation and tedium, or a shopping malaise, in shopping malls in particular. This is a paradoxical point to make, perhaps, for as consumer society has expanded and more and more shops have opened, the sense of repetitiveness or restriction of choice has also often increased. In addition, the increasing globalization of consumption is also leading to an international sense of the same monotony. When thinking of shopping malls in particular, they are in a sense space*less* – one feels lost and out of contact, as if entering a post-holocaust zone. Consequently, the relationship of shopping and identity is complex and not simply a one-way process of construction but often a two-way process of confusion, dislocation and *re*location. For some, particularly those already with a low sense of self-esteem, this literally may mean one has to *buy* something to *be* something. In this context, fashion commodities as the very articulation of 'self-on-the-shelves' are particularly prominent. People are not necessarily dupes or victims, but they are perhaps disempowered.

This leads me to a particularly critical point of shopping and power: to what extent are we active or passive consumers? We are currently presented with an increasingly contradictory picture of ourselves as rational actors making choices concerning everything from provisions to pensions, with producers and service providers apparently tripping over themselves to outwit or outstep us all; while we are equally presented with a picture ourselves as cultural dupes, consumed and sucked into something we do not feel we have any control over whatever, particularly if we are poor or excluded in some way through where we live or the work we do or do not do. What is often invoked here is the notion of consumer choice as a con-trick and an illusion – something we like to think, and what is more 'they' like us to think, we have. The difficulty here is that, in one sense at least, the choices we have are quite real, for in a supermarket society we can, and do, pick and choose, and mix and match, to suit ourselves and our tastes. When presented with endless products that perform the same function for an equivalent cost, we constantly pick up one, so someone wins and someone loses. The choice is limited and strings are pulled, yet shopping is a far more complex process than that represented in the fictional world of *The Stepford Wives*, considered in detail in Chapter 6. Interestingly, the drama of such films comes precisely from the war of power that ensues, and this, in the final instance, is the nature of the contemporary shopping experience.

Conclusions: rapture or torture

Throughout this chapter I have stressed the importance of shopping as an *experience*. This implicitly accepts and promotes a perspective that sees shopping as a personal and subjective activity as opposed to a social and objective, or functional, reality. Although this highlights, I think appropriately, the very interpretive nature of the phenomenon in question, the difficulty is that it also has a tendency to produce a picture of shopping that is one-sided, centred almost entirely on its personal, pleasure-seeking or more simply experiential dimensions, when, in particular, a structural and material reality of limitations still remains for many of the populations of even the most affluent Western societies – let alone those that are less wealthy.

As a result, and to sum up this chapter, this leads me to outline a series of tensions underlying the contemporary nature and development of shopping. It is important to point out that these tensions are not easily resolved, if at all, and reflect what I perceive to be the highly contradictory or paradoxical position of shopping in contemporary society. First, there is a strong sense in which the nature and development of shopping are pulled in two different directions, one towards increased choice and individuation in the sheer proliferation of products, services and outlets, and the other towards a mass culture where, in a sense, options are closed down instead of opened up, and the expansion of shopping, in terms of its commodities and the means to consume them, merely turns into a repetition and not cultural diversity. In addition, this may give some credence to the earlier assertions of the Frankfurt School or other theses of cultural homogenization but it also illustrates a certain social patterning in shopping practice, which is not, in contrast, necessarily nihilistic. Second, this is also reflected in the tension of the local and the global that informs the contemporary experience of shopping as more and more societies are apparently drawn into the same world of commodities while simultaneously experiencing them differently and often juxtaposing them with pre-existing cultural histories or traditions. Third, this leads into a third and fundamental tension of the aesthetic and the material. Although the development of shopping malls in particular has facilitated a highly visual culture stressing the aesthetic significance of goods and services, their material importance remains and primarily undermines the position of some groups or populations while supporting others in a particularly insidious set of processes of inclusion and exclusion that range from surveillance to credit controls and poverty. Fourth, this taps into the highly political dimensions of shopping and its capacity to exploit some groups and empower others in processes of facilitating individual or group expression or oppression, as well as its wider gendered, sexualized and racialized dimensions, and these are points I wish to explore in the next chapter. Perhaps most fundamentally to our discussion here, however, what remains most contradictory and paradoxical in relation to shopping is the nature of the shopping experience itself, rapturous for some people some of the time, particularly those most affluent and with most access, yet often tortuous, tiring and frustrating for many people much of the time. In sum, then, shopping is *neither* rapture *nor* torture, but is rapture *and* torture for most people most of the time.

Suggested further reading

Bowlby, R. (1993) *Shopping with Freud*. London: Routledge – unusual literary investigation of the connection of marketing with psychoanalysis.

Falk, P. and Campbell, C. (eds) (1998) *The Shopping Experience*. London: Sage – useful and fairly up-to-date collection of essays.

Humphery, K. (1998) *Shelf Life*. Cambridge: Cambridge University Press – fascinating and wide-ranging ethnography and cultural history of the supermarket.

Miller, D. (1998) *A Theory of Shopping*. Cambridge: Polity – interesting anthropological ethnography set in north London.

Shields, R. (ed.) (1992) *Lifestyle Shopping*. London: Routledge – ground-breaking collection of mostly poststructural analyses of shopping mall culture.

6
EXPRESSION, OPPRESSION AND THE POLITICS OF CONSUMPTION

Following the discussion of social divisions and social policy in Chapter 4, and the contradictory nature of contemporary experiences of shopping in Chapter 5, this chapter is concerned primarily with the politics of consumption more directly, including its class dimensions and particularly its often paradoxical position in relation to oppressed groups such as women, gay men or lesbians and racial or ethnic minorities.

Prior to this, though, it is worth considering the relationship between consumption and politics more widely. The most immediate point to make is that there is, in a sense, apparently no relationship. This is due primarily to the enormous emphasis traditionally placed on work and production, as opposed to leisure and consumption, as sites of power and resistance. This stems most particularly from Marxist theory and also from the narrow focus of many socialist movements which have often seen consumerism as nothing more than another opiate of the masses. Consumption's relationship with the traditional Left, communism or socialism, then, tends to remain underdeveloped and potentially antagonistic. Consequently, the focus of attention in the study of consumption more academically has tended to shift more towards identity politics which therefore, of necessity, form the primary focus of this chapter. Where consumerist practices have informed politics most widely is in relation to consumer movements and consumer activism, for example around environmentalism or in the formation of co-operatives, and these were considered critically in Chapter 4.

However, perhaps the most elementary form of politics in relation to consumption is omitted from any of these analyses, and that is the politics of social divisions. More essentially, it is important to point out that the most fundamental of all oppressions in relation to consumption is quite simply that of exclusion. This is often coupled, with merciless irony, to the wider processes of exploitation and production. Consequently, those most ruthlessly exploited in producing the goods and services of consumer society, such as those employed in factories in the Third World, or, more relatively speaking, those working at low levels and/or casually in retailing, are precisely those persons or groups with the least capacity to partake in the opportunities of consumer society, namely little time, less money and near-non-existent excess energy. Even the unemployed, although often comparatively poor, have the time and some limited capacity to shop, play sports or simply watch television.

In addition, as consumption escalates in its importance in affluent Western societies, whether as a leisure activity, a series of social interactions or a process of self-definition, exclusion from full participation in the opportunities it offers is also potentially equally costly in terms of undermining self-worth, increasing isolation and, most perniciously, creating a rising sense of at least relative poverty. As advertising endlessly permeates all forms of communication or entertainment, as products and services relentlessly multiply and diversify, and as displays of everything from convenience meals to luxury cars escalate in seductive significance, so the misery of those who cannot afford the commodities, haven't the time to use the services, or simply can't keep up becomes unremitting and interminable (Bauman 1998). The problem then becomes one not of how gender, race, sexuality or even class, as categories or identities, work to include or exclude certain groups but rather how they operate as mechanisms to compound, or perhaps undermine, the more fundamental processes of consumer society. Consequently, this chapter considers the relations of class, gender, sexuality and race to consumption in turn, and then, in the concluding section, discusses the significance of their connections.

Keeping up appearances: class and consumption

Given consumption's monetary importance and consumer society's most fundamental foundations as capitalist society, the question of the relationship of social class to consumption is of primary importance. Despite this, because of the recent tendency to interpret consumption culturally or discursively as opposed to economically or empirically, its connections with social class have often suffered a lack of critical consideration. I am thinking here particularly of the work of Mike Featherstone, which in many ways paved the way for a more poststructural analysis of consumption

(Featherstone 1991). In addition, some of this situation is also a result of the rather dismissive attitude some theorists of social class have taken towards consumption, often seeing its analysis as in some sense undermining or opposing more important questions of work and production, particularly in relation to the perspectives of John Goldthorpe and Gordon Marshall, and echoed more critically in the discussions of Rosemary Crompton and Alan Warde (Goldthorpe 1987; Marshall *et al.* 1988; Warde 1994; Crompton 1996).

This state of affairs is perhaps ironic, for social class has always meant more than economic position, even in the crudest of Marxist terms, invoking the importance of shared values, politics, and the processes of inclusion, exclusion and resistance, to name only some. More particularly, what seems to stick in the craw of many more traditional theorists of social class is the sense that consumption has been argued by some, most notably many post-structural theorists, to be undermining the importance of social class *as an identity* (Bauman 1987, 1988; Saunders 1987; Giddens 1991). Alan Warde in particular is virulently critical of consumption's importance in the formation or maintenance of self or personality (Warde 1994). Consequently, perhaps an increasingly unnecessary tension has started to arise around the question of whether class still constitutes the linchpin of identity in contemporary Western society *or* consumption when, perhaps more accurately, one could easily assert that class and consumption act precisely *in conjunction with* one another to maintain individual and group identities, particularly at the level of status and prestige.

Veblen's often much-derided work still provides one of the building blocks for the study of consumption and class in its important development of the concept of conspicuous consumption (Veblen [1899]1934). It is precisely consumption's significance as a visible indicator of status that links it to wider questions of social class and position. Unlike occupation, the most commonly used indicator of social class, consumption is an essentially visual phenomenon where, from the display of commodities such as clothes, property or cars through to consumption practices such as shopping, dining out or engaging in leisure activities from playing sports to simple conversation with other people, what one is seen in and where one is seen are still what matters most in, quite literally, keeping up appearances (see also Chapter 1).

More importantly, and this is where many of the recent disputes are located, consumption activities may not necessarily co-ordinate with other indicators of social class. For example, many young working-class men, unemployed and often still living at home, were notorious in the 1980s for their outward displays of conspicuous consumption through their adoption of designer-label clothing (Edwards 1997). In conjunction with this, although social class has never correlated particularly directly with financial status, or simply with money, consumption is crucially dependent on economic position. Every aspect of consumption is, to some extent, economically determined according to the simple question of whether one can or cannot afford certain commodities or to partake in particular activities.

This sense of economic determination is, however, limited in predicting the individual choices that are made within financial constraints or, to put it more simply, styles of consumption. Of primary importance regarding the combination of class and consumption in the formation of individual and group identities is the work of Pierre Bourdieu, whose detailed study of the lifestyles of the Parisian middle classes of the 1960s in *Distinction: A Social Critique of the Judgement of Taste* still stands as a modern landmark in more empirical attempts to address the relationship of class and consumption (Bourdieu 1984). Although more contemporary, Bourdieu's work stands in close relation to a more grounded and classically sociological tradition of empirical research which, in some senses, also forms the logical extension to Veblen's much earlier work on *The Leisure Class* already mentioned (Veblen 1934).

The underlying thrust of Bourdieu's analysis was to argue that taste, as exemplified in differing patterns of consumption, from use of hairstyles to choices in dining out, is still socially patterned if not economically determined. To do this he invoked a series of concepts, of which probably the most important was 'habitus'. Habitus, although strongly related to habitat in its widest sense, was not determined by environment but related to a wider series or set of dispositions which were socially and culturally shaped, such as ways of speaking, chosen leisure activities, and overall patterns of living – from the time spent eating out to the reading of particular newspapers.

Of crucial importance in this was the collective and ordered, rather than individual and random, nature of the often small and near unconscious decisions that were taken and, most significantly, their location in a wider framework of socio-economic inequality and maintenance of social position. Consequently, choices of schooling, entertainment or modes of dress were neither open nor neutral, as they performed the primary function of creating or maintaining what he called 'cultural capital', or the overall level of knowhow concerning socially correct and incorrect styles of living, modes of presentation and purchasing decisions (see also Chapter 2).

So, consumption patterns, far from casual adoptions of open or 'postmodern' choice, are perhaps a quite insidious series of social divisions that operate as processes of inclusion and exclusion alike. In conjunction with the concept of cultural capital, the role of what Bourdieu called 'cultural intermediaries', or style experts from magazine editors to image consultants, was also deemed crucial in the maintenance of the privileges of the middle classes. As a result, what Bourdieu's work still demonstrates is that, without necessarily descending into economic determinism, consumption is still all too socially ordered and divisive. Moreover, it forms part of the wider processes of 'symbolic violence' whereby cultural capital becomes precisely a weapon of exclusion. In addition, it is this sense of divisiveness that also underpins discussion of the question of gender and its relationship to consumption.

Gender matters: men, women and consumption

Gender stands as one of the most important and pervasive, but most sloppily conceived aspects of consumption and consumer society. Perhaps it is its very pervasiveness that explains the messiness in making its connections with consumption and in defining just what is gendered in consumer society. Part of the difficulty also lies in the high degree of strongly gendered images and stereotypes surrounding consumption. These include the wayward women of the nineteenth century, neatly encapsulated in the tragic story of Flaubert's self-destructive heroine Madame Bovary, whose marital frustration leads her into costly spending, and the wicked men, including her lover Rodolphe, who try to seduce them into spending yet more of their husbands' money; the movie struggles of *The Stepford Wives* to regain control of their lives, and Gordon Gekko's swaggering greed on *Wall Street* (Flaubert [1857] 1992).

There are, in fact, three key aspects to the gendering of consumption. First, the gendering of objects into sex-specific commodities, from fast executive cars and power drills to jewellery and cosmetics. There is nothing intrinsically masculine or feminine about any of these items, but they resonate with intensely gendered meaning and association. In addition, perhaps the only truly gendered commodities are tampons or similar sex-specific or medical products, as even shaving is a cultural practice and related products apply to each of the sexes. One potential exception is fashion or dress, which does have some, limited, intrinsically gendered connections in terms of its fit to the male or female form, although, as we shall see in Chapter 7, this is often overstated. Second, the gendering of consumption practices, most specifically in the increasingly outdated notion that women shop and men do not. It is, however, still true that whereas it is usually women who trawl the supermarkets and department stores, it is men who tend to disseminate the DIY superstore and have disputes concerning CDs and digital hi-fi technology. Third, and more controversially, there is the gendering of the production of consumption in terms of the masculinity and femininity of design, plus the sexual divisions of production lines and retailing itself, as sweaty men weld things together and sell complicated pieces of technology and women put them in decorative packets and stack them on shelves (Ash and Wright 1998).

Although stereotypes tend to proliferate here also, there is increasingly ample evidence that consumption at the levels of commodities, practices and production alike is indeed strongly gendered, often in conjunction with other factors such as class, race or sexuality (Lury 1996). For example, Victoria de Grazia has provided a fascinating collection of insights into the historical construction of feminine and masculine modes of consumption, while Pat Kirkham has similarly provided a collection of essays on the gendering of commodities, and Mica Nava has recently provided insights into the continued gendering of the practices of consumption (de Grazia 1996; Kirkham 1996; Nava 1996).

Stepford wives and pleasure seekers: women and consumption

If there is one image that springs most powerfully to the popular and feminist mind alike when considering women's relationship to consumption, it is that of the Stepford housewife as popularized in the series of films centred on the part-science-fictional and part-factual story of the residents of Stepford, Connecticut, in the 1970s. The films, and the first one in particular, simply entitled *The Stepford Wives*, tell the story of how middle-class suburban housewives struggle to retain self-worth in the face of an anti-feminist backlash from their husbands. The initial story takes on more dramatic dimensions as it is slowly revealed that the women are being ghoulishly transformed into living zombies of themselves and the climax of the film comes when the valiant heroine, in true psychoanalytic style, is confronted quite literally with the full terror of her own acquiescent, automated and indeed murderous self. The final scene shows her drifting around the supermarket in feminine soft focus discussing recipes for her family with other similarly passive housewives.

Although now somewhat comical in some respects, the film struck a nerve in the popular and feminist consciousness alike and highlighted in particular the importance of housewifery as the nexus uniting consumption with femininity. Following the rise of second-wave feminism, housewifery came under attack as the epitome of passive and patriarchal self-loathing, chaining women to the kitchen sink, economic dependence and isolation. Consumption *per se* also came under attack for encouraging and perpetuating an idealized image of housewifely satisfaction gained from shopping, cleaning and generally pursuing a life of the provision of happiness for others and not for oneself. Ann Oakley's fierce condemnation of housewifery in the UK paralleled Betty Friedan's earlier exposition of middle-class femininity in the US; and the later work of Christine Delphy in particular added a strongly Marxist assault on the role of the contemporary Western and capitalist household in the oppression of women (Friedan 1963; Oakley 1976; Delphy 1984).

This condemnation of consumption's role in relation to the oppression of women seemed nearly complete, but later studies have provided increasingly sophisticated and complex analyses of women's consumer practices and experiences. Janice Winship's ground-breaking analysis of women's reading of women's magazines highlighted the essentially interactive nature of the construction of feminine consumption; and Rachel Bowlby took the argument considerably further, giving it a strongly psychoanalytic dimension, later addressed most directly in the work of Hilary Radner who argued with some force that consumption constitutes a major, if still contradictory, site for the formation of feminine pleasure (Winship 1987; Bowlby 1993; Radner 1995). In vociferous opposition to this, Naomi Wolf launched a fierce attack on the beauty industry for creating anxiety-provoking ideals, often echoed in concerns over anorexia and other eating disorders, which was reflected more empirically in the work of Lisa Adkins who demonstrated that women's appearances still matter disproportionately to their positions at work (Wolf 1991; Orbach 1993; Adkins 1995). A little more historically, Wilson's study of the *flâneuse* highlighted the contradictory and often shadowy world of women as strollers in the city, also echoed in Dowling's study of the construction of femininity in department stores; and Mica Nava has defended women's role in consumption as potentially empowering and often reinforcing of certain skills as part of an overall perspective which emphasizes with some virulence the activity, rather than passivity, of women as consumers (Nava 1992; Wilson 1992; Dowling 1993).

What are we to make of this increasingly contradictory set of perspectives concerning the relationship of women and femininity to the practices of consumption and consumer society more widely? First, perhaps not surprisingly, much would seem to depend on the prior foundations of the perspective in question. Those whose views of women as consumers are most positive are usually those with the most psychoanalytic or poststructural of academic perspectives. For example, Janice Winship, Hilary Radner and Rachel Bowlby are all cultural or textual theorists relying to varying degrees on poststructural or psychoanalytic critiques. Mica Nava also stands at the crossroads of media or cultural studies and wider social theory. Similarly, those who are most negative, such as Ann Oakley, Christine Delphy or Naomi Wolf, tend to adhere to more political or structural traditions within feminism either from more Marxist or polemical standpoints. Consequently, there is perhaps less a contradiction of feminist positions in this discussion and more a reflection of the underlying differences in their foundations.

Second, following the line of Celia Lury, one can argue that the position of women in relation to consumption is accurately reflected as contradictory *per se*, as women themselves are seen as active participants *within* the constraints of their positions (Lury 1996). The difficulty here is that this tends to lead to a rather naive sense of sitting on the fence in not deciding which side of the equation of femininity and consumption matters most. In sum, it is difficult to see how women can occupy quite opposing situations simultaneously. One solution to this conundrum comes in a more sophisticated view of the position of women as complex and dynamic rather than as simple and static. For example, women's positions in relation to consumption may vary enormously according to such factors as class, race or sexuality and, perhaps more importantly, life cycle. Although young and gainfully employed women are increasingly powerful agents in the world of consumption, their positions are undermined enormously through marriage, child-rearing and career interruptions. In addition, one of the key and unresolved issues here concerns the role of appearance and its attendant links to questions of sexuality. Whereas for some feminists make-up and stilettos are precisely the commodification of women's oppression, others see the potential for sexual expression, if not empowerment, in the 'trappings' of feminine appearances (for example, see Vance 1984). These points link strongly to questions of fashion which are addressed in Chapter 7.

Third, this leads to a strong sense in which the position of women in relation to consumption does remain inherently socially determined. Although young, affluent and independent women with inherent good looks may enjoy the sense of power or self-worth they may gain from exercising their rights as consumers; older, poorer, economically dependent, emotionally committed or simply less pretty women may well feel excluded, derided or disinterested. Perhaps oddly, it is also on these points of appearance and social division where the positions of men and women in relation to consumption are most similar, and this is the focus of the next section.

Dandies, lads and the new man: men and consumption

Recent years have witnessed a steadily rising interest in the question of men's relationship to consumption and, more widely, masculinity and consumer society. Most of this interest has focused on a series of apparently unprecedented and diverse developments starting in the mid- to late 1980s. In particular, these included the following: first, the rise of designer fashions for men and the inclusion of menswear collections on the catwalk; second, a series of related markets for specifically male products, particularly in the arena of cosmetics and grooming and ranging from aftershaves to moisturizers; third, the meteoric rise in the UK particularly of increasingly self-conscious and glossy style magazines aimed directly at men as consumers; fourth, the simultaneous rise of advertising targeting men as opposed to women, of which the worldwide cinematic and TV commercials for Levi's 501 jeans remain prime examples; and fifth, the sense in which all of these developments in conjunction were also increasingly constructing men as the objects as well as subjects of consumer desire, sometimes in blatantly sexual ways as in the expansion of pornography for women.

From this rather mixed set of developments certain themes have started to develop more academically. In Rowena Chapman and Jonathan Rutherford's pioneering, if eclectic, collection *Male Order*, the question of men's relationship to consumption was raised primarily in terms of its impact on sexual politics and framed in terms of its consequences for feminism (Chapman and Rutherford 1988). Although the authors clearly differed in their opinions, the overall conclusion was that the aforementioned developments tended to amount to little more than increased competition at the cosmetics counter and not to some kind of sexual revolution. In particular, much work journalistically and academically concluded that what we were witnessing in the 1980s were the same old wolves in designer clothing (Savage 1996).

Later work has tended to raise a different set of concerns more related to the question of the reconstruction of masculinity through consumption primarily for men themselves. Most of this work has tended to stress the significance of a series of increasingly plural and visual codes around masculinity, where men are encouraged to engage with other men as consumers of style, whether in terms of a presentation of self in terms of cuts of suits and logos on trainers or more widely in terms of their consumption of commodities such as cars, hi-fis, holidays and overall lifestyles. In particular, Frank Mort has constructed an analysis that emphasizes such developments as part of an overall cultural history; and Sean Nixon has stressed the visual significance of these patterns of consumption (Mort 1996; Nixon 1996).

As pointed out previously, consumption historically has tended to have been equated with femininity rather than masculinity, at least stereotypically. If one assumes, I think fairly safely, that this perception is increasingly misplaced and that men are increasingly shopping for themselves and others, and that men are increasingly involved in all aspects of consumption from traipsing around supermarkets to enjoying the raptures and passions of fashion, then this does indeed raise a very salient question concerning the reconstruction of masculinity *through* the practices of consumption.

Answers to this question work on several levels. First, in terms of the masculinity equals production and femininity equals consumption matrix, it is important to point out that, even at the supposed peak of its application in the late Victorian era, this was still at least partly an incorrect conception, as men did take part in consumption practices, although differently from women, and working-class women in particular played important roles in production. In addition, men have tended to retain a monopoly over certain modes of consumption, from cars and DIY to participation in many sports activities and social drinking.

More importantly, however, what is at stake here is the confused notion that production and consumption are mutually opposed, when it is perhaps more accurate to see them as complementing one another. For example, in performing a productive role at the office men were, and still are, required simultaneously to consume the appropriate attire, namely the right style of suit and tie, or often to adopt certain lifestyles or take part in appropriate leisure activities, such as games of golf, particularly in terms of their career progression. In addition, production or work, at least in terms of making money, forms the gateway to consumption and, conversely, consumption in terms of opportunity or possession forms one of the main motivations for work or production.

It is, then, in a sense ludicrous to assume that, in playing an active productive role, men were therefore ever excluded from consumption, or vice versa, and what is often at issue here is precisely the secondary and associated notions of activity and passivity that construct such a strong sense of gender difference in production and consumption. In particular, it is the perception of the out-of-control female victim which forms the epitome of the conjunctions of femininity, passivity and consumption (Bowlby 1993; Nava 1996; Humphery 1998). This also helps to explain, at least partly, the suspicion of homosexuality and stereotype of effeminacy that often still attends men seen as too interested in matters of consumption (Campbell 1997b).

Second, men have historically also often played important roles in more passive or feminine forms of consumption, whether as dandies, *flâneurs* or aristocrats. In conjunction with this, what we are perhaps witnessing in the 1980s and 1990s, then, is a contemporary example of a historical set of more contradictory and often gendered processes where, across centuries, particular groups of often affluent, young or sometimes homosexual men have sporadically courted disapproval to live up to their personal ideals.

Third, as is already clear, the relationship of masculinity and consumption in contemporary society is complex, not least because of the significance of social divisions. Although some affluent and often young men may enjoy and play an important part in the reconstruction of their masculinity through consumption, many poorer, older or inappropriately located men are constrained or even excluded in relation to consumption. As a result of all of this, the contemporary reconstruction of masculinity through consumption is neither without precedent nor as new as it seems and is, in addition, a far more limited development, at least in terms of its practice, than is commonly supposed. In addition, as I asserted previously in *Men in the Mirror*, the supposed pluralism of many of these developments is widely open to question, as the images and ideals they present remain focused on an often hard, muscular and certainly youthful sense of material aspiration (Edwards 1997).

How, then, despite these limitations, do we explain the continuance of recent interest in matters to do with men and consumption? One explanation is the apparent expansion of men's involvement in areas of consumption previously defined as 'feminine', at least within the confines of more contemporary history. Although still not without historical precedent, it is the increased participation of men in domains such as fashion and cosmetics that has caused the most furore in popular and academic circles alike. Also constantly lurking under the surface of these discussions is the question of sexuality and for some writers, particularly Mark Simpson, consumption is the arena in which distinctions of heterosexual and homosexual are increasingly 'queer' or confused, as gay men and straight men alike are encouraged to look at themselves and other men as consumers, something seen previously as quite suspect outside of certain artistic, aristocratic or sexually perverse circles (Simpson 1994, 1996).

The difficulty of this perspective is that it still remains all too easy to over-state the case and, more particularly, to attach too much importance to the question of sexuality *per se*. What, perhaps, *is* still evident is that there is an increasing sense of conflation, demographically and economically, in the positions of younger and more affluent gay and straight men alike and, in terms of spending patterns, it is precisely this more socio-economic issue of discretionary income, single status and access to major sites of consumption, from upmarket city stores to voyeuristic cafés, that matters most and not sexual orientation. None the less, there is still a sense in which gay men have provided an unintended pilot study for the wider processes of masculinity and consumption, and this is one of the central questions raised in the next section.

In the pink: gay sexuality and consumption

Gay sexuality, unlike gender or race, is not an intrinsically visual phenom-enon. Of consequence in this, then, is an evaluation of the importance of consumption for minority sexual groups as a primary means of forming, asserting and displaying an identity. Sexual minorities, from gay men to transsexuals, are unusual in this respect, as sexuality, unlike gender or many aspects of race and ethnicity, is not visually recognized without the props of appearance, dress or demeanour. Therefore, a sense of expressing oneself through patterns of conspicuous consumption gains added significance for the gay community as a visual and potentially political act as well as a per-sonal statement.

Over recent years, a series of stereotypes and myths have developed con-cerning the role of the gay community in relation to consumption. The most important and pervasive of these is the idea that gay men in particular, as individuals or in groups or as childless couples, earn the same amount or more than straight men with wives and children to support and therefore have a vastly improved level of discretionary income to spend on themselves or as they please as opposed to on necessities. The professionally employed gay male couple has attracted particular attention in this respect, but there are clearly marked difficulties in making such claims, not least in terms of methodology.

As homosexuality remains a stigmatized identity, open to and often unprotected from discrimination, there are clearly difficulties in construct-ing surveys or research that directly address the question of the relationship of sexual orientation and consumption. The primary exception is surveys conducted through the gay press or similar networks, where the clear limitation is that the sample is formed from a minority, namely an openly scene or press-using part of the gay community, which often excludes the majority of gay men who, for one reason or another, ignore the gay scene and or do not access its press widely. In addition, all samples are inherently unrepresentative as the population itself is unknown because there is no electoral roll, household survey or census that covers, or that can even successfully or honestly cover, sexual orientation. On consideration of only some of the difficulties of conducting studies into sexual orientation and consumption, it is quite staggering, then, that so much is so often concluded from so little.

In addition, a second consideration centres on the lack of recognition of the diversity of the gay community. The assumption that all gay men are white, middle-class and high-earning professionals with few financial commitments is clearly a false perception stemming at least partly from the distortion that comes from the high visibility of some parts of the gay community, often those who are young, affluent and professional, and the invisibility of others, often those who are older, poorer or rurally located. A linked factor here is that high-earning, childless couples are equally often straight, as opposed to gay, and that to assume that gay men do not have financial commitments from either their primary, or in some cases secondary, families is also empirically suspect.

Perhaps most importantly, however, whatever status professional, affluent or middle-class gay men may attain, it remains open to discrimination and is effectively quite insecure. Contentiously, and a little less clearly, it is also asserted in some circles that the myth of the affluent gay male consumer is sometimes used to support the suppression of civil rights on the pretext that the gay male community is comparatively *un*oppressed. Nevertheless, what is clear is that a certain sector of the gay male community which *is* affluent and which *can* openly support its sexual orientation without fear of discrimination through consumption *is* still of primary importance, past and present, in understanding the relationships of sexuality, masculinity and consumer society.

Of associated importance is the perception of the gay male community as trend setters or, in marketing terms, innovators. One suspects strongly, once again, that although certain sectors of the gay male community are first in the queue for some new products, particularly when witnessing the consumption of fashion goods, this hardly applies to the entire community or the entire range of commodities. For example, although there are no prizes for guessing that it probably was gay men who were the first to go to work in the latest suited styles, there are no guarantees that they figure significantly as first-time buyers of new washing powders! The reasons for this development would appear twofold: first, as already stated, appearances have an added importance for the gay community in terms of the formation and expression of identity; and second, gay men, in not trying to live up to the ideals and stereotypes of heterosexual masculinity, which still tend to include a disdain for dandyism, are more open to the impact of the marketing of fashion-related commodities.

More recently, some sectors of the gay community, particularly in the US, have also started to assert the potential power of the pink economy to improve the political position of the gay community. This is seen, moreover, to work on three levels: first, it is asserted that gay commerce forms an increasingly important market in itself and in competition with similar markets; second, the infiltration and promotion of some lesbians and gay men in major corporations is seen to influence policy decisions inside and outside of the organizations concerned; and third, that all lesbians and gay men have the power to both boycott and support commercial enterprises and political organizations through the cash register and the ballot box respectively.

Impressive as these arguments may at first seem, the transformation of fairly limited economic power into far more widespread political power is clearly more complex. In particular, few companies which have successfully targeted a gay market have developed or supported anti-discriminatory practices or legislation, at least outside of their own employment policies. Similarly, the practice of purchasing vetoes, although unhelpful, is unlikely to cripple most concerns, whose markets are far wider than those explicitly or implicitly developed around the gay community. It is therefore true to say that there is little reason to assume that if a company provides products or services suited to, or even targeted at, the gay community that it necessarily supports the gay community politically: or, to put it simply, selling the product or service remains a sufficient end in itself in most cases.

Conspicuous by their absence in this discussion, though, are lesbians. Lesbians are often assumed to be the second-rate consumers of the gay community because of the economic discrimination they face as women as well as lesbians. The clear problem here is that being lesbian and being a woman, like being gay and being a man, are inseparable, and the lesbian is a type of woman in a particularly ambiguous position often similar to her gay male counterpart. More particularly, an important point is that consumption does not have the same political ramifications for lesbians as it does for gay men precisely because of the equation of shopping and spending with femininity. Consequently, lesbians are more likely to *oppose* conspicuous consumption. As a result, gay men do not often have the same economic standing or privileges as straight men, and lesbians, conversely, are often more likely to work full-time with fewer financial commitments than heterosexual women. A recent Channel 4 television survey in the UK, the results of which were shown on *Out* in 1994, confirmed that while lesbians earned on average 10 per cent less than gay men, they equally earned up to one-third more on average than their heterosexual female equivalents. In other words, the economic gender differential between lesbians and gay men seems to be considerably less than that between heterosexual men and women. It is important not to overstate this point for all the reasons already mentioned in relation to the gay community more generally, but it would seem that the notion of the impoverished and oppressed lesbian is as mythical, or as meaningful, as the stereotype of the high-spending guppy. What all of this tends to add up to is a clear targeting of affluent and secure gay male consumers who are equally clear in their lifestyle consequences and purchasing preferences. In sum, then, the primary importance of this is to form the foundations for marketing policies around sexual orientation and not to set light to the gunpowder of political revolution.

In black and white: the colours of consumption

If gay sexuality remains a problematic and misrepresented subject in studies of consumption, this pales into insignificance when compared with the overwhelming 'whitewash' or lack of racial awareness in most investigations of consumer society, theoretically and empirically. The lack of fully ethnically and racially informed analyses of consumption is, on the whole, quite appalling, and most major studies of consumption are wide open to accusations of racism. Most importantly, this is perhaps surprising as consumer society is quite clearly and specifically for the most part white, Western society.

In the first instance, then, how are we to explain this situation? Apart simply from racism on the part of many theorists and researchers in the area, much of the explanation lies paradoxically in the very whiteness of consumer society itself, which tends to render the contributions and role of racial and ethnic minorities invisible, at least beyond the level of the highly visible world of subcultural style. Dick Hebdige's highly influential, if problematic, analysis of subcultural style in *Subculture: The Meaning of Style* (1979) provided the basis for an analysis of consumption as a political phenomenon which then tapped into later studies of specific patterns of consumption in racial or ethnic minorities. He attempted a semi-semiotic analysis of style and its significance for subcultures and, in particular, punk, asserting that it disrupted dominant codes of communication, understanding and common sense:

> Style in subculture is, then, pregnant with significance. Its transformations go against nature, interrupting the process of normalisation. As such, they are gestures, movements towards a speech which offends the silent majority, which challenges the principle of unity and cohesion, which contradicts the myth of consensus.
>
> (Hebdige 1979: 18)

Hebdige's work followed heavily on the heels of Stan Cohen, Stuart Hall and Paul Willis, all of whom attempted essentially Althusserian analyses of various phenomena under the auspices of the new deviancy theory (Cohen

1972; Hall and Jefferson 1976; Willis 1977). Consequently, teddy boys and Bowie-ites were seen as reacting equally against the dominant culture and against a society that structurally subordinated them in relation to economic position, unemployment, housing and so on. Processes such as 'bricolage', whereby mainstream symbols were reassembled to form differing and often counter-cultural meanings as in the example of the mods' reconstruction of the stoic conservatism of the suit and tie into a sexualized iconography, are thus perceived as political. All of these style cultures were then seen as 'noise' or 'interference' in the semiotics of a dominant culture that ultimately incorporated these movements into the culture on two levels: first, through the commodification of subcultural signs into mass-produced objects as, for example, in punk safety pins seen on the catwalk; and second, through the labelling and social control of subcultural activities as deviant through the state and the media.

The immediate difficulty with this perspective lies in the assumption of a division of dominant ideology or culture from subordinate ideology or subculture, further problematized by the dominant culture's implied one-way control of its subcultures, when it could be argued that the reality is more fragmented, less hegemonic and also more mutually influential. Hebdige did to some extent acknowledge the variation in degrees of resistance and conservatism in the styles involved. However, he never escaped the sense of separation, if not divorce, of 'dominant culture' from subordinate or 'subculture'.

More problematic still was his constant interpretation of style according to class, and coupled with this there was a serious neglect of gender and race in defining meaning. This gender dimension was addressed later in Angela McRobbie and Mica Nava's *Gender and Generation* (1984), a feminist collection of essays that provided a successful critique of femininity as constructing and constructed through consumption, and also in McRobbie's *Zoot Suits and Second-hand Dresses* (1989). This second collection also raised the significant factor of racial and ethnic variation in the use and interpretation of street style and fashion. From the Zooties of the 1940s in their dressed-for-success suits and the pinstripe hipsters of the 1950s to the later revival of Rastafarianism and dread-locked reggae culture in the 1970s and 1980s, and even the current crusade of techno-rappers, racial and ethnic minorities have had a long, varied and influential history of association with various patterns or styles of consumption.

In his most recent analysis of style cultures entitled *Street Style: From Sidewalk to Catwalk*, published to accompany the 'Street Style' exhibition at the Victoria & Albert Museum in London, Ted Polhemus also points to the contemporary tendency to plunder the past in faster and faster succession as a 'supermarket' of style where one is a mod one day, a punk the next and a raver in the evening, with an equal sense of parody or authenticity in each case (Polhemus 1994). This perspective, he asserts, also ties in with the theory and practice of postmodernity, yet the difficulty with this is that while style cultures have constantly proliferated, their relationship to wider society often remains slippery and rather confined to students, unemployed youth and disco dancers. The end result is that street style tends to end up plundering and parodying itself rather than anything else. This also starts to open up the question of the connections of racism and consumer society more widely and/or structurally.

One important study of the interweaving of race and consumer society is, however, provided in the work of Anne McClintock, who argues from an essentially historical and economic perspective that the expansion of consumer capitalism relied heavily on the incorporation of imperialism into commerce. For example, much of the advertising of the early twentieth century demonstrated a strongly racialized and racist set of processes of representation on several levels (McClintock 1994). First, racial and ethnic minorities were often portrayed as exotic or were given overtones of otherness, and this process simultaneously normalized white populations and justified their privileged positions. Second, whiteness was increasingly equated with notions of cleanliness and goodness that in turn tended to endorse imperialism. Perhaps most importantly, and third, racial and ethnic minorities were also increasingly portrayed as slaves in happy servitude, which directly undermined their exploitation. These processes were particularly evident in relation to products imported from other countries, including tea and cocoa, or where commodities had strong associations of cleanliness such as soaps or washing products. These twin processes of consumerism and imperialism were then seen to form what McClintock calls 'commodity racism', where consumerism is perceived to depend on imperialism as much as imperialism does on consumerism.

The underlying thrust of this analysis is pursued further in the work of Susan Willis who, from a more structural Marxist perspective, asserted that the development of consumer capitalism crucially depended on the mutual processes of standardization, in terms of producing goods, and differentiation, in terms of selling or marketing them (Willis 1990). Racism then came to inform the latter of these processes in marking out differences in association among similar products, particularly at the level of racialized advertising.

Somewhat neglected in each of these analyses is the equally strong sense in which the production of consumption was also racialized and, more importantly, is increasingly so under conditions of international trade and globalization. Annie Phizacklea's study of the fashion industry's increasing reliance on racialized exploitation of labour in Third World countries is a case in point (Phizacklea 1990). Also of common importance here is the sense in which these processes are not only racialized but gendered, as it is both black and Asian *women* who are represented as exotic and other or as happy servants in advertising for Western commodities, and Eastern, Oriental or African-Caribbean *women* who are ruthlessly exploited in producing such goods in developing countries. Perhaps more importantly still, it is primarily the adoption of particular subcultural styles as modes of resistance by black *men*, from logo to DJ cultures, which tends to inform studies of consumption's importance in opposition to racism – which leads us neatly on to the other side of the equation.

Paul Gilroy, while accepting the essential premise of imperialism's importance in the formation of modern consumer society, tends to argue against the work of McClintock and Willis, seeing consumption as a fundamental mode of opposition or resistance for racial and ethnic minorities (Gilroy 1987, 1993). This is seen to work on several levels: first, in relation to racial and ethnic minorities' reworking of time and space where, for example, 'night time' is seen as the 'right time' to outwardly work, produce and consume in direct inversion of white Western traditions of day-time working and night-time privacy; second, at the level of collective resistance through ritual and the overall processes of affirmation in shared consumption practices, for example in relation to music or food; and third, in the tendency of racial and ethnic minorities to implode or undermine strict Western definitions and separations of art from life and high culture from low culture.

This tends to lead Gilroy on to an increasingly poststructural or postmodern terrain in common with the work of Stuart Hall (Hall 1976, 1992, 1997). This poststructural drift of Gilroy's work is also reflected in much contemporary work around racial and ethnic minority consumption patterns and uses of style essentially as a form of resistance to racism, often stressing the importance of (mis)representation (see, for example, Cosgrove 1989; Bhaba 1990; Mercer 1994; Hall and Du Gay 1996). Apart from the clear importance attached to the analysis of the mechanisms of racism and the means of resisting them, much of this literature is centred on an increasingly 'postmodern' understanding of identity politics, aptly summarized by Bauman: 'Indeed, if the modern "problem of identity" is primarily how to construct an identity and keep it solid and stable, the postmodern "problem of identity" is primarily how to avoid fixation and keep the options open' (Bauman 1996: 18).

The underlying thrust, politically and academically, of such an analysis, and as it is consequently applied to consumption and race, is to attempt to *de*legitimate and destabilize any hegemonic or dominant, essentialist or static, notion of identity and to, as it were, 'shake the foundations' of white, Western certainties set up following the Enlightenment and industrial colonialism. Consequently, the alternative consumer practices and style cultures of ethnic minorities are precisely endorsed as a form of resistance in the wider scheme of anti-racist identity politics.

There is clearly some appeal to the popular and academic mind alike in such an analysis. However, I would also like to raise a series of serious limitations to this perspective. First, it is difficult to distinguish with any real clarity what is or is not 'black' from 'white' and furthermore whether one appropriates or mimics the other or vice versa. Moreover, Eastern and Oriental cultures are often neglected in these analyses, yet they are clearly of significance to our understanding of consumption practices. This may also have the unintended consequence of reconstructing racism in the form of privileging one form of ethnocentrism over another, at least in terms of the attention it receives. It is perhaps more accurate to suggest that what we are witnessing here are processes of consumption which are essentially cyclical and interactive, reflecting a constant cycle of appropriation in two or more directions. In addition, this tends to seriously undermine any notion of *intrinsic* resistance through styles of consumption, and much depends on an increasingly perilous concept, as well as practice, of dominant culture as separate from minority or oppressed practices. Second, the constant and increasingly nefarious hijacking of black, Oriental or Asian patterns of consumption, from Indian food and Sari dresses to rap music and sportswear, is undermined in essentially poststructural analyses of consumption, as is the wider importance of the racialization of production itself, as already outlined. Third, and perhaps most importantly, what all of the aforementioned work on the racialized aspects of consumerism and consumer society tends to lead to is an unresolved tension of action and structure which is rarely addressed let alone explained. In most of these analyses, racial and ethnic minorities are represented as *either* the victims of consumption *or* its victors, passive dupes in racial exploitation and stereotyping or active agents of their own destinies which then impact drastically on the wider society. Quite clearly, neither picture alone is particularly accurate, and it is perhaps more appropriate to talk of racial and ethnic minorities as victims and victors of consumer society alike, often quite simultaneously, although this still leaves us with the wholly unaddressed question of how this sense of tension is reconciled, resolved or simply explained.

One potential way forward comes in the work of Richard Dyer. Dyer, already famed for his analysis of the representation of sexualities in media studies, turns his attention to the construction of whiteness in his work *White* (Dyer 1997). It is an insightful analysis which replaces the sting that poststructural identity politics was in danger of losing through turning its analysis full circle to face itself. He writes: 'As long as race is something only applied to non-white peoples, as long as white people are not racially seen and named, they/we function as a human norm. Other people are raced, we are just people' (Dyer 1997: 1). Thus, whiteness, like masculinity, functions fundamentally and powerfully as an unconscious norm that is threatened most when questioned directly. This leads Dyer to an analysis of the 'embodiment' of whiteness through Christianity, biological and genealogical notions of 'race', and imperial enterprise culture. Although the foundations of whiteness often fall apart on close inspection, its power lies in its appeal as an ideal and in its internal contradictions in constructing endless 'others' to deflect it from itself. These 'others' of course include racial and ethnic minorities, yet they also incorporate the vectors of gender and sexuality, for white dominance is ultimately indistinct from masculinity or hetero-sexuality. It is at this point that the underlying interplay and complexities of the politics of consumer society are particularly apparent.

Conclusions: expression, oppression and the politics of consumer society

From the preceding discussion it is clear that whatever consumer society is or is not, it is not neutral or apolitical. Importantly, this provides an additional illustration of the ways in which consumer society does not in reality or practice live up to its ideology of consumer sovereignty. This formed the focus of my discussion in Chapter 4 from an overall perspective of social divisions. Gender, race, sexuality and class are all clearly social div-isions, but the difficulty is that they do not work or operate in any simplistic or one-dimensional fashion but rather through complex and multiple means that are, on closer inspection, somewhat contradictory.

More particularly, I started this chapter by asserting that the most funda-mental aspect of the politics of consumer society is a politics of inclusion and exclusion, which often has socially divisive consequences clearly echoed in concerns relating to social class. The politics of consumption are not simply explained in relation to social class, however, and are, more importantly, com-pounded through the operations of such processes as gender, race or sexuality.

Although these different facets of consumer society have equally different implications, one factor that they all have in common is the underlying sense in which they are all caught up in wider processes of expression or oppres-sion. Class, race, gender and sexuality, in their potential importance to the formation or maintenance of individual and group identities, all have the capacity to provide modes of expression for particular people or groups, often giving them a sense of unity and resistance to wider processes of dis-crimination or inequality. Thus, practices of conspicuous consumption in particular provide the aspiring middle classes with the means to form an identity and to maintain or develop a particular status or standing in society. Conversely, however, the same practice operates to exclude others and to reinforce the underlying divisiveness of the overall social situation. In ad-dition, gender, race and sexuality, as sometimes more focused or specific con-cerns, often operate to unite certain populations in opposition to others. It is at this level, then, that the politics of self or group expression are in complete conjunction or collusion with a wider politics of oppression and division.

Consumption's particular importance in these processes is that it tends to provide a particularly visual means through which identity is maintained and status is undermined, reinforced or increased. In this sense, the practice of consumption is as profoundly nefarious and insidious as it is open and carefree. Added to this, advertising and marketing tend to work to perpetuate, recreate and even add caveats and divisions to an already socially divisive situation (see also Chapter 3). At this level, the social and economic processes of consumption in their capacity to individuate and consolidate, quite equally and frequently simultaneously, are particularly paradoxical at a more political level. Moreover, consumption, perhaps uniquely, has the capacity to exploit or empower oppressed groups and individuals alike and it is to these populations that consumption seems to matter most.

More academically, though, the politics of consumer society are complicated further through the tendency to separate differing aspects or processes that are in practice often indistinct. Thus, to assert that class in some sense matters more than gender or vice versa, or that the oppression of racism is somehow more fundamental than that of sexuality, is to neglect the conjunction of all of these factors. To put this most clearly, no individual or group occupies any one position according to class, race, gender or sexuality independently of its status in relation to the other three. Therefore, the importance of class is refracted through the processes of sexuality, race, gender and so on. The position of gay men in relation to consumption, for example, is different from that of lesbians precisely because they are men, and again varies significantly according to questions of class or race.

In addition, one can add such factors as economic position, age or physical appearance into the equation until the politics of consumption seem to drown in a sea of variations. One way out of this sense of relativism is to examine the precise importance of particular conjunctions of class, race, gender and sexuality and to see some of these connections as of greater priority in relation to consumption than others. Thus, the relationship of class and gender is often particularly important in studying the position of women in relation to consumption; whereas one may point out that the importance of class is undermined in relation to the positions of gay men which, in relation to consumption, tend to share certain features in common, such as comparatively higher discretionary income. Similarly, the position of racial and ethnic minorities in relation to consumption is clearly strongly associated with wider questions of cultural heritage and style. Underlying this discussion, however, is the question of just what *is* particularly important concerning the meanings and impact of styles of consumption or, perhaps more fundamentally, what makes consumer society different from other forms of society, and it is to these questions that I turn in the next chapter.

Suggested further reading

Attfield, J. and Kirkham, P. (eds) (1989) *A View from the Interior*. London: The Women's Press – fascinating, if eclectic, collection on feminism and design, including an analysis of women's relationship to the production of consumption.

Dyer, R. (1997) *White*. London: Routledge – intriguing and sensitive new slant on the importance of race to identity politics.

Lury, C. (1996) *Consumer Culture*. Cambridge: Polity – student friendly, if overly style driven, review of identity politics and consumption.

Saunders, P. (1987) *Social Theory and the Urban Question*. London: Unwin Hyman – interesting, if contentious, re-evaluation of the relationship of social class to consumption.

Simpson, M. (1994) *Male Impersonators*. London: Routledge – light-hearted and journalistic, though nonetheless insightful exploration of masculinity, sexuality and 'queer' consumerism.

7
CONSUMING PASSIONS – FASHION AND CONSUMER SOCIETY

Fashion, as an apparently high-speed and high-greed phenomenon, seems to epitomize many aspects of contemporary consumer society. Consequently, it continues to feature in many studies of consumption, past and present (Veblen 1934; Bourdieu 1984; Fine and Leopold 1993; Mort 1996; Corrigan 1997). Perhaps ironically, however, full-scale academic attention to the world of fashion remains primarily located within the domains of art and design (see, for example, Amy de la Haye's *The Cutting Edge*, 1997). One exception is Elizabeth Wilson's now somewhat out-of-date work *Adorned in Dreams*; updated in Jennifer Craik's more recent *The Face of Fashion*, which also extended the study of fashion to include its more cultural dimensions and a consideration of men's dress; while Naomi Wolf's *The Beauty Myth* still constitutes one of the most powerful feminist indictments of the fashion industry's impact on women (Wilson 1985; Wolf 1991; Craik 1994). Similarly, studies of men's dress and style as an example of the reconstruction of masculinity through consumption have also started to appear (Mort 1996; Nixon 1996; Edwards 1997).

Despite its clearly apparent salience to studies of consumer society, this state of affairs is not surprising, as fashion in essence is still concerned with art and design. The clear difficulty, however, is still one of definition, as studies of consumer society which consider fashion as a *prima facie* example of at least some of the features of (post)modern consumption are discussing fashion precisely as a *phenomenon* and not fashion more simply as *adornment*. In addition, confusion also emerges around separating fashion as *style*, for example in talking of what is in or out of fashion, from fashion as *dress*, or clothing. Further contortions are raised around considerations of *haute couture*, which some people still consider the truest and most undiluted form of fashion owing to its purer emphasis on art and design, versus street style and mass-produced clothing, which some argue conversely shows how styles are not only reproduced but created at street level and then exploited upwards not downwards through the class system (Simmel 1904; McCracken 1985; Polhemus 1994). What is more, the situation has more recently gained confused distinctions as designer clothing, following its profusion in the mid- to late 1980s, is itself increasingly mass produced and copied. For example, the styles of the UK high street giant Next frequently offer watered-down variants on catwalk designs often produced at immense speed. More importantly, and academically, art historians tend to complain that social scientists do not pay sufficient attention to the details of design or dress itself; while writers on consumption similarly criticize historians of art or design for their elitism in failing to recognize fashion's wider significance. As I have discussed elsewhere, there is some validity to each of these perspectives; yet, nevertheless, it is fashion as a phenomenon and its wider relationship to consumer society that form the focus of interest in this chapter (Edwards 1997).

In this respect, I wish to assert that there are three key dimensions to the relationship of fashion to consumer society. First, an analysis of fashion highlights some of the central contradictions in the relationship between production and consumption, as fashion is simultaneously one of the most exploitative and underdeveloped forms of production, which contrasts sharply with its luxurious and hyper-cultivated importance as a mode of consumption. Second, the study of fashion also informs much of the wider relationship of the individual and the commodity, from specific questions of conspicuous consumption to wider concerns of overall product signification. Third, and perhaps most importantly, fashion seems to epitomize many of the more political elements of consumer society, from racial exploitation to sexual expression, and its centrality in perpetuating and undermining social divisions almost simultaneously is particularly important in this respect. Importantly, then, this chapter develops some of the prior, and particularly political, themes of earlier chapters while moving towards an analysis of the relationship of consumer society and postmodernity, which is presented in Chapter 8. Consequently, this chapter has three central sections considering each of these questions in turn, and the concluding piece discusses the overall importance of fashion to the study of consumer society.

From rags to riches: fashion and the production of consumption

The fashion industry has historically always stood out as one of the worst offenders in exploiting its workers through low rates of pay and appalling working conditions. In particular, the so-called 'rag trade', which grew out of the sweat shops of the late eighteenth and early nineteenth century, had a notorious reputation for its near-slaughterous exploitation of its workers (Fine and Leopold 1993). Interestingly, in relation to the UK more particularly, the formation of sweat shops was also a critical component in the move towards industrialization. Fashion, far from representing some minority or elitist practice, consequently often proved central in the expansion and development of industrial capitalism. More importantly, many of these practices continue today, with their accompanying exploitation, although in different places. In particular, there is increasing evidence that improved working conditions in many Western societies, alongside increasingly advanced mechanisms of transport and marketing, have led to the development of increasingly racialized as well as gendered patterns of oppression in parts of Asia and the Third World particularly (Attfield and Kirkham 1989; Phizacklea 1990; Craik 1994).

One may well question quite why fashion *per se* has earned such a reputation. There are several dimensions to answering this question. First, fashion, as dress and as style, is second only to food and household goods in its speed of turnover. This is partly a result of the fact that clothing, particularly underwear as opposed to outerwear, has a fairly short life history and, more importantly, coupled with this it is caught up in the relentless cycles of fashion and display which endlessly undermine its capacity to last socially and materially. Second, fashion as an industry is in some senses crudely technologically if not economically determined. Until the invention of the spinning jenny in the late eighteenth century and the sewing machine, patented by Singer in 1851, all clothing was, of necessity, hand made. In addition, although many other products from cars to computers are increasingly mechanized, if not almost automated, in their modes of production, clothing remains, owing to its variety and detail, dependent on people and not machines at least in terms of tailoring, cutting and sewing if not the manufacture of textiles themselves. Most of the advances in technology related to fashion, from mail-order systems to marketing information, have in fact added to the need for increased cheaper and multiple modes of production. Or, to put it more simply, most of the technological progression in fashion has come in relation to its consumption rather than its production. Third, and perhaps most oddly, it is the very necessity of fashion, at least in terms of its role as dress, that stimulates demand. Fundamentally, clothing forms one of the three main elements of survival along with shelter and food and, in addition, as children grow and adults gain or lose weight or need different modes of dress for different purposes in differing climates from playing sports to working with chemicals, the demand for clothing is constantly sustained.

In addition, this sense of fashion's importance as a particular mode of production is juxtaposed with its significance as a form of consumption. As already mentioned, fashion is second only to food and household goods in terms of the speed of its consumption. This is partly explained as a result of necessity, as clothing wears out and needs replacing more quickly than many other commodities such as cars, electrical items or furniture. Some aspects of physical adornment, including hair styling and physical cleansing, remain fundamentally necessary, yet the wider explanation for the consumption of fashion as *dress* lies in its intrinsic connection with fashion as *style*. To put it more simply, the main motivation in most Western capitalist societies for consuming fashion goods and discarding or getting rid of functionally adequate clothing lies in the desire to maintain a sense of style and/or to keep up to date. Added to this, the motivation to mutate is inherent within the operations of the fashion industry, namely in its six-monthly seasonal turnover that renders anything six months old, or even less, as somehow lacking in style or status. The fashion industry justifies this wasteful and, on the face of it, slightly daft situation as a reflection of climatic requirements, or the idea that one needs different, usually cooler and more leisurely clothing in spring and summer as opposed to autumn and winter when one needs warmer and often more work-oriented clothing. Although there is some, very limited sense in this, most climates do not fit into two seasonal types and the advent of centrally heated workplaces, transportation and homes, coupled with escalating worldwide travel, increasingly renders any such distinctions redundant. Indeed, today at least, the only true reason for the fashion industry's seasonal turnover is stimulation of demand. Climates and seasons are themselves then turned into stimulants of demand as marketing devices, giving them, in postmodern terms, an almost hyper-real significance.

This leads us on to a second dimension to the consumption of fashion, namely its capacity to stimulate demand. Fashion is quite unique in its capacity as a mode of dress and phenomenon of style alike to render functionally and practically perfectly satisfactory commodities wholly unworthy or redundant on grounds of style alone. Clothing is a particularly strong example of this process and justified to some extent economically, as a new shirt for example is more easily afforded than a new hi-fi system, yet it does not stand alone, as the rising status which accompanies new cars, often only afforded through the expansion of credit, increasingly testifies (see also Chapter 3). A central issue in this is the increasingly negative equation of oldness with low status, or even dirtiness, as highlighted in some more historical studies of consumer society, and there is some consensus that the gradual decline of various patterns of inheritance, including the patina system through the eighteenth and nineteenth centuries, accompanied the increasing valuing of newness as a status asset. However, there remains significant dispute concerning the extent to which these processes were demand driven or supply led, or in adjudicating the degree of emphasis on consumption or production respectively (McKendrick *et al.* 1982; Campbell 1987; Fine and Leopold 1993).

A third dimension to fashion's particular importance as a mode of consumption is its connection with questions of self and identity. It is also this factor which explains the process of fashion*ing* an expanding array of commodities, from interior design to cars in particular, all of which are increasingly equated with some aspect, or aspects, of personality. For example, executive cars are marketed precisely according to managerial imagery, and the highly stylized and stripped-down interior designs of Sir Terence Conran are then moulded into a reflection of an equally minimalist and modern personality.

On top of this, as part of the wider processes of lifestyle advertising, different products are increasingly clustered together to reinforce certain notions of status and personality. For example, designer suits are associated with fast cars, which are linked to status-conscious hi-fi systems and similar technology, giving their usually male owners strong connotations of careerism, monetary success and commodified sexual charisma. Much of this process centres on the need to stimulate and orientate demand in often saturated markets. Consequently, there is often little technical difference or advantage in choosing one hi-fi system over another, and therefore the creation of what is called in marketing terms a 'unique selling proposition' is essential. For example, BMW and Audi cars are both sold according to their high levels of 'Germanic' engineering, yet the association of Audi cars with a quiet, superior refinement, something played on in their advertising, differentiates them sharply from the far louder and sportier, if not now infamously 'naff show-off' qualities of BMWs.

Following on from this example, fashion as a particularly personal phenomenon directly associated with the individual visually is even more open to such creations of product personality. Consequently, Armani suits have strong connotations of Italian sexuality whereas Boss suits are more strongly, and Germanically, associated with the world of business and commerce. This is, very partially, centred on design, as Armani suits are designed for a slimmer, smaller 'Southern European' frame whereas Boss suits are cut considerably more broadly for the 'Northern European' frame. Far more importantly, though, the capacity of fashion marketing and advertising to reinvent itself seems almost limitless. The German designer label Hugo Boss is also an excellent example of this process. In the 1980s, Boss became near synonymous with stylish and successful corporate masculinity, using models with particularly chiselled jawlines to sell equally shoulder-widening and chest-expanding suits for the aspiring yuppie. Following the recession of the early 1990s, and with it the attendant shifts in attitudes towards the styles of the late 1980s, Hugo Boss started to make losses materially and, more importantly, symbolically. To solve the problem, 'Boss' begat 'Hugo' and built a diffusion line of clothing targeted at a younger, trendier and more casual market. A heavily advertised fragrance with the same name was also launched to match its new image. Such campaigning, combined with, and boosted by, various footballers strongly publicizing a love of Boss single-breasted suits in particular, turned the company's fortunes around and reinstated its sense of kudos as the trendy but smart label for young men with style.

Consequently, appearances are increasingly seen to constitute personality in an insidious relationship of equating how one *looks* with how one *is*. This is a process that is open to positive and negative consequences alike, from parody and masquerade to deception and misunderstanding. In addition, the role of dress in creating social admiration or outright castigation, often according to context, is particularly striking. Adorning oneself in expensive clothing in socially caring or politically correct circles is to risk raising hackles; yet it is a functional requirement and a measure of esteem in many media and image industries. This sense of fashion's significance precisely as a process of signification is considered critically in the next section.

What are you looking at? Fashion and signification

Fashion has had a long history of association with questions of signification or the meanings associated with commodities. A primary example is the work of Thorstein Veblen, who, in studying the practices of the American middle classes at the turn of the century, noted the particular importance of dress and fashion as means of signifying status (Veblen [1899]1934). As a form of personal adornment, fashion was seen as unusually important in the overall process of conspicuous consumption, for it displayed an individual's status visually, directly and independently of context in some senses. For example, in simply walking along the street, clothing and adornment form a visual statement of status that depends neither on interaction nor place, unlike one's car or home, which one needs to witness someone using to make any association with them. Fashion, then, remains quite unique in its apparent capacity to communicate individual status or association with the person.

This factor has led some commentators to perceive fashion precisely as a form of communication. For example, Alison Lurie has provided a psychologically driven study of dress, from style and colour to detail and cut, quite literally as a language; and Malcolm Barnard has developed the perspective further in a more postmodern analysis of what he calls the 'undecidability' of fashion. Peter Corrigan has similarly pointed towards the contradiction of the increased uncertainty and dynamism of meanings and associations around clothing, coupled with the simultaneous persistence in seeing fashion as a mode of communication (Lurie 1981; Barnard 1996; Corrigan

1997). Thus, these writers tend to conclude that fashion could, and should, start to fall apart as means of communication, yet, ironically, it escalates in its significance as the confusion increases over its social meanings. Other writers have, however, criticized such ideas, highlighting fashion's ineffectiveness as a mode of communication, its differences from linguistic associations, or its more nefarious consequences in perpetuating stereotypes (Wilson 1985; Finkelstein 1991; Edwards 1997).

What are we to make of this paradox? It would seem that fashion is a particularly accident-prone form of communication. For example, the wearing of smart or formal clothing is often associated with working in commerce or having corporatist aspirations, yet such dress may simply apply to a particular occasion such as a night out or an interview for work or merely express a preference for looking smart on the part of its wearer. Similarly, the meanings of fashion are context related and while a suit and tie might look status conscious when driving a car on a motorway, they look equally out of place when washing it. Significantly, people consistently misread or differ in their interpretations, as the display of designer clothing for some may mean 'cool' while for others it means 'poser'. Despite all of this, people do still endlessly read things into how others dress or adorn themselves and there is increasing evidence that appearances matter in everything from dating to getting promoted, particularly in the United States (Spillane 1993). More importantly, in an increasingly media-driven and image-centred consumer society this is hardly surprising, and likely to increase, not decrease, in its significance. Consequently, the rise of image consultancies for every purpose, from increasing sexual attractiveness to winning votes, is a case in point, as is the proliferation of fashion media in itself, from TV programmes to style magazines.

The connection of fashion to wider questions of image or representation and, more precisely, the role of the media in escalating the importance of individual appearance and the overall significance of the visual is often central in many more postmodern analyses of style and consumer society. Although no full-length study of fashion's connections to postmodernity yet exists, issues of style and design have figured largely in analyses of postmodernism, partly due to the wider connection of questions of art and design to issues of society and politics in the theory of postmodernity (see also Chapter 8).

Of primary importance in making such connections is the work of Jean Baudrillard, for whom dress and fashion form primary examples of the 'commodity sign' which works as an axiom where the processes of commodification and signification come together (Baudrillard 1972, 1983). His secondary argument that the sign value is increasingly autonomous of the commodity value is also highlighted in the ludicrous cost of *haute couture*, as is the desire for 'authenticity' in the construction of 'classics' and the increasing difficulty individual designers face in trying to differentiate their designs from their imitators. More importantly, this also ties up with wider societal processes of 'reproduction' and 'simulation' and their implied impacts of uncertainty and confusion concerning social values, as the significance of fashion and dress is seen as increasingly out of control and anarchic. The processes of reproduction and simulation refer, in particular, to the importance of the media and similar visual cultures in reproducing goods so effectively that the simulation, or visual representation of commodities, gives greater significance or status than the actual goods or services themselves. Moreover, this is then seen to lead to increasing confusion and uncertainty concerning what is real or authentic, in turn rocking the foundations of tradition and social values; a vision which, in its most extreme form, is almost apocalyptic.

However, the ultimate vision of fashion as postmodern implosion comes in the work of Arthur and Marilouise Kroker, whose hysteria concerning everything from Eurythmics videos to Calvin Klein advertising, for example, teeters on self-parody:

> Indeed, if fashion cycles now appear to oscillate with greater and greater speed, frenzy and intensity of circulation of all the signs, that is because fashion, in an era when the body is the inscribed surface of events, is like Brownian motion in physics: the greater the velocity and circulation of its surface features, the greater the internal movement towards stasis, immobility, and inertia.
>
> (Kroker and Kroker 1988: 45)

A little more seriously, Fredric Jameson makes some similar applications of postmodernity theory to the study of fashion in terms of his concept of 'depthless culture', for the fascination of fashion is often seen as the fascination of surfaces, of reflections, of packaging, and of seduction (Jameson 1984). In addition, for some feminists these processes have had more positive consequences and led to the disruption of gendered traditions in fashion, as: 'the dichotomy whereby fashion is identified with women and oppositional style with masculine subcultures was erased in postmodern fashion' (Evans and Thornton 1989: 74). This also starts to raise the question of the extent to which fashion potentially starts to undermine social divisions of gender, race or sexuality, and this forms the focus of the next section.

Express yourself: fashion and social divisions

On the face of it, fashion is often seen as self-selected or as part of an overall process of individual choice and expression; yet these decisions concerning personal dress and appearance are often deeply constrained within, and also reproduce and recreate from without, a never-ending series of social divisions according to class, age, gender, race and sexuality, to name only some. More importantly, it is precisely fashion's importance as a phenomenon of conspicuous consumption that facilitates these processes.

Fashion's connections to wider questions of class, status and social standing are of clear significance and fairly well documented. I have already mentioned Veblen's analysis of dress in his study of conspicuous consumption in the previous section (Veblen 1934). More recent and complex is Pierre Bourdieu's analysis of fashion in relation to his documentation of the workings of taste (Bourdieu 1984). In some senses, this is clearly the cutting edge of fashion's significance. The rendering of some forms of adornment as vulgar and trashy, while others are valorized as unique, chic and indicative of individual good judgement, expresses particularly successfully some of the most immediate and subjective impact of fashion's importance, past and present.

What is perhaps less clear is quite where questions of fashion, taste and social divisions ended up in the now somewhat notorious 1980s. The rise of designer cultures highlighted a key contradiction often present in fashion, namely the sense in which its adoption is equally meritocratic (if you have the money you can have the look) and socially divisive (if you haven't you can't). Interestingly, this contradiction was further complicated in relation to the question of gender. Although designer clothing for women mostly connoted career progression and independence; for men flashy suits and endless labels often suggested 'ill-breeding on the make' or badly behaved city boys at best. This gendered problematic is mostly explained by reference to the wider positions of the sexes: while women's status was, and still is, often judged according to questions of visual taste, men's position remains more defined in relation to occupational position where a highly competitive pecking order is often enacted. Consequently, disdain for the primarily male yuppie was deeply intertwined with a sense of the potential undermining of more traditional and patriarchal systems of class and status. Thus, fashion in the 1980s was often a primary site where questions of class and gender came together.

In terms of gender, fashion also has an immediate and important impact in sexing the person. For example, the common Western practice of seeing pink as appropriate for female babies and blue as suitable for males is merely the tip of the iceberg in terms of the way dress and adornment are gendered. In addition, a series of sex-typed dualisms is set up through which masculinity and femininity in terms of appearance are often reinforced. Thus, dark colours, hard outlines and coarse textures are generally equated with masculinity; whereas lighter colours, softness and smoothness are usually associated with femininity. More importantly, some items of clothing are themselves quite specifically sex-typed, particularly skirts, which are still seen as unequivocally feminine, at least when they are not some form of national dress as in the case of the kilt; or the suit and tie, which still resonates strongly with associations of masculinity. Many items of clothing are also strongly gendered in their emphasis of male and female physical forms. For example, the modern man's suit fairly uniformly tends to widen shoulders; while in its feminine form it simultaneously tends to narrow the waist. The skirt also alludes to female sexuality and men's access to it. Similarly, processes of transvestism, although important, are precisely transgressive due to their crossing of gendered associations.

In addition, a series of historical mutations in most Western societies have led to the further tendency to sex-type processes of self-presentation. For example, make-up and most cosmetics, high heels, stockings and a miscellany of underwear remain almost exclusively feminine; while for men in general the options of personal adornment, despite some expansion in recent times, remain more limited. The underlying tendency in this process is to equate masculinity with restraint and practicality and femininity with expression and decoration, as in the case of Flügel's concept of the Great Masculine Renunciation (Flügel 1930). This situation is often easily overstated, however, as men's dress has periodically displayed peacock-like tendencies, as in the case of the dandies, many more subcultural styles from mods to rockers, or the general Armani-suited and designer-glitz looks of the 1980s. Women's dress has similarly undergone periods of relative restraint, as in the inter-war example of utility wear or the contemporary tendency towards downplayed femininity and grunge.

The degree of fudge involved in gendered display through fashion and dress does, however, remain severely limited, as men are still seen to exude sartorial elegance or casual raunchiness not frivolous decoration or perfumed display, and suffer negative and uneasy responses if they are perceived as too over-the-top, effeminate or plain narcissistic. Some authors have questioned the potential for change in this situation in the light of the enormous expansion of interest in men's fashion in most Western societies since the mid- to late 1980s, often accompanied by a series of wider developments encouraging increased conspicuous consumption (Simpson 1994; Mort 1996; Nixon 1996). The yuppie with his sharp suit, fast car and Filofax was a case in point, alongside the rise of designer styles in sports adopted in many male youth cultures. Although the increasing attention paid to men's appearances in everything from style magazines to gym cultures is without contention, these developments tend to remain limited to, and indeed targeted at, a demographically specific group of younger, often single men with high discretionary incomes (Edwards 1997).

If men's fashion is an increasingly contested terrain of definitions of masculinity, at least in some circles, then women's fashion has progressively polarized and fragmented in the wake of second-wave feminism. As outlined in Chapter 6, second-wave feminism provided a fundamental critique of femininity as an essentially unnatural and constraining construct that reflected and perpetuated women's oppression or, more simply, men's power over women. The importance of fashion as part of a wider process of forming and indeed imposing femininity on women was similarly challenged as oppressive or patriarchal. In particular, stiletto heels, stockings and short skirts alongside cosmetics and complex hairstyles came under attack as, on the one hand, male defined and designed to titillate and, on the other, as thoroughly impractical and hampering to women's independence. Early radical feminist critiques of femininity often summed up this position (Firestone 1970; Greer 1970; Brownmiller 1984). On top of this, the slightly later and rising importance of sexuality in feminist movements increasingly started to polarize feminist opinion on some of these issues, often mixed in with questions of sexual violence or pornography (Griffin 1979; Dworkin 1981; Vance 1984).

Most importantly, the centrality of women's own responses to fashion and sexuality shifted the terrain of feminist discourse away from a simple condemnation of femininity and more towards a sense of contradiction often centred on the question of pleasure. The particular sense in which women may still enjoy the trappings of femininity from make-up and perfume to short skirts and high heels, whether as a form of playfulness and experimentation or to experience prevailing modes of seductive power when adopted or dropped on women's as opposed to men's terms, opened a paradox of choice within constraint. More specifically, later feminist-directed analyses of women's fashion variously asserted a sense of multiplicity and complexity in contravention of earlier feminist attempts to simply equate femininity and fashion with women's oppression (Wilson 1985; Kidwell and Steele 1989; Craik 1994). Similarly, many more empirically driven studies of young women and girls' adoption and rejection of prevailing styles as presented in magazines and stores alike suggested a greater degree of complexity in women's responses (McRobbie and Nava 1984; Winship 1987; Nava 1992). However, rising concerns in relation to anorexia and similar eating disorders, particularly in the United States, have directly or indirectly refuted such claims, insisting on the overriding importance of women's victimization through images of fashion, femininity and slimness (Orbach 1979; Wolf 1991).

How are we to resolve this situation in relation to fashion and feminism? One solution is to adopt an increasingly poststructural or postmodern perspective which questions the certainties of fashion, dress and its meanings for women or society more widely. Evans and Thornton assert in *Women and Fashion: A New Look* that the drift towards postmodernity has increasingly undermined fashion's importance in reinforcing gender difference (Evans and Thornton 1989). Thus, gender difference *per se* has become something to play with as part of the overall fashion system. More empirically, the move towards increased narcissism and style aimed at a male market and the rejection of certain ideals of femininity among some groups of women have added to this sense of gender implosion. Although there is some sense in which there is evidence for such assertions, fashion remains one of the most central means through which gender difference is reinforced rather than challenged. In addition, drag cultures in particular, despite increasing salience in poststructural gender theory, remain extremely limited minority practices (Butler 1990).

On top of this, many more poststructural perspectives on fashion tend to underestimate the tyranny of ideals in appearances that still dominates many women's lives and is increasingly encroaching on the experiences of some groups of primarily younger men. More importantly, the proliferation of media outpourings on style, coupled with the rise of the so-called super-models, has, in all likelihood, added to the sense of pressure outside the fashion industry as well as inside it. The furore that accompanied the display of 'heroin chic', where the woefully thin, pale and sickly looks which often accompany drug addiction were turned into a cutting-edge look in certain designer collections and leading style magazines in the early to mid-1990s; and conversely the sensationalism that accompanied model Sophie Dahl's rise to eminence as a UK size 16, clearly demonstrated the continued pre-occupation with the ideals of thinness inside and outside the world of modelling. Similar concerns are increasingly raised in relation to the pressure placed on some young men to look muscular and/or slim, with, in particular, a 'six-pack' or flat stomach. Although the emphasis on appearances for males has a long way to go to equal that aimed at females, the rising use of steroids to enhance muscular development, use of dietary controls in aid of physique and increased rates of anorexia in young men rather undermine some claims that such developments are merely aids to healthy living.

Consequently, the key point that emerges here is that although fashion styles themselves may plunder and parody gender, the bodies they adorn are increasingly subject to ruthless surveillance, which also reinforces gender difference. Therefore, as thousands of women undergo yet another diet regime in order to look more like 'ideal women', their male counterparts are increasingly doing sit-ups and going to the gym in order to look more like 'ideal men'. The irony, then, at least in relation to gender, is that fashion and style, far from expressing personal or individual ideals, increasingly confirm the tyranny of gendered differences and the pressure of appearances.

One may well ask at this juncture whether this situation alters when considering sexuality or race as opposed to gender. One clear difference, at least in Western society, is that gender, unlike race or sexual orientation, does not tend to fully constitute a minority status. Fashion, as part of personal identity and appearances, then gains a particular importance in the social as well as individual visibility of both sexual and racial minorities. This is particularly important for sexual minorities, as sexual orientation, unlike gender or race, is itself unrecognized without the aid of dress, style or demeanour. The difficulty here, however, is that sexual minorities may or may not choose to display their sexuality. For example, it is not at all unusual for gay men in particular to drastically tone down the extent to which they 'look gay' in certain contexts, most significantly at work. Consequently, the gay male office worker may well transform his entire appearance when going to a gay venue, changing clothing, accessories and even hairstyle. Interestingly, the distinction is not quite so rigid for lesbians, where the boundaries between 'looking lesbian' and 'looking feminist' have become a little blurred. The problem that emerges from this discussion is that fashion and appearance for sexual minorities are used to conceal sexual orientation as well as to display it, perhaps equally if not more so, and, on top of this, some sexual minorities may also choose *not* to conform to prevailing representations that come from within their minority groups as much as from without, perceiving these as limiting rather than as liberating.

In addition, when looking at the content and meaning of different styles associated with sexual minorities, it is immediately apparent that factors of sexuality are strongly connected to questions of gender. Until the 1970s, the prevailing visual code concerning homosexual men was one of varying degrees of effeminacy, whether in the form of drag or camp cultures, excessive narcissism or some kind of idiosyncrasy as in the case of Quentin Crisp. In the wake of moves towards greater tolerance and increased openness, the now notorious macho gay image was created, consisting of tight, button-fly Levi's, vests, varying degrees of leather and denim, and some use of near-sadomasochistic accessories, from caps and jock-straps to chains and belts. Although debates ensued as to the seriousness of such imagery, such bodily adornment remained blatantly both sexualized and gendered in primarily masculine terms as well as being white, Western and often North American (Blachford 1981; Adam 1987; Gough 1989). It is not my intention to discuss these styles in detail, yet what remains apparent is the sense in which gay male style has never really escaped connection to questions of gender and masculinity (Edwards 1994). Similarly, debates have raged in relation to lesbianism concerning the persistence of butch and femme dichotomies (Vance 1984; Bristow and Wilson 1993; Harwood *et al.* 1993). Much of this persistence in either case is explained partly as a result of never-ending stereotyping and counter-stereotyping of sexual minorities and partly as an outcome of lesbians and gay men's own sexual investment in such images.

More recently, attention has shifted more towards the relationship of sexual minorities and consumption more widely. This was discussed in detail in Chapter 6. However, what remains of interest here is the sense in which fashion is seen to retain a particular importance for gay men. Interestingly, this does not seem to apply to lesbians who are often perceived as relatively disinterested in matters of style. Once again, the explanation for this situation lies in connections to questions of gender, as it is gay men's perceived gender rather than sexual deviance as narcissists that stands out, and similarly it is some lesbians' rejection of traditional definitions of femininity that causes social consternation. In addition, the overall visual emphasis of much of gay male culture, coupled with a clear awareness of fashion's role in constructing the sexual attractiveness of men, tends to explain their apparently significant interest in it, rather than the more mythical notion of enormous discretionary income which may apply equally well to any other professionally employed and childless group. To conclude, then, the relationship of fashion to questions of sexuality is clearly still significant but also far more complex and often contradictory than any simple notion of its equation with identity politics may imply.

When turning attention to questions of race and fashion, a similar situation is apparent, as many prevailing perspectives on racial and ethnic minorities and their use of style heavily emphasize its importance in identity politics (Hebdige 1987; McRobbie 1989; Willis 1990; Hall 1992; Gilroy 1993). Most of these writers stress the importance of style in undercutting more hegemonic notions of culture, whether through processes of parody and mimicry or sheer pluralism. Although some sympathy with such perspectives is necessary to avoid victimizing racial and ethnic minorities, many of these developments are far more limited in terms of their spread and far more complex in terms of their importance than these often wildly overstated viewpoints will allow. What stands out in particular is the limitation of oppositional racial and ethnic minority styles to youth cultures, and the frequent conflicts of assimilation and separation that develop across different generations. For example, many young Asian women will adopt Westernized styles while their mothers retain more traditional dress. Similarly, the popularity of sports apparel among many black male youth groups illustrates a process of appropriation of Western ideals as much as it does one of minority alliance. In addition, most of these styles are produced under conditions of mass Western racialization rather than minority invention (Phizacklea 1990). In addition, Western designers regularly plunder Eastern styles for inspiration. In conclusion, then, the relationship of race and fashion is often complex and contradictory and, although it maintains an importance in the formation and maintenance of racial and ethnic identities, this is hardly the whole story.

In sum, whether in relation to gender, sexuality or race, fashion is often seen to reinforce social divisions often at the level of identity politics. In particular, though, the sense of contradiction and complexity which comes into play when analysing fashion's importance to minority groups opens up fashion's wider connections to questions of consumption. Whether in terms of the production of fashion goods or their use and interpretation of styles, the sense of power and inequality at work, often in differing directions, is never very far away. None of this, however, quite explains fashion's own phenomenal importance in consumer society, and for an answer to this question, we need to address a different dimension of its significance.

Conclusions: consuming passions

During this chapter, I have primarily considered three key dimensions to the importance of fashion in consumer society: first, as a site of extreme contrasts in terms of its outmoded and exploitative modes of production juxtaposed with its often wasteful and extravagant significance as a form of consumption in affluent Western society particularly; second, its highlighting of the importance of consumption practices and display as forms of social communication or signification; and third, its more political dimensions as a site in the simultaneous formation of individual and collective identities and social divisions. However, none of these dimensions, despite their clear salience to the theory and practice of consumer society, quite taps into or explains fashion's more particular importance as a mode of consumption or perhaps, more widely, as a series of associated commodities.

Fashion, in the sense of dress and personal adornment, is quite unique in its significance as, in essence, a second skin. It is this dimension that helps to explain its closeness, its intimacy, and the often deep-seated and personal investment placed in it. Although for some people, perhaps many, in consumer society, fashion often seems trivial and unimportant, this disinterest and disengagement is conversely often as significant as keenness and fascination, because these responses are equally caught up in an often self-reinforcing process of acceptance and rejection, fashion and anti-fashion, or fashion destruction and fashion recreation.

The importance of dress and adornment is quite literally three-dimensional as an expression of self in relationship to society, as an aesthetic or artistic form, and as a tactile or sensual experience. For example, the wearing of an evening dress, heels and scent if female and similarly a smooth lounge suit, dress shirt and polished shoes if male, not only communicates socially a certain, often sexual, maturity and portrays a particular aesthetic ideal, it also creates in its wearer a physical set of sensations. Few, if any, commodities in consumer society can manage, even in their most perfect forms, to do so much so immediately for the individual and for the society around them. Some other examples might include luxurious foods, music or the so-called third skin of the car, considered critically in Chapter 3, yet none of these has the power, the immediacy or indeed relative longevity, of responses to fashion. In sum, then, fashion has come to represent a simultaneously psychological, social and sometimes highly erotic experience or, in short, a passion. It is perhaps not surprising, then, that clothing and other forms of personal adornment make up a disproportionate importance in the worlds of shoplifting and shopping addiction alike, for fashion alone touches the metaphorical G-spot, as it were, of consumer society. Importantly, it is also this more experiential dimension to fashion that tends to underpin its relationship with the theory of postmodernity, which forms the focus of the final chapter.

Suggested further reading

Ash, J. and Wilson, E. (eds) (1992) *Chic Thrills: A Fashion Reader*. London: Pandora – topical collection of essays on fashion.

Craik, J. (1994) *The Face of Fashion*. London: Routledge – probably the most comprehensive book of fashion and feminism; also includes work on the exotic, the body and masculinity.

McRobbie, A. (ed.) (1989) *Zoot Suits and Second-Hand Dresses*. Basingstoke: Macmillan – wide range of cultural essays on fashion and music.

Mort, F. (1996) *Cultures of Consumption*. London: Routledge – interesting, if uneven, cultural history of masculinity and men's fashion.

Phizacklea, A. (1990) *Unpacking the Fashion Industry*. London: Routledge – sobering account of the changing nature of exploitation in the fashion industry.

8
CONSUMER FUTURES - CONSUMER SOCIETY AND POSTMODERNITY

The primary purpose of this chapter is to explore the relationship of post-modernity and consumer society. There is a common, though often implicit, sense of association of the theory and practice of consumer society with the theory and practice of postmodernity, particularly in more poststructural studies of consumer culture. The key difficulty here, however, is one of definition, as theorists of postmodernity and postmodernism, on occasions at least, openly resist all forms of categorization, and the recent plethora of works on consumption has often added to this sense of openness, if not confusion, concerning definitions of consumer society conceived variously as a modern form of material culture, a contemporary process of social transformation, or as a series of economic systems of provision and exchange (see respectively Miller 1987; Fine and Leopold 1993; Sulkunen *et al.* 1997).

Consequently, in the first section of this chapter it is my foremost intention to attempt to define and delineate, at least in essence, the most important elements of postmodernity and the key characteristics of contemporary consumer society. In the second section I will seek to investigate the extent to which the concepts and practices of consumer society and postmodernity are indeed congruent or different. Finally, in the third section, I shall provide a heuristic critique of the work of such writers as Jean Baudrillard, Fredric Jameson, Scott Lash and John Urry as vehicles for the study of the relationship of postmodernity and consumer society more widely. In summary, I intend to demonstrate that although postmodern society is of consequence consumer society, consumer society is not necessarily postmodern society. Perhaps more importantly, this chapter returns us to some of the earliest themes of this text while raising the central question of the future of consumer society.

The question of definition: conceptions of consumer society and postmodernity

> Yet the term 'postmodernism' is more strongly based on a negation of the modern, a perceived abandonment, break with or shift away from the definitive features of the modern, with the emphasis firmly on the sense of the relational move away.
>
> (Featherstone 1991: 3)

As outlined in Chapter 1, definitions and conceptions of consumption remain an open question. Much of the concern centres on two somewhat differing notions of consumption as a more contemporary matter of aesthetic style or as a more historical development in industrial capitalism. The former tends to emphasize, not surprisingly perhaps, its more cultural and stylistic aspects, seeing it as a contemporary phenomenon crucially dependent on a series of postwar developments such as rising living standards, the development of shopping malls and other environments through which shopping is recreated as a leisure activity, and fuelled through the rise of advertising and visual media more widely (see, for example, Featherstone 1991; Lury 1996; Mort 1996). Analyses driven through the concerns of the latter tend to emphasize conversely more historical, and linked to this, mostly more economic aspects to consumption, often allying its expansion to wider developments in mass production, increased openness in class positions or similar systems of stratification, or to overall changes in social values where luxury and newness are increasingly associated as markers of social status over wealth and inheritance (see, for example, McKendrick *et al.* 1982; Campbell 1987; Fine and Leopold 1993).

There are, of course, many ways in which these two aspects or perspectives on consumption interlink as qualitatively different dimensions of essentially the same series of developments. None the less, there remains a sense in which the degree of *emphasis* placed on economic history, or conversely contemporary style cultures, leads to a tension concerning what is seen as the *key driving force* of modern consumer society. Interestingly, this sense of contrast in perspective echoes, and indeed underpins, much of the sense of conflation or difference in outlooks on consumer society and theories of postmodernity, as we shall see in succeeding sections. The definition of consumer society used here remains the one that I outlined in the Introduction, namely one that sees consumer society as an economic and political phenomenon *as well as* a more social and cultural one.

Despite the aforementioned sense of tension in studies of consumption, I now wish to unpack some of the more empirical foundations underpinning perspectives on consumer society in an attempt to start to define its salience to the study of postmodernity. Consumer society is, most simply, defined as society which is importantly, and in all likelihood also increasingly, organized around the concept and practice of consumption. Thus, in essence, people are seen to spend more time and more money consuming, whether at the level of leisure activities from the arts and sports to holidays and dining out, or more directly in terms of shopping and purchasing goods and services to suit various aspects of their lives. Moreover, and somewhat more contentiously, one may also assert that this also interlinks with the wider construction of personal and social identities around consumption practices, from assertions of status through adoptions of certain styles, or through using various modes of consumption, from shopping to playing sport, as primary mechanisms through which social relationships are formed and maintained. As mentioned in Chapter 2, some more theoretically traditional or classical scholars still tend to reject the assertion that consumption is increasingly significant in the construction of individual and social identities, seeing class in particular as still retaining an overriding importance (Warde 1994; Campbell 1995; Crompton 1996).

In addition, some academics see consumption's importance as tapping into wider concerns relating to the overall commodification of everyday life, whereby nearly all social activities and individual needs – from spiritual happiness to social status – are marked out and met through patterns of spending and consumption. Many of these assertions are implicitly or explicitly offset against the converse notion that production, or work, has decreased in importance. Most of the evidence for this centres on the decline in manufacturing, increased unemployment and the supposed collapse of traditional class politics (see, for example, Harvey 1989; Beck *et al.* 1994; Bauman 1998).

As highlighted in previous chapters, there is much controversy and counter-critique of such assertions, particularly from more Marxist perspectives (Callinicos 1989). However, this is perhaps to miss the point, because to conceive of production and consumption as somehow opposing elements, similar in essence to a pair of scales where if one goes up the other must go down, is itself fundamentally misguided. Indeed, as I have argued earlier, production and consumption are for the most part mutually maintaining, as, at its simplest, production provides the means for consumption and consumption if nothing else provides a motivation and justification for production.

In addition, one might also assert that production and consumption are increasingly intertwined where the worlds of work and leisure often collude into an overall miscellany of 'lifestyle' (Chaney 1996). For example, most professional and particularly financial industries invoke a strong sense of allegiance that extends out of the workplace into social life, sports and modes of dress and appearance inside and outside the office. Similarly, many dull and routine occupations are ameliorated through common experience inside and outside the workplace. In summary, then, the fundamentally economic and social sense in which consumption is seen to increase in its prevalence and importance feeds simultaneously into wider questions of politics and culture.

As I have already stated, there is no one theory or definition of post-modernity and this is due partly to the resistance to categorization that often comes from within the theoretical enclave of postmodernity *per se*. This opposition has several aspects, of which the first comes from the critique of meta-narratives or grand theories of society where perspectives such as Marxism in particular are criticized for producing increasingly inept and totalizing theories that attempt to explain the entire development, and indeed predict the future, of modern society (see particularly Lyotard 1984). Second, postmodernity theory has often constructed itself around an increasingly inchoate notion of looking around corners where, to put it more simply, if we knew what it was it wouldn't be what it is (Harvey 1989). In this sense, the theory of postmodernity is strongly predicated on the notion of not knowing and not defining itself, or its thesis is precisely its *anti*thesis. The tendency here, though, is to collapse into a sense of such intense relativism that postmodernity is, or is not, entirely what one likes and the question of definition is avoided rather than answered. Criticisms of this stance aside, however, I would assert strongly that as time has passed, and the theory of postmodernity has progressed, it has increasingly gained clarity and concreteness, whether intended or unintended, as to what it is and what it is predicated on in economic and political as well as social and cultural terms. Some theorists have, furthermore, asserted that postmodernity has, ironically, come to create its own meta-narrative out of its own critique of those associated with modernity (Ritzer 1991).

More importantly, in the first instance, it is necessary to conceptually separate, at least artificially, some of the key concepts commonly linked to postmodernity. Postmodernity is primarily a theory of society similar in kind, if not in content, to a theory of modernity. Indeed, postmodernity is often defined precisely in terms of what it is not, namely modernity, implying a radical shift away from something old as much as any kind of move towards something new. What is of central significance is that the theory of post-moder*nity* is not simply conflated with postmoder*nism*, which is usually a more specific term relating to developments in cultural, aesthetic and artistic forms; most particularly in architecture, literature and various visual media where practices of pastiche, parody and a wider plundering of the past are often incorporated stylistically.

This is not to imply that the concepts of postmodernity and postmodernism do not in practice interlink, conflate or operate in parallel. In particular, the tendency of the theory of postmodernity to emphasize the increasing importance of cultural and visual phenomena and the clear social implications of changing modes of presentation within the documentation of postmodernism are clear demonstrations of enormous similarity. Perhaps more importantly, however, these overlaps still do not *necessarily* constitute a simple *equation* of the two concepts of postmodernity and postmodernism.

Similarly, the theory of postmodernity is often conflated with poststructural theory. Poststructural theory tends to have two key dimensions, the first concerning the primary importance of language and textuality, including its more psychoanalytic ramifications as exemplified in the work of Lacan and Derrida, and the second concerning the use of discursive analysis as a tool for understanding society more widely and, most importantly, situating various ideas and theories used to explain its development, itself in turn most strongly associated with the work of Foucault (Lacan 1966; Foucault [1969] 1974, 1977, 1978; Derrida 1982). Although the theory of postmodernity tends to share a similar sense of relativism, it is not fundamentally and of necessity in contradiction with wider theories of social and economic development. For example, some authors have pointed to the potential alliances of Marxist and postmodern theory in relation to consumption, yet little such association links poststructuralism to any more classical theory of society. Martyn Lee's *Consumer Culture Reborn* is a vigorously scholarly exploration of precisely this conflation of Marxism with developments in the theory of postmodernity, ultimately postulating the need for a new and more sophisticated form of historical materialism (Lee 1993).

Similarly, most postindustrial theory, which focuses on a series of particular economic developments including the rise of multinational corporations, global trading and flexible working and production methods as indicative of a qualitatively different and therefore postindustrial era, feeds into many more economic dimensions of the theory of postmodernity, yet perhaps remains only a part of it. In addition, the foundational ideas of postindustrial theory developed decidedly earlier than those of postmodernity, particularly in relation to such issues as the separation of ownership and control. More contemporary developments in postindustrial theory have, however, focused more strongly on the importance of consumption and its relationship to wider theories of reflexivity, particularly in the work of Scott Lash and John Urry which I will consider shortly (Lash and Urry 1987, 1994).

Interestingly, one of the central ironies of much contemporary or postwar social theory is the fact that theories of postmodernity, poststructuralism and postindustrialism have often developed alongside and in tandem with theories of modernity, structuralism and industrialism and have not simply followed on in any linear way, although both sets of theories materialized under the shadow of the more classical sociological traditions of Marx,

Weber and Durkheim. Thus, although the ideas of writers such as Daniel Bell, Ralph Dahrendorf or Alain Touraine may well inform the theory of postmodernity more widely, this does not lead to any direct identification of these authors with any theoretical perspective other than postindustrialism (Dahrendorf 1959; Touraine 1969; Bell 1974, 1976).

Having discussed some of the factors affecting the definition of postmodernity more theoretically, I now wish to consider some of the more empirical elements underpinning some of its most important claims. I must point out immediately that it is not my intention to resolve controversies concerning what is, in essence, a highly contentious series of assertions. In addition, my discussion of these ideas is used wholly to start to illustrate the degree of congruence and difference in the claims of most postmodern theory and that of consumer society, which I wish to consider directly in the next section. More practically, I wish to discuss these claims under four headings of economic, social, political and cultural factors. These are, of course, artificial distinctions that are strongly interlinked in concept as well as practice.

To consider economic factors first, the theory of postmodernity is strongly predicated on the assumption that consumption is an increasingly important part of economic and social life alike and that the scales of production and consumption are, in a sense, increasingly tipping in favour of consumption as an overall societal organizing device. Aforementioned difficulties of distinction aside, this is supported through the claim that consumption takes up more and more of the time and money of most Western populations particularly and, as a consequence of this, a greater part of industry and commerce is centred on its continued development. The rise of the service sectors and the comparative decline of more traditional manufacturing industries is also a case in point. On top of this, various more postindustrial claims are also invoked in relation to the use of increasingly global and flexible working methods at all levels typified by short run and often racialized production methods and the increased use of commissioning and fixed-term contracts. Somewhat more speciously, many theorists of postmodernity also add that technology, and information technology particularly, is creating an 'information society' where knowledge is taking over from economic position as a primary form of power or that it is indeed now the primary mechanism through which status and wealth are attained (Lyotard 1984; Lash and Urry 1987, 1994; Beck et al. 1994).

Politically, much of the theory of postmodernity has developed in the wake of a perceived collapse in traditional Left or socialist politics, particularly in the light of the decline of the former Soviet Union and political disruption in Eastern Europe. More specifically, the rise of many Right-wing and neo-Conservative governments in the 1980s throughout Europe and in the United States, under the auspices of Thatcherism and Reaganism particularly, has fuelled a wider sense of political fragmentation. Another, more economic, dimension to this question comes in the form of neo-liberalism, discussed in Chapter 4. This is, in sum, often also linked to the parallel rise of many more social movements from feminism to environmentalism that started to radically undermine any exclusively class-centred analysis of political resistance. Linked to this also is a wider thesis of increased individualism and concern with the formation and dissolution of identity politics around such factors as race, gender and sexual orientation. In addition, some commentators have also seen enormous positive potential in such disruption of any traditional political order and have focused instead on various notions of radical pluralism (Weeks 1985; Rutherford 1990; Giddens 1991).

This sense of pluralism also tends to inform the more social dimensions to the theory of postmodernity, where the emphasis is placed strongly on questions of diversity, particularly in the light of the growing globalization of society in the wake of increased geographical mobility, travel and information technologies. This sense of globalization is often juxtaposed with a sense of localism, because while commodities and experiences, from Coca-Cola to package holidays, increasingly render the world more and more the same, these events are in turn experienced differently at a local level (Howes 1996). More broadly, everyday life is also seen as being increasingly aestheticized, or subject to questions of image and style, and thereby commodified or marketed (Featherstone 1991). The rise of multiple means through which Western populations purchase such immeasurable and intangible qualities as happiness, love and a sense of wellbeing – whether through aromatherapy potions, health farms or dating agencies – is an example of one dimension of such commodification. More politically, much controversy has centred on the increased privatization of health, education and welfare provision, particularly in the UK (see Chapter 4). This is itself often linked to a perceived decline in state provision if not in state control, as policing, surveillance and security are now frequently growth industries inside and outside the modern state, whether in the form of closed-circuit television in town centres or in the tagging of offenders and those doing community service (see Chapter 5).

These more social questions are almost inseparable from a wider problematization of the role of culture more generally. Culture in this sense is defined fairly specifically in terms of the role of the media industries, from the arts, TV and cinema to advertising, marketing and image consultancies. The theory of postmodernity tends to argue that this cultural and aesthetic dimension is increasingly determining of, as well as determined by, more concrete economic, social or political factors. Consequently, it is this emphasis placed on the importance of culture as a forceful realm of concepts and practices *per se* that perhaps lies at the epicentre or is, in a sense, the essence of postmodern theory in relation to late-twentieth-century society (Jameson 1991). A primary example of this is Scott Lash's influential *Sociology of*

Postmodernism, which is almost wholly concerned with questions of style, aesthetics and visual culture (Lash 1990).

The theory of postmodernity has itself suffered severe criticism in recent years, so much so that it has almost become the *bête noire* of many of the social sciences. Most of this criticism, although often unfocused and scattered widely, remains centred on three key assertions: first, that most of the more empirical claims of the theory of postmodernity are easily overstated and that their validity is limited to certain sectors of the population, namely the affluent and Western; second, and more politically, that as an overall perspective it suffers from a highly descriptive form of liberalism that never quite succeeds in providing a critique of its own assertions and development; and third, and most damning of all, that it in truth offers very little that is 'new' at all. In relation to consumption, such criticisms are upheld across a spectrum of perceptions and theorists, including Rosemary Crompton, Daniel Miller, Don Slater and Alan Warde (Miller 1987, 1997; Warde 1994; Crompton 1996; Slater 1997).

As I have already stated, it is not my intention to answer these criticisms or to try to resolve the conflicts that have developed. Nevertheless, an analysis of what the theory of postmodernity taps into more widely remains worthy of discussion here or, to put it more simply, a sense of its pulse is still important to our consideration of consumer society and requires further investigation. In addition, as I shall start to argue in the next section, it is not so much a question of what postmodernity is or is not, or does or does not include in its discussion, which is most significant to our exploration, it is more a question of its sometimes implicit and often diffuse sense of *direction* that requires more detailed consideration.

Consumer society and postmodern society: congruence and difference

Having discussed at some length the key elements of a consumer society in concept and practice, as well as many of the central assertions and dimensions of the theory of postmodernity, it is now time to start to unpack their connections and separations.

The connections of theory and perspectives of consumer society and postmodernity are perhaps more immediately apparent than their differences. In the first instance, they share a common concern with the increasing significance of consumption as a way of life and as an organizing, if not necessarily a driving, feature of contemporary society. Similarly, they also link consumption's increasing importance to wider developments in the overall aestheticization and commodification of everyday life whereby more and more aspects of daily living are quantified monetarily and wrapped up, sometimes literally, in the visual cultures of the media, advertising and marketing. More significantly still, perhaps, they invoke, implicitly and explicitly, a strong perception of consumption practices as increasingly constitutive of personality and social identity, whether in terms of group practices and the maintenance of status or in the light of a more psychoanalytic and unconscious sense of wish fulfilment and fantasy. More poststructural or postmodern studies of shopping, for example, often highlight in particular its more psychoanalytic and fantasy-driven dimensions (Shields 1992). It is also at this point that parallels with cultural studies more widely are apparent, as analyses of consumer society and postmodernity, intentionally or unintentionally, tap similarly into an emphasis on cultural and aesthetic forms and practices as an increasingly influential factor in the development of contemporary society.

As a consequence of this, the degree of congruence linking conceptions of consumer culture and postmodernity seems significant, but this is equally suspect when more economic conceptions of consumer society are invoked. For example, a more Marxist or Weberian perspective on consumption as developed variously in the works of Neil McKendrick, Colin Campbell or Ben Fine and Ellen Leopold creates a sharply contrasting picture with that painted by postmodernity (McKendrick *et al.* 1982; Campbell 1987; Fine and Leopold 1993). Although the theory of postmodernity has a tendency at least to see consumption primarily as a contemporary and more cultural or aesthetic phenomenon, more traditional views of consumer society lend it an enormous historical precedence and an overwhelmingly strong economic *dimension* if not necessarily an industrial or productive *determination*. More importantly, many more recent analyses of consumer practices have added to the sense in which consumption remains socially divisive and economically determined in relation to such factors as class, age and gender and, perhaps more fundamentally, is still perceived as mundane (Keat *et al.* 1994; Edgell *et al.* 1996; Miller 1998).

In addition, significant academic conflict has developed around the assertion that consumption is increasingly important in the formation or maintenance of personal or social identities, particularly when this is used to undermine more traditional analyses of the importance of social class particularly (see Chapter 2). Some authors have pointed more specifically to the ways in which consumption patterns are often still strongly related to questions of social class or wider social divisions which, in turn, still remain more fundamental to the construction of identity (Cahill 1994; Warde 1994; Crompton 1996).

Perhaps more importantly, the theory of postmodernity remains a far wider and more all-encompassing perspective than any of those associated with consumption. Consumption in this sense is only ever a part or an aspect to the theory of postmodernity, yet no theory of postmodernity that does not pay significant attention to the question of consumption ever seems complete. Thus, while postmodern society is necessarily consumer society, consumer society is not necessarily postmodern. However, what is opened up here is the question of the *direction* in which developments in consumer society are headed, or, to put it more simply, the question is not whether consumer society is or is not postmodern now, but is consumer society simply not postmodern *yet*?

Utopia, dystopia and postmodernity

In order to consider the question of the direction of the development of consumer society and its relationship to postmodernity more directly, it is useful to look in some detail at the work of some of the most eminent scholars of postmodernity and consumer culture alike, including Jean Baudrillard, Fredric Jameson, and Scott Lash and John Urry. Given the often free-floating nature of the definition of postmodernity, and indeed any theorist of postmodernity, this is a necessarily selective discussion that is not intended in any way to be exhaustive or all-encompassing, but to be suggestive and exploratory. More importantly, the intention is primarily heuristic as opposed to definitive. In relation to the question of the future of postmodern consumer society, I will also start to draw a distinction between dystopian and Utopian perspectives. The distinction is derived partly from the work of Kaplan (Kaplan 1988).

As a cultural critic and social philosopher, Baudrillard has become what one might call *l'enfant terrible* of contemporary theory, partly because of his in some respects oversimplified association with postmodernism. Although it is true that much of his later work has taken his earlier ideas to the extremes sometimes associated with postmodernism, it is important to point out that he started his academic life as an essentially neo-Marxist semiotician. In addition, it is some of his earlier rather than later ideas that are most important for our study of consumption. These are summarized usefully in two excellent edited collections (Poster 1988; Baudrillard 1990).

Certain problems are also particularly apparent when attempting to assess the importance of Baudrillard's ideas and theories. In the first instance, like many of his French and other European contemporaries, his work is subject to translation which leads to both difficulties in making exact equations in meaning across differing languages and long delays in publication. In relation to Baudrillard's work, this is particularly problematic as some of his major works have yet to be published in full in English although they were published in part some time ago. In some cases, this gives his work a near-anachronistic status and it particularly applies to the publication of *The Consumer Society* in 1998, originally published in French in 1970 (Baudrillard 1998). Second, in common with some of his postmodern contemporaries, Baudrillard frequently seems to refuse to define his terms of reference, often writing in a wilfully open-ended style, littered with hyperbole and inflammatory statements, as we shall see shortly. Third, this leads to an added difficulty of glossing over inherent contradictions or points of resistance in his theorizing, often leaving his ideas wide open to multiple interpretation and/or castigation. Nevertheless, his influence and importance, particularly in the study of consumption, should not be underestimated (Poster 1988).

Mostly for the above reasons, Baudrillard has also become a near symbol of postmodernity in himself, loved and loathed with similar levels of emotional hysteria across the academic community. Most of the controversy has centred on his later work concerning the so-called 'death' of social meanings through endless simulations and processes of hyper-reality. Put most simply, his later writings seem to imply at least that, due to repeated and multiple representations of reality, the end is nigh for society as we know it. I will consider these issues shortly. However, much of Baudrillard's earlier work, which was in fact concerned with consumer society much more directly, has suffered some academic neglect, at least until the full English publication of *The Consumer Society: Myths and Structures*, originally published as *La Société De Consommation* in 1970 (Baudrillard 1998). Although problematic in its almost anachronistic status it is worth considering this work in some detail as, I will assert, it sheds significant light on the foundations and directions of much of the theory of postmodernity in relation to consumer society which has developed subsequently. Baudrillard starts thus:

> There is all around us today a kind of fantastic conspicuousness of consumption and abundance, constituted by the multiplication of objects, services and material goods, and this represents something of a fundamental mutation in the ecology of the human species. Strictly speaking, the humans of the age of affluence are surrounded not so much by other human beings, as they were in all previous ages, but by objects.
>
> (Baudrillard [1970]1998: 25)

Apart from the irony that this was first written nearly 30 years ago, various dimensions to Baudrillard's more recent ideas and indeed those of many other theorists of postmodernity are immediately apparent. Most importantly, the emphasis is placed heavily on the importance of consumption as indicative of a trend towards a new era characterized in terms of an alternative regime of meaning and understanding, communication and interaction. There is inherent in this a twin legacy coming from an anthropological, and particularly Saussurian, interpretation of signs and meanings on the one hand; and a more classically economic reading of the age of affluence on the other, as exemplified by the influence of Galbraith in particular (Galbraith 1958; Saussure 1974).

On top of this, and spliced in with it, is a more implicit political concern with the implications for power and resistance often derived from various forms of contemporary Marxism. Most fundamental in this for our discussion is the sense in which consumption *per se* is *not* the focus of study for Baudrillard or any other theorist of postmodernity, but is the *vehicle* through which wider statements concerning the status of signifying meanings can be analysed. Thus, it is not surprising that Baudrillard's own attention has drifted so strongly in this very direction more recently. More importantly, consumer society is analysed precisely as a society of signs and signifiers. Therefore, the practice of consumption is seen primarily as the manipulation of signifying meanings to various individual and social ends.

What is also apparent at this point are the political implications of this position. These are, in essence, socially divisive and enmeshed with questions of status and position. At this point, consumption remains tied up with production, and the criticism that *all* the theory of postmodernity somehow immediately and automatically 'throws out' questions of production is fundamentally a misinterpretation. Baudrillard makes this point most clearly:

> This does not mean that our society is not firstly, objectively and decisively a society of production, an order of production, and therefore the site of an economic and political strategy. But it means that there is entangled with that order an order of consumption, which is an order of the manipulation of signs.
>
> (Baudrillard [1970]1998: 33)

However, the difficulty with this perspective is that the analysis of the relationship of production and consumption remains underdeveloped and open to interpretation. In addition, Baudrillard was eventually to overturn it in favour of a model of seduction (Baudrillard [1979] 1990). It also renders consumption as a primarily stylistic and social phenomenon still tied up with production and equally not a material or economic condition but rather a sign system not entirely dissimilar to language. Thus, consumption practices in Baudrillard's world view are not so much concerned with possessing or belonging but *communicating*. This linguistic parallel is indeed problematic, as a number of commentators have pointed out previously (see particularly Campbell 1995). More importantly, it is perhaps the point at which any simple conflation of studies of consumer society and postmodernity starts to come unstuck, as while some theorists of consumption would accept these premises, particularly Mike Featherstone or Celia Lury, others such as Daniel Miller or Ben Fine and Ellen Leopold ostensibly would not (Miller 1987, 1995; Featherstone 1991; Fine and Leopold 1993; Lury 1996).

In the light of this model, Baudrillard then considers such contemporary phenomena as time, the body and advertising as examples of his overall schema. It is perhaps open to question exactly how appropriate, complete or successful these analyses are, but what concerns us here is the way in which they are used by Baudrillard to build up an increasing sense of implosion and, ultimately, societal self-destruction. This conception of consumption as an all-consuming phenomenon wasting away from within is summed up near the end of the text: 'Our society thinks itself and speaks itself as a consumer society. As much as it consumes anything, it consumes itself as a consumer society, as idea' (Baudrillard [1970]1998: 193). In addition, consumer resistances, or discourses of *anti*-consumption, themselves defined primarily in terms merely of self-parody, are also seen to play into the same mythical structure, seeming to imply that there is no way out and we have reached a modern-day Armageddon.

In *For a Critique of the Political Economy of the Sign* (1972), Baudrillard argues that signs are so increasingly commodified and commodities so increasingly signified that any sense of distinction is increasingly redundant and they come together to form the commodity sign. The importance of this conception is clearly apparent in contemporary Western society, as few commodities these days are not free from additional and overladen significations; and few signifying meanings do not have some kind of material or commodified example. This applies most clearly to luxury goods, such as designer fashions or expensive cars, but can also apply to many more staple items such as the more upmarket appeal of freshly made wheatgerm loaves over ready-sliced convenience packs.

The more difficult and contentious question concerns the assertion that such meanings operate increasingly independently of wider economic or political determinations. In addition, the most immediate criticism here is that all significations have their price, as fancy fashions, luxury items or even upmarket supermarket goods usually cost more in the first place. On top of this, though, there is a sense that, although the status of commodities may have an economic determination, the more complex and wider nuances of meanings attached to many items do not, particularly in fairly monopolist or oligopolist markets. For example, washing powders in the UK form an essentially oligopolist market dominated by Lever Brothers and Procter & Gamble, where prices are held constant but the distinction in meaning between Ariel as somehow 'modern, independent and high tech' versus Persil as particularly 'traditional, family oriented and whiter than white' makes the world of difference in terms of product significations. In addition, though, what they have in common is a higher status value than equivalent cheaper products. As a result, it is an open question as to how far one takes the increasing so-called autonomy of sign values, as there is clearly a sense in which they are still economically related if not determined.

Underlying this discussion, however, is a set of implicitly more poststructural assumptions concerning the nature and development of contemporary Western society. These focus particularly on the importance of the media in forming image cultures and undermining any direct link or connection of commodities and signification in opening up an increasingly complex, and indeed wide, landscape of meanings. Mixed in with this is the confusion of the 'real' with the 'imaginary', together with the contemporary quirks and contradictions of constructed or faked authenticity. One contemporary example is the promotional connotations surrounding Levi's 501 jeans seen as the original and authentic product and yet surrounded in mythic and iconic sex appeal (Edwards 1997).

At this juncture, it is worth clarifying the definition of the imaginary, which does not, as one may assume, particularly apply to the imagination but to the Lacanian notion of unconscious processes, or visual fantasies. For Baudrillard, these 'imaginings' are then also constructed and manipulated around commodities, particularly in advertising. These more psychoanalytic dimensions to consumption and sign systems are explored most fully in *The Mirror of Production* (Baudrillard 1975). It is also at this point that Baudrillard's break with Marxism starts to become more apparent. The more political dimensions to this are also increasingly explicit, and indeed pessimistic, when they are explored more directly in *Symbolic Exchange and Death* (Baudrillard [1976]1993). Here Baudrillard asserts that it is death alone that offers any symbolic escape from an increasingly totalizing sign system. Similarly, resistance in the form of political radicalism is undermined and the wider context of the decline of the traditional class-affiliated Left and the student protests in Paris of May 1968 are particularly apparent.

Yet, perhaps paradoxically, it is also this sense of implosion into meaninglessness that underlies Baudrillard's increasingly grandiose claims attached to the processes of 'reproduction' and 'simulation' whereby commodities become almost decommodified in the production of copies, fakes and suggestions of greater and greater illusion, ideas developed in his more recent works and tending to start with *Simulacra and Simulations* (Baudrillard 1983). In essence, the underlying principle of these processes is the rising rate of turnover or exchange in the production of commodities and indeed commodity signs, where products and their associations are increasingly outmoded, replaced and parodied. In addition, this is in turn founded on a system of 'seduction' rather than production as the system of generating symbolic meaning itself displaces any sense of more concrete reality. Thus, commodities themselves are no more than signs in a sign system that is itself increasingly self-referential and divorced from material production (Baudrillard 1979).

The ultimate example of these processes comes in the concept of 'hyperreality' where the media or technologically driven simulation or reproduction of products, services or even events becomes experienced as more 'real' than its actual or tangible reality. The increasing absurdity of car advertising is a good example of this process, whereby the meanings attached to an Audi – in which yuppie-styled anti-hero Freddie's rejection of the car becomes the car's rejection of him and by implication also attacks the quintessentially yuppie-driven BMW – add new, and essentially inverse, dimensions to the classical marketing notion of product personality; and the new age promotion of the Ford Ka almost renders the car itself redundant (see also Chapter 3).

In addition, it is this increasingly chaotic sense of social change that leads Baudrillard into his own wilderness of the destabilization of meanings and the postulation of 'the death of the social', whereby the human subject is now replaced by, and indeed inseparable from, a commodified object world whereby the subject–object relationship has essentially become reversed and commodities themselves are invested with social meaning. Underlying this is the objectification of the human body in particular, which is a recurrent theme in Baudrillard's work, alongside his development of the notion of 'fatal strategies', where the object–subject relationship has become so reversed as to invest the object with both a thinking and driving logic of its own from which the world must be perceived. The conundrum then becomes one of understanding the world from the point of view of the object, not the subject, and consequently the human subject is constantly prey to the fatal (fated *and* deadly) strategies of the object (Baudrillard 1990).

As if this were not enough, Baudrillard's critique of not only advertising but the television news itself as hyper-real fuelled an even greater sense of feverishness in the wake of the Gulf War. What is more, Baudrillard's nihilism now increasingly extends to a critique of theory itself, rejected in favour of travelogues, essays on art and aesthetics, and photography (Baudrillard 1989, 1990; Zurbrugg 1997). Paradoxically, however, this apocalyptic vision of capitalist implosion, epitomized almost literally in the form of world warfare, returns us full circle to the passive dupes of consumer culture encapsulated in the work of the Frankfurt School, which was considered critically in Chapter 1. Ironically, then, the free-floating world of signs and meanings has become the ultimate Orwellian Big Brother of social control.

It is worth comparing Baudrillard's prognoses here with those of Fredric Jameson, whose reappraisal of contemporary Marxist theory is welded more directly to his discussion of postmodernity. Never particularly far away in this discussion are the connections of developments in consumer society to wider questions of culture and capital. Jameson's article 'Postmodernism, or the Cultural Logic of Late Capitalism' has proved particularly influential in relation to these questions and his analysis is premised importantly on the assertion that developments in aesthetics, culture or postmodernism are not necessarily separate from developments in economics or capitalism. They are, rather, indicative of a particular late or high point reached in capitalism, defined most concretely in relation to the formation of multinational companies and, more pervasively, in international patterns of production and consumption where, in empirical terms, commodities are derived organically from the resources of one country, manufactured in another frequently to reduce costs, and sold, marketed or promoted in a series of others often to maximize profits. He points out:

> What has happened is that aesthetic production today has become integrated into commodity production generally: the frantic economic urgency of producing fresh waves of ever more novel-seeming goods (from clothing to airplanes), at ever greater rates of turnover, now assigns an increasingly essential structural function and position to aesthetic innovation and experimentation.
>
> (Jameson 1984: 56)

Jameson's main concern, then, is to unpack his thesis of postmodernity primarily in relation to the question of culture. First, Jameson asserts that high culture, defined as traditionally more elite, middle-class or academic pursuits including the theatre, art, and literature, is now increasingly confused with low culture, defined as more working-class or mass entertainment including popular music, television and some sports. Of particular importance here is the push towards popularizing various art forms, from well-publicized exhibitions to media transmissions of classical concerts, combined with certain developments in the arts themselves which have questioned the very definition of art, for example in the work of Andy Warhol.

Although some controversy still surrounds these assertions, as access to various cultural interests, such as the opera or the ballet, is still often shrouded in snobbery and exclusivity not least in the high ticket prices, the far more open point concerns his second notion of the development of 'a new depthlessness', defined as a culture of the image or 'simulacrum' centred on a 'weakening of historicity', or loss of history, and an increasingly schizophrenic (in the Lacanian sense) way of relating to the arts, leading to a stronger emotional engagement which he terms 'intensities' (Jameson 1984: 58). Interestingly, this applies as well to commodities surrounded in glossy packaging, seductive display and in store ambience as to the arts, where Hollywood glitz, stardom and special-effects cinema in particular have come under fire.

What is partly at stake here is a question of pejorative judgement in potentially deeming such developments as somehow 'worthless', but a wider issue concerns the implied sense of political apathy that ensues. A primary example here is the work of Andy Warhol whose images of the Coca-Cola bottle or Campbell's soup can which, in Jameson's terms, '*ought* to be powerful and critical political statements' yet, by implication, clearly are *not* (Jameson 1984: 60, original emphasis). Jameson also argues that this parallels an increasing fragmentation as opposed to alienation, in the classical Marxist sense, of the human subject. Thus, when combined with his prognoses on the 'loss' of a 'radical past' or even history itself through the rise of nostalgia and a 'well-nigh libidinal historicism', Jameson's prognosis on the future seems as gloomy as Baudrillard's implied 'death of the social'

(Jameson 1984: 66). This ties up rather well with Baudrillard's more apocalyptic points and leads Mike Featherstone to derive an underlying sense of, if not implicit thesis of, a convergence or 'logic of consumerism', as if all Western capitalist societies are somehow undergoing transformation or a drive towards a certain condition of what one might call cultural homogenization due in part to the rise of multinational production and services (Featherstone 1991).

However, Jameson remains implicitly more optimistic in seeing the shift towards postmodernity as primarily a challenge to our prevailing conceptions of time and space. In an analysis of the city and architecture that is not a world away from Simmel's notion of the blasé in the metropolis or Benjamin's analysis of the *flâneur* in the arcades, Jameson sees space as precisely the most fundamental social concern of contemporary society, taking over, in essence, from time and temporality (see Chapter 1). Consequently, to put it more simply, one's place in time or history has turned into one's place in space or the city as an organizing feature of identity and meaning, or what he calls 'cognitive mapping' (Jameson 1984: 89). Therefore, the challenge is to *re*-cognize our understanding of ourselves and the world around us. Much of this article is then unpacked, through a process of dense and near-literary style review, in Jameson's full-length reworking of its key elements in *Postmodernism, or, the Cultural Logic of Late Capitalism*, incorporating a detailed discussion of the role of video, architecture, linguistics, Utopia, the market and nostalgia (Jameson 1991).

The work of Scott Lash and John Urry manages, quite distinctively, to weld together some of these more sweeping themes of the theory of postmodernity to a form of comparative and empirical study, particularly of the UK, US, Germany and Japan. This was first posited in *The End of Organized Capitalism* (1987) and developed significantly in *Economies of Signs and Space* (1994), and multiple collaborations have resulted in equally multiple spin-offs (see, for example, Beck *et al.* 1994). It is also worth making it immediately apparent that these theses are grandiose in the extreme and much lies out of the scope of a work on consumption, but it remains important to outline some of their most central claims. In the first instance, they adopt a primarily tripartite model of capitalist development which characterizes early industrial capitalism as 'liberal', or locally and regionally centred, later industrial capitalism as 'organized', or national in focus, and contemporary capitalism as 'disorganized', or internationally driven. In addition, mapped on to this is the further dimension of (post)modernity, as organized capitalism is mostly associated with modernity and disorganized capitalism with postmodernity, and indeed postindustrialism. Consequently, their work as a whole is dedicated to the unpacking and sophistication of what appears in the first instance as a fairly crude set of equations and categories.

Summarizing the key differences in the movement towards disorganized capitalism and postmodernity is necessarily difficult and contentious, but the following might offer themselves as fundamental. First, disorganized capitalism is characterized by greater reflexivity on all levels. Consequently, individuals and institutions alike are increasingly self-aware, less certain of their foundations, and sensitive to their limits and internal dynamics. Second, disorganized capitalism sees a move towards the creation and production of an economy of signs as opposed to commodities. This sign system is seen to fall into roughly two forms: cognitive or informative and aesthetic or image-driven. Third, this then sees a growing interconnection of consumption, as opposed to production of work, with questions of identity, in which issues of choice, loss of the constraints of tradition or ascription, and negotiation of risk are increasingly critical. Fourth, this then ties in with a wider dimension of an overall aestheticization of culture and move towards more visual forms of consumption, of which theme parks and tourism as purely voyeuristic activities are prime examples. Fifth, and finally, this is allied to the development of a more information-driven or service-centred society and an international and global economy in terms of production and consumption, and time and money alike, all of which are increasingly cross-cultural.

There are clear parallels here with both Baudrillard and Jameson's work outlined earlier, as well as Anthony Giddens' wider study of reflexivity (Giddens 1991, 1992). However, what tends to mark out a point of difference is the degree of optimism with which Lash and Urry view these developments:

> It is to claim that the sort of 'economies of signs and space' that become pervasive in the wake of organized capitalism do not just lead to increasing meaninglessness, homogenization, abstraction, anomie and the destruction of the subject. Another set of radically divergent processes is simultaneously taking place. These processes may open up possibilities for the recasting of meaning in work and in leisure, for the reconstitution of community and the particular, for the reconstruction of transformed subjectivity, and for heterogenization and complexity of space and of everyday life.
>
> (Lash and Urry 1994: 3)

Despite this, they also retain some sense of social divisions in the formation of an underclass around consumption informed by the work of Wilson on ghettos in the United States (Wilson 1991).

What emerges from this for our discussion of consumption and postmodernity is an increasing sense of *consensus* concerning the *nature* of the developments involved compared with an equal *disparity* in the perception of the *outcomes* of such processes. Baudrillard's vision of consumer society is, in particular, best described as 'dystopian' in its sense of impending doom and destruction. Some academics are severely critical of this sense of nihilism, and more culturalist critics are often significantly more positive or

'Utopian' concerning the direction and outcome of contemporary consumer society, seeing it as offering an increasing potential for openness, plurality and pleasure on various levels (Featherstone 1991; Shields 1992; Lury 1996). Much of this conflict or difference in perspective on consumer society here centres on interpretations of its more political implications. For Baudrillard, and to some extent Jameson, both of whose ideas are drawn on heavily in the work of Arthur and Marilouise Kroker, the increasing importance of consumer culture represents a strong sense of social control through capitalism whereby the consumer is rendered increasingly fragmented, confused and passive (Baudrillard [1970]1998; Jameson 1984; Kroker and Cook 1988; Kroker and Kroker 1988). However, some feminists in particular have highlighted a more active role of consumer culture in opening up spaces for women's empowerment (Nava 1992; Bowlby 1993; Radner 1995). Similarly, although more reserved, Lash and Urry also remain rather more positive, or at least open-ended, in terms of their predictions for the future of a 'postmodern' consumer society (see also Chapter 6).

In either case, however, most if not all of the attention centres on notions of consumption as related to style cultures, aesthetics and identity and, in particular, the importance of forms of consumption which are located essentially as leisure activities. As a result, consumer society under the auspices of postmodernity is characterized and defined by certain key features: first, an overall rise in the significance of sign value over use value in relation to commodities, or, to put it more simply, when purchasing items their visual and social connotations are increasingly significant while questions of their functionality and use are less important; second, consumption as a monetary and aesthetic practice alike is seen to take over and define more and more elements and features of contemporary society, from the formation of personal identities to the creation of social cohesion or order; and third, and most contentiously, these two elements are then seen to lead to an increasing sense of fragmentation, openness and uncertainty in relation to social life and social meanings. Whether this in turn then leads to a centripetal implosion into nothingness or the positive development of wider forms of expression is open to question. Consequently, Utopian and dystopian postmodernity, like Utopia and dystopia, are ultimately two mutually reinforcing and self-defining sides of the same coin.

The sense in which consumer society is in any true accordance with dystopian or Utopian notions of postmodernity remains open to question. In addition, empirical investigation into the importance of consumption practices for Western populations would, at present at least, seem not to support an adoption of either perspective. Instead, there is a sense in which consumption is seen as an increasingly socially significant yet still fundamentally fairly mundane activity that is strongly patterned in its importance according to such factors as social class, race, gender and sexuality, to name only a few (Crompton 1996; Campbell 1997b; Miller 1998).

In considering the relationship of postmodernity to consumer society, then, the key distinction therefore perhaps rests on separating forms of consumption that are essentially mundane, routine and necessary, of which supermarket shopping and use of household services are prime examples, from forms of consumption that are exotic, spontaneous and luxurious, of which wandering around shopping malls for something to do and taking holidays in foreign destinations are significant cases in point. The primary question here, however, centres precisely on the staying power of this distinction itself. Although traipsing around a local supermarket to do one's weekly shop for provisions may still have all the appeal of pulling teeth, the sense of growing encroachment of consumption's more wild, exotic and luxuriant dimensions is ever increasing in its pervasive importance. For example, many convenience foods in particular are marketed as tasters of far-away cultures, and conditioners for one's laundry are promoted as transformers of personal mood using emotive terms such as 'vitality' and 'spring'. An important factor here is the extent to which commodities are still defined as necessary or luxury. Consequently, convenience foods and laundry conditioners alike still have connotations of extravagance because of their inessential status, and there is little sense of the exotic one can conceivably put into the marketing of a pint of milk! Despite this, there is little true sense of immunity here, as even staple items such as tea, bread and even vegetables become wrapped up, sometimes literally, in notions of health, status and prestige, often invoking connotations varying from foreign sensuality to local freshness.

What is often of particular significance here is the association of such processes with the wider thesis of the aestheticization of everyday life. That everyday life is increasingly centred on the visual, or on images primarily produced in the mass media of television, cinema and advertising, is not in question. Of greater controversy are the links with consumption as a primary mechanism in these processes. Many commodities, although not necessarily all, are increasingly sold according to their sign value, a significant factor in which is their visual function. However, to assert that this is then linked to wider developments in social institutions such as the family or state, or indeed that it starts to form the mainstay of social organization or social life, seems increasingly centred on a series of decidedly 'postmodern' assumptions that return us full circle to the start of this chapter.

In conclusion to this discussion then, one might make the following assertions. First, conceptions and practices of consumer society and postmodernity do conflate in various senses and particularly in relation to more exotic or luxury forms of consumption. This does not mean, though, that there is any simple equation to be made between consumer society and postmodern society, and one may still conclude that while the increasing significance of consumption practices and meanings may well characterize a postmodern society, consumer society is not necessarily, and certainly not in its entirety, postmodern society. Second, if one defines a postmodern consumer society in terms of increased sign value over use value, consumerism's operation as a means of forming and maintaining personal and social identities, and the overall aestheticization and commodification of everyday life, it is in all likelihood the case that consumer society is moving in the direction of postmodernity. Third, however, this remains a limited or finite development and its social, economic and political implications are still open to question and essentially a matter of speculation. In addition, it is precisely this sense of social divisiveness that holds down some of the more high-flown aspects of consumer society.

However, it seems imperative not to underestimate the extent to which Western, and increasingly non-Western, populations are drawn into a more postmodern world of consumption on some level, even if only in terms of their exposure to visual advertising and marketing cultures. Although it is all too easy to disprove and undermine the present empirical realities of postmodernity, this is perhaps to miss the point, for the question is not one of where we are now but of where we are going, and postmodernity, whether utopian or dystopian in its outcomes, looms ever larger in the seas of consumer society and it remains the role of social scientists to look ahead and navigate the waters.

Conclusions: consumer futures

In assessing the future development of consumer society, little is certain. Despite this, some elements of its direction would seem without contention. The first and most fundamental of these is the expansion of consumption as concept and practice into more and more areas of everyday life. Health, education and welfare provision across Northern and Western Europe, to name only some examples, have all increasingly come into the realm of consumption as goods and services sold and marketed like any other product. Second, and in conjunction with this, the increasing aestheticization and commodification of more and more aspects of society opens up a series of questions concerning the conflation of consumption and postmodernity. There is perhaps now little controversy concerning the move towards an essentially image-driven society where sign value increasingly takes over from use value as a primary mechanism for organizing patterns and meanings of consumption. In addition, there is clearly much opportunity for pleasure and expression in many consumer practices in contemporary society, particularly for those who are most affluent and with most access to its amusements and gratifications. More politically, there is perhaps some limited sense of democracy in its sense of openness to anyone with the money to spend on its products and services.

However, more controversially, there is little sense in which such developments are unequivocally egalitarian or emancipatory. One may well assert conversely that such developments are highly socially divisive, often excluding the most economically insecure such as the low paid, elderly or single parents; while the most affluent are constantly presented with an ever-widening array of temptations to spend. Importantly, the sense in which such processes compound or undermine more traditional forms of social division remains open to question. In addition, the creation of a plethora of mutually exclusive lifestyle categories seems paradoxically to reinforce the economic inequalities it seems to undermine; while simultaneously confusing any sense of simplicity in its connection to patterns of inequality around class, race, gender or sexuality. Essentially, in consumer society, human life is increasingly and superficially organized according to questions of income and access, in turn rendering underlying factors of inequality not less important, but less *apparent* (see Chapter 4).

Perhaps more significantly, there seems little political potential to resist such developments other than through the setting up of some forms of more collective or co-operative exchange, as the tendency of contemporary patterns of consumption to individualize every activity into a lifestyle miscellany seems endless. More perniciously, the sense in which consumer society sets itself up as a kind meritocratic, and indeed democratic, 'open shop' where everyone is welcome, as long as they can demonstrate their capacity to spend, masks any sense of social or economic exploitation so effectively as to render itself, intentionally or unintentionally, politically stupefying (Bauman 1998).

This starts to tap into the Utopian and dystopian dichotomies of postmodernity, where contemporary society is seen as heading towards a state of rapturous individualized expression or sliding over a precipice into complete emptiness. It is all too easy to overstate the significance of such developments in either direction, as Western and non-Western populations alike were never so passive as to not even see what was coming or to form some resistance if only through lack of interest. Most significantly perhaps, it is the persistence of many consumer practices, particularly shopping itself, as mundane, routine and even dull that tends to undermine many of the more extravagant claims of the theory of postmodernity. Yet, it is equally easy to miss its significance in a wave of empirical counter-claims. The problem remains one of charting the waters of contemporary consumer society, for postmodernity is as real and as menacing as a mass of ice in the distance, and an outright rejection of its significance is as dangerous as a head-on collision with its hidden depths.

Suggested further reading

Baudrillard, J. ([1970]1998) *The Consumer Society*. London: Sage – early, yet still perhaps definitive, work on postmodernity and consumer society.

Featherstone, M. (1991) *Consumer Culture and Postmodernism*. London: Sage – landmark collection of essays on the relationship of consumer society and postmodernity.

Howes, D. (ed.) (1996) *Cross-cultural Consumption*. London: Routledge – useful collection of essays on globalization and consumption.

Lash, S. and Urry, J. (1994) *Economies of Signs and Space*. London: Sage – obfuscatory writing style but a major bridge between empiricism and postmodernity.

Lee, M. J. (1993) *Consumer Culture Reborn*. London: Routledge – rather neglected yet rigorous analysis of Marxist theory and consumer society in the light of more postmodern theory.

CONCLUSION: HUNGER AND DESIRE IN CONSUMER SOCIETY

'Choose life . . .'

Throughout this work, I have emphasized three key themes in relation to the theory and practice of consumer society. First, I have stressed that consumption is a multifaceted phenomenon encompassing a series of experiences from household shopping to holiday voyeurism in arcades. In addition, consumer culture *per se* may also equally apply to practices as diverse as leisure and viewing, as well as spending. Second, consumerism as an ethos and a practice is expanding in its importance at a near-exponential rate to incorporate everything from health and insurance to education and recreation. The privatization of state services in the UK is a most eminent example of this condition. Third, and most significantly, despite its expansion, consumer society remains socially divisive, often adding to existing dimensions of oppression around class, gender or race or constructing new forms of stratification according to income, credit status and physical access.

Although it is perhaps extremely difficult to encompass all of these elements of the theory and practice of consumer society in any one study or analysis, it remains necessary to retain an awareness of their importance. Despite the recent, and sometimes meteoric, rise in interest in consumption in academic and popular circles alike, all too often the focus has centred on a single dimension of consumer society, most commonly the significance of affluent, aesthetic consumer style cultures, to the exclusion of other key aspects of its development or contemporary salience. Most particularly, it is consumer society's construction of its own poor, as it were a consumer underclass, that sometimes comes under least scrutiny. Conversely, shop-aholicism as a more cultural and psychological phenomenon has come into the spotlight of increasing inspection. This situation is perhaps curious for in increasingly affluent Western society, a sense of at least relative depri-vation is used quite explicitly to stimulate demand and, ironically, an expan-sion in the importance attached to consumption must also necessitate an increasing experience of poverty. Coupled with this is the sense in which the analysis of consumption still tends to remain dissociated from the entire world of production on which it so fundamentally depends.

Most of these apparently slightly contradictory developments are explained through the rise of poststructural theory and its spillover into cultural studies, popular culture and the media. Indeed, as outlined in Chapter 1, earlier analyses of consumer society were often more Marxist, economic or social historical in their emphasis (McKendrick *et al.* 1982; Campbell 1987; Benson 1994). What all this tends to lead to is an increas-ing sense in which neither consumption nor its study is clearly defined. Con-sequently, in the next section, I wish to focus on this question of definition and, more importantly, start to investigate the relationship of sociology to consumer society.

Sociology and consumer society

As already outlined in the Introduction, academic interest in consumption has expanded in recent years. This expansion has often reflected the increas-ingly dynamic and fluid state of the social sciences in the wake of the rise of wider cultural and poststructural questions. Attention to consumer society and studies of consumer culture alike have taken many forms and dimen-sions, raising further issues concerning the meanings of consumption for individual psychology on the one hand, and opening up discussion of the future of Western society on the other. These questions have in turn often invoked connections with an equal diversity of wider concerns, from mod-ernity and postmodernity to anthropology and economic history, and from popular culture and psychoanalytic interpretation to social policy and con-sumer activism (see, respectively: Slater 1997a and Featherstone 1991; Miller 1998 and Fine and Leopold 1993; Shields 1992 and Bowlby 1993; and Cahill 1994 and John 1994).

The origins of the analysis of consumer society lie, for the most part, in the confines of economic history and early studies of modernity (Simmel 1904, 1990; Veblen 1934; Adorno and Horkheimer 1973; Benjamin 1973; Marx 1975). As is clearly apparent, however, the study of consumer society is now essentially multidisciplinary, developing across the full spectrum of the social sciences and some of the humanities, including anthropology, social history, economics, psychology, cultural studies and literature as well as sociology. Positive as such a plethora of studies may seem, particularly in the light of its apparent openness, such a *multi*disciplinary development of interests is easily, and often incorrectly, confused with an *inter*disciplinary analysis of issues. Some writers have already started to rein in, rather than ring in, these changes whereas others have attempted to throw the net ever wider (see Edgell *et al.* 1996; Lury 1996; Sulkunen *et al.* 1997; Miller *et al.* 1998).

What this tends to lead to is a strong sense of diffusion, if not confusion, concerning what, exactly, the central issues are in the study of consumer society. Although the study of shopping in particular is sometimes more precisely and more definitely focused on concrete locations, social practices and their interpretations, most of the study of consumer society is general, theoretical and sometimes grandiose as opposed to specific, empirical and self-critical. Consequently, there is a need to hold down the study of consumer society theoretically as well as empirically and the wide coverage of this text is a further reflection of the often high-flying pitch of studies of consumer society.

More importantly, this opens up a further question of definition concerning what consumer society actually *is*, and moreover what consumption actually *means*, as everything from patterns of eating and drinking to shopping practices and the interpretation of cultural texts has, as it were, thrown itself into the arena of consumer culture. I have endeavoured to answer this question in the Introduction, and again in relation to the study of postmodernity, but neither a frank discussion of this question of definition nor a full exposition of the issues it involves truly exists. Where conflict and dialogue have ensued is in relation to cultural versus economic interpretations as a matter of emphasis in determining the foundations and directions of consumer society more widely. This itself is in danger of entering a state of impasse which seems as unhelpful as it is inaccurate, as consumption is all too clearly a cultural practice *and* an economic phenomenon.

What this seems to lead to then, is a requirement for a multifaceted, if not necessarily multidisciplinary, study of consumer society that seeks to address, if not encompass, its differing dimensions. This would seem well located to develop empirically and theoretically, primarily in the social sciences and sociology. The poststructural drift of many more recent analyses of consumer society has already started to come under fire from some more empirically or materially grounded scholars (Campbell 1997b; Slater 1997a; Miller 1998). What is still lacking, however, is a clearer sense of defining the differing dimensions of consumption, their relationships, and particularly their implications. The necessary critique of the extremes of some forms of Critical Marxism in particular has, it seems, yet to come full circle, and a certain knee-jerk reaction to the raising of such questions still exists. It is, however, vital to recognize that consumer society, even an aesthetic consumer culture, is as economic and political as it is social and cultural, and as divisive and exploitative as it is diverse and democratic. Ultimately, the reign of the sovereign consumer, apparently at liberty to pick and choose as well as to buy and sell in the open shop of the free market, has yet to be dethroned; and there is, perhaps paradoxically, little consumer democracy under a consumer monarchy.

Hunger and desire

The contemporary world of consumer society is now commonly associated, in academic and popular culture alike, with the social psychology of desire. This is hardly surprising given the massive allure of packaging and promotion, seduction and advertising, that now surrounds everything from designer fashion to fast cars and from cans of paint to personal cleansing. The rise of voyeuristic practices in shopping malls and the glamour of style magazines also merely adds to the sense in which consumption, and consumer society, is simply desiring society.

The key difficulty here, however, is that this is really only half of the story and, perhaps more importantly, merely the icing on the cake, the decoration on the wall, or the window dressing for the commodities themselves. As I have pointed out repeatedly, consumer society remains socially divisive: inclusive and inviting of the affluent, mobile and able; exclusive of the poor, the isolated and the impaired. In addition, it remains divided according to questions of location, class, age, gender, race and sexuality, to mention only some measures of oppression.

More importantly, the concept of desire, at least as it is applied to consumer society, assumes some level of agency and autonomy, while the free-floating window shopper still stands at its conceptual apex. The concept of hunger, conversely, implies need, and often an insatiable need of some kind, whether for food or some more emotional stimulant that is often only partially, if at all, under the control of the individual. In addition, the notion of hunger also draws on the emotive imagery of the starving, the exploited and the Third World, and these are equally valid dimensions of consumer culture and the contemporary human condition. These two sides, then, of the same matrix of human experience also make up the dual, and often contradictory, nature of consumer society.

People may well, then, drift along arcades looking to fulfil any whim, particularly if they are in the social and economic position to do so; yet they may equally struggle around the supermarket in need of food with limited income, or work strenuously to produce the goods they may later purchase themselves. This sense of division and contradiction, and particularly its more oppressive dimensions, remains missing from many, though not all, contemporary analyses of consumer society. Despite the immense expansion of popular and academic interest in consumption, its politics as opposed to its theory and practice remain for the most part out of sight. Consequently, in the final instance, it is worth remembering that a consumer society is made up of people consuming; and, whether for food, or love, or shelter, people consume when they are hungry. Consumer society is, then, not only desiring society, it is hungry society.

REFERENCES

Adam, B. D. (1987) *The Rise of a Gay and Lesbian Movement*. Boston, MA: Twayne Publications.

Adkins, L. (1995) *Gendered Work: Sexuality, Family and Labour Market*. Buckingham: Open University Press.

Adorno, T. W. and Horkheimer, M. (1973) *Dialectic of Enlightenment*. London: Allen Lane.

Adorno, T. W. and Horkheimer, M. (1993) The culture industry: enlightenment as mass deception, in S. During (ed.) *The Cultural Studies Reader*. London: Routledge.

Aldridge, A. (1994) The construction of rational consumption in *Which?* magazine: the more blobs the better, *Sociology*, 28(4): 899–912.

Arendt, H. (ed.) (1973) *Walter Benjamin: Illuminations*. London: Fontana.

Armstrong, S. (1996) Catch 'em young, *The Sunday Times*, Culture: 10.

Barnard, M. (1996) *Fashion as Communication*. London: Routledge.

Baudrillard, J. (1972) *For a Critique of the Political Economy of the Sign*. St Louis, NY: Telos Press.

Baudrillard, J. (1975) *The Mirror of Production*. St Louis: Telos Press.

Baudrillard, J. ([1976] 1993) *Symbolic Exchange and Death*. London: Sage.

Baudrillard, J. ([1979] 1990) *Seduction*. London: Macmillan.

Baudrillard, J. (1983) *Simulacra and Simulations*. New York: Semiotext(e).

Baudrillard, J. (1989) *America*. London: Verso.

Baudrillard, J. (1988) The system of objects, *Art Monthly*, 115: 5–8.

Baudrillard, J. (1990) *Revenge of the Crystal: Selected Writings on the Modern Object and its Destiny, 1968–1983*. London: Pluto Press.

Baudrillard, J. ([1970] 1998) *The Consumer Society: Myths and Structures*. London: Sage.

Bauman, Z. (1987) *Legislators and Interpreters: On Modernity, Postmodernity and Intellectuals.* Cambridge: Polity.

Bauman, Z. (1988) *Freedom.* Milton Keynes: Open University Press.

Bauman, Z. (1990) *Thinking Sociologically.* Oxford: Blackwell.

Bauman, Z. (1996) From pilgrim to tourist – or a short history of identity, in S. Hall and P. du Gay (eds) *Questions of Cultural Identity.* London: Sage.

Bauman, Z. (1998) *Work, Consumerism and the New Poor.* Buckingham: Open University Press.

Beck, U., Giddens, A. and Lash, S. (1994) *Reflexive Modernization.* Cambridge: Polity.

Bell, D. (1974) *The Coming of Post-Industrial Society.* New York: Basic Books.

Bell, D. (1976) *The Cultural Contradictions of Capitalism.* New York: Basic Books.

Benjamin, W. (1973) *Illuminations.* London: Fontana.

Benson, J. (1994) *The Rise of Consumer Society in Britain, 1880–1980.* London: Longman.

Berthoud, R. and Kempson, E. (1992) *Credit and Debt: The PSI Report.* London: Policy Studies Institute.

Beveridge, W. (1942) *Social Insurance and Allied Services: A Report by Sir William Beveridge,* Cmd. 6404. London: HMSO.

Bhaba, H. (ed.) (1990) *Nation and Narration.* London: Routledge.

Blachford, G. (1981) Male dominance and the gay world, in K. Plummer (ed.) *The Making of the Modern Homosexual.* London: Hutchinson.

Bourdieu, P. (1984) *Distinction: A Social Critique of the Judgement of Taste.* London: Routledge & Kegan Paul.

Bourdieu, P. (1989) *Outline of a Theory of Practice.* Cambridge: Cambridge University Press.

Bowlby, R. (1993) *Shopping with Freud.* London: Routledge.

Bristow, J. and Wilson, A. (eds) (1993) *Activating Theory: Lesbian, Gay, Bisexual Politics.* London: Lawrence & Wishart.

Brownmiller, S. (1984) *Femininity.* New York: Simon & Schuster.

Buck-Morss, S. (1989) *The Dialectics of Seeing: Walter Benjamin and the Arcades Project.* Cambridge, MA: MIT Press.

Butler, J. (1990) *Gender Trouble: Feminism and the Subversion of Identity.* London: Routledge.

Cahill, M. (1994) *The New Social Policy.* Oxford: Blackwell.

Callinicos, A. (1989) *Against Postmodernism: A Marxist Critique.* Cambridge: Polity.

Campbell, C. (1987) *The Romantic Ethic and the Spirit of Modern Consumerism.* Oxford: Blackwell.

Campbell, C. (1995) The sociology of consumption, in D. Miller (ed.) *Acknowledging Consumption.* London: Routledge.

Campbell, C. (1997b) Shopping, pleasure and the sex war, in P. Falk and C. Campbell (eds) *The Shopping Experience.* London: Sage.

Certeau, M. de (1984) *The Practice of Everyday Life.* London: University of California Press.

Chaney, D. (1996) *Lifestyles.* London: Routledge.

Chapman, R. and Rutherford, J. (eds) (1988) *Male Order: Unwrapping Masculinity.* London: Lawrence & Wishart.

Chartered Institute of Marketing (1993) *Certificate Fundamentals and Practice of Marketing*. London: BPP Publishing.

Cohen, S. (1972) *Folk Devils and Moral Panics: The Creation of Mods and Rockers*. London: Martin Robertson.

Corrigan, P. (1997) *The Sociology of Consumption: An Introduction*. London: Sage.

Craik, J. (1994) *The Face of Fashion: Cultural Studies in Fashion*. London: Routledge.

Crompton, R. (1996) Consumption and class analysis, in S. Edgell, K. Hetherington and A. Warde (eds) *Consumption Matters: The Production and Experience of Consumption*. Oxford: Blackwell.

Dahrendorf, R. (1959) *Class and Class Conflict in an Industrial Society*. London: Routledge & Kegan Paul.

Delphy, C. (1984) *Close to Home*. Cambridge: Hutchinson.

Derrida, J. (1982) *Margins of Philosophy*. Chicago, IL: University Of Chicago Press.

Dodd, N. (1994) *The Sociology of Money: Economics, Reason and Contemporary Society*. Cambridge: Polity.

Douglas, M. (1996) *Thought Styles: Critical Essays on Good Taste*. London: Sage.

Dowling, R. (1993) Femininity, place and commodities: a retail case study, *Antipode*, 25(4): 295–319.

Doyal, L. and Gough, I. (1991) *A Theory of Human Need*. Basingstoke: Macmillan.

Du Gay, P. (1996) *Consumption and Identity at Work*. London: Sage.

Dworkin, A. (1981) *Pornography: Men Possessing Women*. London: The Women's Press.

Dyer, R. (1997) *White*. London: Routledge.

Edgell, S., Hetherington, K. and Warde, A. (eds) (1996) *Consumption Matters: The Production and Experience of Consumption*. Oxford: Blackwell.

Edwards, T. (1994) *Erotics & Politics: Gay Male Sexuality, Masculinity and Feminism*. London: Routledge.

Edwards, T. (1997) *Men in the Mirror: Men's Fashion, Masculinity and Consumer Society*. London: Cassell.

Evans, C. and Thornton, M. (1989) *Women and Fashion: A New Look*. London: Quartet.

Ewen, S. (1976) *Captains of Consciousness: Advertising and the Social Roots of the Consumer Culture*. New York: McGraw-Hill.

Ewen, S. (1988) *All Consuming Images: The Politics of Style in Contemporary Culture*. New York: Basic Books.

Falk, P. (1994) *The Consuming Body*. London: Sage.

Falk, P. (1997) The Benetton-Toscani effect: testing the limits of conventional advertising, in M. Nava, A. Blake, I. Mackury and B. Richards (eds) *Buy this Book: Studies in Advertising and Consumption*. London: Routledge.

Falk, P. and Campbell, C. (eds) (1997) *The Shopping Experience*. London: Sage.

Featherstone, M. (1991) *Consumer Culture and Postmodernism*. London: Sage.

Fine, B. and Leopold, E. (1993) *The World of Consumption*. London: Routledge.

Finkelstein, J. (1991) *The Fashioned Self*. London: Polity.

Firestone, S. (1970) *The Dialectic of Sex: The Case for Feminist Revolution*. New York: Bantam.

Fiske, J. (1989a) *Reading the Popular*. London: Unwin Hyman.

Fiske, J. (1989b) *Understanding Popular Culture*. London: Unwin Hyman.

Flaubert, G. ([1857] 1992) *Madame Bovary*. Harmondsworth: Penguin.

Flügel, J. C. (1930) *The Psychology of Clothes*. London: Hogarth Press.

Ford, J. (1988) *The Indebted Society: Credit and Default in the 1980s*. London: Routledge.

Ford, J. (1991) *Consuming Credit: Debt and Poverty in the UK*. London: CPAG.

Foucault, M. (1974) *The Archaeology of Knowledge*. London: Tavistock.

Foucault, M. (1977) *Discipline and Punish: The Birth of the Prison*. London: Tavistock.

Fowles, J. (1996) *Advertising and Popular Culture*. Thousand Oaks, CA: Sage.

Friedan, B. (1963) *The Feminine Mystique*. London: Victor Gollancz.

Friedman, M. (1948) A monetary and fiscal framework for economic stability, *American Economic Review*, 38(3): 245–64.

Friedman, M. (1968) The role of monetary policy, *American Economic Review*, 58: 1–17.

Frisby, D. and Featherstone, M. (eds) (1997) *Simmel on Culture: Selected Writings*. London: Sage.

Frith, S. (1983) *Sound Effects: Youth, Leisure and the Politics of Rock*. London: Constable.

Gabriel, Y. and Lang, T. (1995) *The Unmanageable Consumer: Contemporary Consumption and its Fragmentation*. London: Sage.

Galbraith, J. (1958) *The Affluent Society*. Boston, MA: Houghton Mifflin.

George, V. and Wilding, P. (1994) *Welfare and Ideology*. Hemel Hempstead: Harvester Wheatsheaf.

Giddens, A. (1991) *Modernity and Self-Identity: Self and Society in the Late Modern Age*. Cambridge: Polity.

Giddens, A. (1992) *The Transformation of Intimacy: Sexuality, Love and Eroticism*. Cambridge: Polity.

Gilroy, P. (1987) *There Ain't No Black in the Union Jack*. London: Unwin Hyman.

Gilroy, P. (1993) *The Black Atlantic: Modernity and Double Consciousness*. London: Verso.

Goffman, E. (1976) *Gender Advertisements*. New York: Harper & Row.

Goldman, R. (1992) *Reading Ads Socially*. London: Routledge.

Goldthorpe, J., Lockwood, D., Bechhofer, F. and Platt, J. (1968a) *The Affluent Worker: Industrial Attitudes and Behaviour*. Cambridge: Cambridge University Press.

Goldthorpe, J., Lockwood, D., Bechhofer, F. and Platt, J. (1968b) *The Affluent Worker: Political Attitudes and Behaviour*. Cambridge: Cambridge University Press.

Goldthorpe, J., Lockwood, D., Bechhofer, F. and Platt, J. (1969) *The Affluent Worker in the Class Structure*. Cambridge: Cambridge University Press.

Goldthorpe, J. H. (1987) *Social Mobility and Class Structure in Modern Britain*, 2nd edn. Oxford: Clarendon Press.

Gough, J. (1989) Theories of sexuality and the masculinization of the gay man, in S. Shepherd and M. Wallis (eds) *Coming on Strong: Gay Politics and Culture*. London: Unwin Hyman.

Grazia, V. de with Furlough, E. (eds) (1996) *The Sex of Things: Gender and Consumption in Historical Perspective*. Berkeley, CA: University of California Press.

Griffin, S. (1979) *Rape: The Power of Consciousness*. San Francisco, CA: Harper & Row.

Habermas, J. (1976) *Legitimation Crisis*. London: Heinemann.

Hall, S. (1980) Encoding/decoding, in S. Hall *et al.* (eds) *Culture, Media, Language*. London: Hutchinson.

Hall, S. (1992) The West and the rest, in S. Hall and B. Gieben (eds) *Formations of Modernity*. Cambridge: Polity.

Hall, S. (ed.) (1997) *Representation: Cultural Representation and Signifying Practices*. London: Sage.

Hall, S. and Du Gay, P. (eds) (1996) *Questions of Cultural Identity*. London: Sage.

Hall, S. and Jefferson, T. (1976) *Resistance Through Rituals: Youth Subcultures in Post-war Britain*. London: Unwin Hyman.

Harvey, D. (1989) *The Condition of Postmodernity*. Oxford: Blackwell.

Harwood, V., Oswell, D., Parkinson, K. and Ward, A. (eds) (1993) *Pleasure Principles: Politics, Sexuality and Ethics*. London: Lawrence & Wishart.

Haye, A. de la (ed.) (1997) *The Cutting Edge: 50 Years of British Fashion 1947–1997*. London: V & A Publications.

Hayek, F. A. von (1944) *The Road to Serfdom*. London: Routledge & Kegan Paul.

Hebdige, D. (1979) *Subculture: The Meaning of Style*. London: Routledge.

Hebdige, D. (1987) *Cut'n'Mix: Culture, Identity and Caribbean Music*. London: Comdia.

Hoch, P. (1979) *White Hero, Black Beast: Racism, Sexism and the Mask of Masculinity*. London: Pluto Press.

Howes, D. (ed.) (1996) *Cross-Cultural Consumption: Global Markets, Local Realities*. London: Routledge.

Humphery, K. (1998) *Shelf Life: Supermarkets and the Changing Cultures of Consumption*. Cambridge: Cambridge University Press.

Jameson, F. (1984) Postmodernism, or the cultural logic of late capitalism, *New Left Review*, 146: 53–93.

Jameson, F. (1991) *Postmodernism, or, the Cultural Logic of Late Capitalism*. London: Verso.

Jhally, S. (1987) *The Codes of Advertising: Fetishism and the Political Economy of Meaning in Consumer Society*. London: Francis Pinter.

John, R. (ed.) (1994) *The Consumer Revolution: Redressing the Balance*. London: Hodder & Stoughton.

Kaplan, E. A. (1988) *Postmodernism and its Discontents: Theories, Practices*. London: Verso.

Keat, R., Abercrombie, N. and Whiteley, N. (eds) (1994) *The Authority of the Consumer*. London: Routledge.

Kellner, D. (1995) *Media Culture: Cultural Studies, Identity and the Politics Between the Modern and the Postmodern*. London: Routledge.

Kidwell, C. B. and Steele, V. (eds) (1989) *Men and Women: Dressing the Part*. Washington, DC: Smithsonian Institution Press.

Kirkham, P. (ed.) (1996) *The Gendered Object*. Manchester: Manchester University Press.

Kroker, A. and Cook, D. (1988) *The Postmodern Scene: Excremental Culture and Hyper-Aesthetics*. London: Macmillan.

Kroker, A. and Kroker, M. (1988) *Body Invaders: Sexuality and the Postmodern Condition.* London: Macmillan.

Lacan, J. ([1966] 1977) *Ecrits: A Selection.* London: Tavistock.

Langman, L. (1992) Neon cages: shopping for subjectivity, in R. Shields (ed.) *Lifestyle Shopping: The Subject of Consumption.* London: Routledge.

Lash, S. (1990) *Sociology of Postmodernism.* London: Routledge.

Lash, S. and Urry, J. (1987) *The End of Organized Capitalism.* Cambridge: Polity.

Lash, S. and Urry, J. (1994) *Economies of Signs and Space.* London: Sage.

Lee, M. J. (1993) *Consumer Culture Reborn: The Cultural Politics of Consumption.* London: Routledge.

Leiss, W. (1976) *The Limits to Satisfaction: An Essay on the Problem of Needs and Commodities.* Toronto: University of Toronto Press.

Leiss, W., Kline, S. and Jhally, S. (1986) *Social Communication in Advertising: Persons, Products, and Images of Well-Being.* London: Methuen.

Leyshon, A. and Thrift, N. (1997) *Money/Space: Geographies of Monetary Transformation.* London: Routledge.

Lockwood, D. (1958) *The Blackcoated Worker.* London: Allen & Unwin.

Lukács, G. (1923) *History and Class Consciousness.* London: Merlin Press.

Lurie, A. (1981) *The Language Of Clothes.* London: Heinemann.

Lury, A. (1994) Advertising – moving beyond the stereotypes, in R. Keat, N. Abercrombie and N. Whiteley (eds) *The Authority of the Consumer.* London: Routledge.

Lury, C. (1996) *Consumer Culture.* Cambridge: Polity.

Lyotard, J. F. (1984) *The Postmodern Condition.* Manchester: Manchester University Press.

McClintock, A. (1994) Soft-soaping empire: commodity racism and imperial advertising, in G. Robertson, M. Mash, L. Tickner *et al.* (eds) *Travellers' Tales: Narratives of Home and Displacement.* London: Routledge.

McCracken, G. (1985) The trickle-down theory rehabilitated, in M. Solomon (ed.) *The Psychology of Fashion.* Lexington, MA: Lexington Books.

McCracken, G. (1988) *Culture and Consumption: New Approaches to the Symbolic Character of Consumer Goods and Activities.* Indiana: Indiana University Press.

McDowell, L. (1997) *Capital Culture: Gender at Work in the City.* Oxford: Blackwell.

McKendrick, N. (*et al.*) (1982) *The Birth of a Consumer Society.* London: Europa.

McRobbie, A. (ed.) (1989) *Zoot Suits and Second-hand Dresses: An Anthology of Fashion and Music.* Basingstoke: Macmillan.

McRobbie, A. and Nava, M. (eds) (1984) *Gender and Generation.* London: Macmillan.

Maffesoli, M. (1989) The sociology of everyday life (epistemological elements), *Current Sociology*, 37(1): 1–16.

Marcuse, H. (1964) *One-dimensional Man: Studies in the Ideology of Advanced Industrial Society.* London: Routledge & Kegan Paul.

Marshall, G., Rose, D., Newby, H. and Vogler, C. M. (1988) *Social Class in Modern Britain.* London: Unwin Hyman.

Marx, K. (1975) *Early Writings.* Harmondsworth: Penguin.

Mercer, K. (1994) *Welcome to the Jungle: New Positions in Black Cultural Studies.* London: Routledge.

Miller, D. (1987) *Material Culture and Mass Consumption*. Oxford: Blackwell.

Miller, D. (ed.) (1995) *Acknowledging Consumption: A Review of New Studies*. London: Routledge.

Miller, D. (1997) Could shopping ever really matter?, in P. Falk and C. Campbell (eds) *The Shopping Experience*. London: Sage.

Miller, D. (1998) *A Theory of Shopping*. Cambridge: Polity.

Miller, D., Jackson, P., Thrift, N., Holbrook, B. and Rowlands, M. (1998) *Shopping, Place and Identity*. London: Routledge.

Mishra, R. (1981) *Society and Social Policy: Theories and Practice of Welfare*. London: Macmillan.

Mishra, R. (1984) *The Welfare State in Crisis*. Brighton: Wheatsheaf.

Mort, F. (1996) *Cultures of Consumption: Masculinities and Social Space in Late Twentieth-Century Britain*. London: Routledge.

National Consumer Council (1990) *Credit and Debt: The Consumer Interest*. London: HMSO.

Nava, M. (1992) *Changing Cultures: Feminism, Youth and Consumerism*. London: Sage.

Nava, M. (1996) Modernity's disavowal: women, the city and the department store, in M. Nava and A. O'Shea (eds) *Modern Times: Reflections on a Century of English Modernity*. London: Routledge.

Nava, M. (1997) Framing advertising: cultural analysis and the incrimination of visual texts, in M. Nava, A. Blake, I. MacRury and B. Richards (eds) *Buy this Book: Studies in Advertising and Consumption*. London: Routledge.

Nava, M., Blake, A., MacRury, I. and Richards, B. (eds) (1997) *Buy this Book: Studies in Advertising and Consumption*. London: Routledge.

Nixon, S. (1996) *Hard Looks: Masculinities, Spectatorship and Contemporary Consumption*. London: UCL Press.

Oakley, A. (1976) *Housewife*. Harmondsworth: Penguin.

Offe, C. (1984) *Contradictions of the Welfare State*. London: Hutchinson (edited by J. Keane).

Offe, C. (1985) *Disorganized Capitalism: Contemporary Transformations of Work and Politics*. Cambridge: Polity (edited by J. Keane).

Office for National Statistics (1998) *Social Trends 28*. London: The Stationery Office.

Orbach, S. (1979) *Fat is a Feminist Issue*. London: Hamlyn.

Orbach, S. (1993) *Hunger Strike: The Anorexic's Struggle as Metaphor of our Age*. Harmondsworth: Penguin.

Outhwaite, W. (ed.) (1996) *The Habermas Reader*. Cambridge: Polity.

Packard, V. (1957) *The Hidden Persuaders*. London: Longmans, Green and Co.

Phizacklea, A. (1990) *Unpacking the Fashion Industry*. London: Routledge.

Polhemus, T. (1994) *Street Style: From Sidewalk to Catwalk*. London: Thames & Hudson.

Poster, M. (1988) *Jean Baudrillard: Selected Writings*. Cambridge: Polity.

Radner, H. (1995) *Shopping around: Feminine Culture and the Pursuit of Pleasure*. London: Routledge.

Randall, G. (1993) *Principles of Marketing*. London: Routledge.

Reynaud, E. (1983) *Holy Virility: The Social Construction of Masculinity*. London: Pluto.

Ritzer, G. (1991) *Metatheorizing in Sociology*. New York: Lexington.

Rowlingson, K. (1994) *Moneylenders and their Customers*. London: Policy Studies Institute.

Rowlingson, K. and Kempson, E. (1994) *Paying with Plastic: A Study of Credit Card Debt*. London: Policy Studies Institute.

Rutherford, J. (ed.) (1990) *Identity: Community, Culture, Difference*. London: Lawrence & Wishart.

Saunders, P. (1987) *Social Theory and the Urban Question*. London: Unwin Hyman.

Saussure, F. de (1974) *A Course in General Linguistics*. London: Fontana.

Savage, J. (1996) What's so new about the new man? Three decades of advertising to men, in D. Jones (ed.) *Sex, Power and Travel: Ten Years of Arena*. London: Virgin.

Schudson, M. (1993) *Advertising: The Uneasy Persuasion: Its Dubious Impact on American Society*. London: Routledge.

Shields, R. (ed.) (1992) *Lifestyle Shopping: The Subject of Consumption*. London: Routledge.

Simmel, G. (1904) Fashion, *International Quarterly*, 10.

Simmel, G. (1950) The metropolis and mental life, in K. Wolff (ed.) *The Sociology of Georg Simmel*. London: Collier Macmillan.

Simmel, G. (1990) *The Philosophy of Money*. London: Routledge.

Simpson, M. (1994) *Male Impersonators: Men Performing Masculinity*. New York: Routledge.

Simpson, M. (1996) *It's a Queer World*. London: Vintage.

Slater, D. (1997a) Consumer culture and the politics of need, in M. Nava, A. Blake, I. MacRury and B. Richards (eds) *Buy this Book: Studies in Advertising and Consumption*. London: Routledge.

Slater, D. (1997b) *Consumer Culture and Modernity*. Cambridge: Polity.

Smith, A. (1838) *An Inquiry into the Nature and Causes of the Wealth of Nations*. Edinburgh: Black.

Spillane, M. (1993) *Presenting Yourself: A Personal Image Guide For Men*. London: Piatkus.

Sulkunen, P., Holmwood, J., Radner, H. and Schulze, G. (eds) (1997) *Constructing the New Consumer Society*. Basingstoke: Macmillan.

Tench, D. (1994) Consumer protection legislation, in R. John (ed.) *The Consumer Revolution: Redressing the Balance*. London: Hodder & Stoughton.

Tolson, A. (1977) *The Limits of Masculinity*. London: Tavistock.

Tomlinson, A. (ed.) (1990) *Consumption, Identity, and Style: Marketing, Meanings, and the Packaging of Pleasure*. London: Routledge.

Touraine, A. (1971) *The Post-Industrial Society*. New York: Random House.

Vance, C. S. (ed.) (1984) *Pleasure and Danger: Exploring Female Sexuality*. London: Routledge & Kegan Paul.

Veblen, T. ([1899]1934) *The Theory of the Leisure Class: An Economic Study of Institutions*. New York: The Modern Library.

Warde, A. (1994) Consumption, identity formation and uncertainty, *Sociology*, 28(4): 877–98.

Warde, A. (1994) Consumers, identity and belonging – Reflections on some theses of Zygmunt Bauman, in R. Keat, N. Abercrombie and N. Whiteley (eds) *The Authority of the Consumer*. London: Routledge.

Warde, A. (1996) Afterword: The future of the sociology of consumption, in S. Edgell, K. Hetherington and A. Warde (eds) *Consumption Matters: The Production and Experience of Consumption*. Oxford: Blackwell.

Weeks, J. (1985) *Sexuality and its Discontents: Meanings, Myths and Modern Sexualities*. London: Routledge & Kegan Paul.

Wernick, A. (1991) *Promotional Culture: Advertising, Ideology and Symbolic Expression*. London: Sage.

Williams, F. (1989) *Social Policy: A Critical Introduction – Issues of Race, Gender and Class*. Cambridge: Polity.

Williams, R. (1980) Advertising: the magic system, in R. Williams (ed.) *Problems in Material and Culture*. London: Verso.

Williamson, J. (1978) *Decoding Advertisements: Ideology and Meaning in Advertising*. London: Marion Boyars.

Williamson, J. (1986) *Consuming Passions: The Dynamics of Popular Culture*. London: Marion Boyars.

Willis, P. (1977) *Learning to Labour: How Working Class Kids get Working Class Jobs*. Farnborough: Saxon House.

Willis, S. (1990) I want the black one: is there a place for Afro-American culture in commodity culture?, *New Formations*, 10: 77–97.

Wilson, E. (1985) *Adorned in Dreams: Fashion and Modernity*. London: Virago.

Wilson, E. (1992) The invisible flâneur, *New Left Review*, 191: 90–110.

Wilson, W. J. (1991) Public policy/research and the truly disadvantaged, in C. Jencks and P. Peterson (eds) *The Urban Underclass*. Washington, DC: Brookings Institution.

Winship, J. (1987) *Inside Women's Magazines*. London: Pandora Press.

Winward, J. (1994) The rationale and forms of government intervention, in R. John (ed.) *The Consumer Revolution: Redressing the Balance*. London: Hodder & Stoughton.

Wolf, N. (1991) *The Beauty Myth: How Images of Beauty are used against Women*. London: Vintage.

Zukin, S. and Dimaggio, P. (1990) *Structures of Capital: The Social Organization of the Economy*. Cambridge: Cambridge University Press.

Zurbrugg, N. (1997) *Jean Baudrillard: Art and Artefact*. London: Sage.

INDEX